Happiness and Economic Growth

Studies of Policy Reform

Series Editors

Daniel Cohen and François Bourguignon

This series brings new and innovative policy research to the forefront of academic and policy debates.

It addresses the widest range of policies, from macroeconomics to welfare, public finance, trade, migration, and the environment. It hosts collaborative work under the auspices of CEPR, CEPREMAP, and the Paris School of Economics.

Titles Published in the Series

The Economics of Clusters

Gilles Duranton, Philippe Martin, Thierry Mayer, and Florian Mayneris

Cultural Integration of Immigrants in Europe

Edited by Yann Algan, Alberto Bisin, Alan Manning, and Thierry Verdier

Happiness and Economic Growth: Lessons from Developing Countries

Edited by Andrew E. Clark and Claudia Senik

Happiness and Economic Growth

Lessons from Developing Countries

Edited by

Andrew E. Clark and Claudia Senik

OXFORD
UNIVERSITY PRESS

OXFORD
UNIVERSITY PRESS

Great Clarendon Street, Oxford, OX2 6DP,
United Kingdom

Oxford University Press is a department of the University of Oxford. It furthers the University's objective of excellence in research, scholarship, and education by publishing worldwide. Oxford is a registered trade mark of Oxford University Press in the UK and in certain other countries

First Edition published in 2014

Published in the United States of America by Oxford University Press
198 Madison Avenue, New York, NY 10016, United States of America

British Library Cataloguing in Publication Data
Data available

Library of Congress Control Number: 2014940455

ISBN 978–0–19–872365–3

Contents

List of Contributors

Yann Algan is Professor of Economics at Sciences Po, Paris. He is also a fellow at CEPR and IZA and is co-head of CEPREMAP's macroeconomic program. His research interests are public economics, political economy, experimental economics, and macroeconomics. He is the author of *La Société de défiance* (2012) (with Pierre Cahuc) and *Cultural and Economic Integration in Europe* (Oxford University Press, 2010) (with Alberto Bisin, Alan Manning, and Thierry Vierder) and has published in top economic journals such as *American Economic Review, Quarterly Journal of Economics, Economic Journal,* and *Journal of European Economic Association.* He was awarded Best French Young Economist in 2009, has been a visiting professor at MIT (2007) and Harvard (2008), and is co-director of the Sciences Po Master's course in Economics and Public Policy.

Andrew E. Clark holds a PhD from the LSE. He is CNRS Research Professor at the Paris School of Economics, and previously held posts at Dartmouth, Essex, CEPREMAP, DELTA, the OECD, and the University of Orléans. His work has used job and life satisfaction scores, and other psychological indices as proxy measures of utility. His research has addressed relative utility or comparisons (to others like you, to your partner, and to yourself in the past), and the use of long-run panel data in collaboration with psychologists to map out habituation to life events (such as job loss, marriage, and divorce).

Richard A. Easterlin is currently University Professor and Professor of Economics, University of Southern California. He is a member of the National Academy of Sciences and a Distinguished Fellow of the American Economic Association. He is also a Fellow of the American Academy of Arts and Sciences, the Econometric Society, and the Institute for the Study of Labor (IZA), and is a former president of the Population Association of America, Economic History Association, and Western Economic Association International. He is the author, among other things, of *Happiness, Growth and the Life Cycle* (2010), *The Reluctant Economist* (2004), *Growth Triumphant: The 21st Century in Historical Perspective* (1996), and *Birth and Fortune: The Impact of Numbers on Personal Welfare* (1980; 2nd edn 1987), and editor of *Happiness in Economics* (2002). His current research is on the association between economic growth, public policy, and subjective well-being.

Ada Ferrer-i-Carbonell is a tenured scientist in the Institute for Economic Analysis (IAE-CSIC) in Barcelona and Barcelona Graduate School of Economics' Deputy Director for Academic Programs. She is Research Fellow at IZA, Barcelona GSE, and MOVE, and an associate editor of the *Journal of Economic Behavior and Organization*. Ada has PhDs in Economics from Rensselaer Polytechnic Institute (United States, 2003) and the Tinbergen Institute (University of Amsterdam, 2003). Her current interests are in the area of welfare analysis (through subjective well-being measures), including health, inequality, and risk attitudes. She has published (with Bernard Van Praag) *Happiness Quantified: A Satisfaction Calculus Approach* (Oxford University Press, 2004).

Sarah Flèche is a PhD student from the European Doctoral Program (EDP), jointly organized by the Paris School of Economics and the London School of Economics. Her research interests include economics of happiness, health and institutional studies. She has an M.A. degree in economics from the Ecole Normale Supérieure. From 2010 to 2013, she was a consultant at the OECD and was involved in a research program on new measures of well-being.

Ramani Gunatilaka has been working as a development economist in Sri Lanka and the region since graduating from the Universities of London and Oxford in 1992–3. She received a PhD in Applied Econometrics from Monash University, Australia in 2006 for her thesis on income distribution in Sri Lanka after economic liberalization. She is a member of the Faculty of Graduate Studies, University of Colombo, Sri Lanka. Her research has concentrated on poverty alleviation, rural development, microfinance, and labor market issues in Sri Lanka, Afghanistan, and the Maldives, and on the determinants of subjective well-being in China.

Carol Graham is Leo Pasvolsky Senior Fellow at the Brookings Institution and College Park Professor at the University of Maryland. She has been a Vice President at Brookings and a Special Advisor to the Vice President of the Inter-American Development Bank. Graham is the author of numerous books—most recently *The Pursuit of Happiness: An Economy of Well-Being* (Brookings, 2011) and *Happiness Around the World: The Paradox of Happy Peasants and Miserable Millionaires* (OUP, 2009)—and has published articles in a range of journals including the *World Bank Research Observer, Health Affairs, Journal of Economic Behavior and Organization, Health Economics,* and *Journal of Socio-Economics*. Her work has been reviewed in *Science, The New Yorker,* and the *New York Times,* among others. She has an A.B. from Princeton, an M.A. from Johns Hopkins, a PhD from Oxford University, and three beautiful children.

John Knight is Emeritus Professor of Economics and Emeritus Fellow of St Edmund Hall in the University of Oxford. He has conducted research on

African countries and on China, mainly on issues such as human resources, poverty, and subjective well-being. His recent books include *Towards a Labour Market in China* (2005) and *China's Remarkable Economic Growth* (2012; both Oxford University Press). He holds a Leverhulme emeritus fellowship, is a visiting professor at Beijing Normal University, and is the academic director of the Oxford Chinese Economy Programme.

Stéfan Lollivier is now working in the French Institute of Statistics as director of a program in charge of the implementation of a register of dwellings. He was previously Director of Demographic and Social Statistics in the same institute (2004–11) and Director of the Ecole Nationale de la Statistique et de l'Administration Economique (ENSAE, 1999–2004). In 2010–11, he co-chaired the European Task Force about Quality of Life in charge of the implementation of the Stiglitz recommendations. Recent publications include a chapter in *The Econometrics of Panel Data* (3rd edn: Springer Verlag, 2008), ed. Matyas and Sevestre, with M. Lechner and T. Magnac (2008) and a paper about unemployment in the *International Economic Review* with Laurence Rioux (2010).

Martin Ravallion holds the inaugural Edmond D. Villani Chair of Economics at Georgetown University, prior to which he was Director of the World Bank's research department. He has advised numerous governments and international agencies on poverty and policies for fighting it, and he has written extensively on this and other subjects in economics, including three books and 200 papers in scholarly journals and edited volumes. He is President-elect of the Society for the Study of Economic Inequality, a Senior Fellow of the Bureau for Research in Economic Analysis of Development, a Research Associate of the National Bureau of Economic Research, USA, and a non-resident Fellow of the Center for Global Development. Among various prizes and awards, in 2012 he was awarded the John Kenneth Galbraith Prize from the American Agricultural and Applied Economics Association.

Paul Seabright is Professor of Economics at the Toulouse School of Economics and Director of the Institute for Advanced Study in Toulouse. He has taught at the Universities of Oxford and Cambridge and at the Ecole Polytechnique in Paris. His book *The Company of Strangers: A Natural History of Economic Life* (2nd edn, Princeton 2010) was shortlisted for the 2005 British Academy Book Prize. His most recent book *The War of the Sexes: How Conflict and Cooperation Have Shaped Men and Women from Prehistory to the Present*, was published by Princeton in 2011.

Claudia Senik is Professor of Economics at the Paris School of Economics and the University Paris-Sorbonne. She is also a member of the IZA and of the Institut Universitaire de France. Educated at the Ecole Normale Supérieure, she received her PhD from EHESS. Her main research areas include happiness studies, political attitudes, and post-transition economies, with a special interest in the subjective welfare effects of income growth and income distribution. She is also involved in a research program on well-being at work.

Conal Smith is head of the Well-being and Household Conditions section in the OECD Statistics Directorate. The section focuses on methodological work on measures of well-being, such as the recently released OECD Guidelines on Measuring Subjective Well-being. Before joining the OECD, Conal managed the Social Conditions directorate at Statistics New Zealand from 2008 to 2010, which was responsible for the development and analysis of New Zealand's social statistics programme. Conal has an extensive background in policy, having worked for the New Zealand Ministry of Social Development and other government agencies since 1996. He managed the social outcomes unit within the Strategic Social Policy Group from 2004 to 2008, and held a position as principal analyst before that. His policy career includes work on economic growth, savings, welfare, retirement income, and labour market policy.

Xiaobo Zhang is a Distinguished Professor of Economics at the National School of Development, Peking University, and a senior research fellow at the International Food Policy Research Institute (IFPRI). His research fields are Chinese economy and development economics. He has published widely in top economics journals, such as *Journal of Political Economy, Journal of Development Economics, Journal of International Economics*, and *Journal of Public Economics*. His recent books include *Governing Rapid Growth in China: Equity and Institutions* (Routledge, 2009), *Regional Inequality in China: Trends, Explanations and Policy Responses* (Routledge, 2009), *Narratives of Chinese Economic Reforms: How Does China Cross the River?* (World Scientific Publishing, 2009), and *Oxford Companion to the Economics of China* (OUP, forthcoming). He is a co-editor of *China Economic Review*. He was selected as the president of the Chinese Economists Society from 2005 to 2006.

Ekaterina Zhuravskaya received a PhD in economics from Harvard in 1999. Betweem 1999 and 2010 she was a professor at the New Economic School (Moscow). In 2010, she joined EHESS and the Paris School of Economics. Her articles on political and institutional economics have appeared in top international journals including *American Economic Review, Quarterly Journal of Economics, American Economic Journal: Applied Economics, American Economic Journal: Microeconomics, Journal of European Economic Association, Journal of Economic Literature, Journal of Public Economics, Journal of Business, American Law,* and *Economics Review*. In 2001, the World Economic Forum in Davos named her Global Leader for Tomorrow. In 2006, she received a gold medal in a Global Development Network award competition.

List of Figures

List of Tables

Introduction

Andrew E. Clark and Claudia Senik

Happiness economics has undergone a remarkable and rapid change, moving from something of a curiosity to a well-known and, we believe, legitimate field of research. This is reflected in the constantly mounting volume of articles and research findings that have accumulated over the past twenty years, thanks in part to the increasing availability of surveys that contain subjective well-being information. At the same time, the debate over the best measure of well-being "beyond GDP" has spread far outside of academia and reached policy makers, international organizations, and statistical offices.

For economists, one of the resulting central questions has been the economic foundations of happiness, in particular the relationship between income growth and well-being. This is a question of primary importance for both developed and emerging countries. It now seems incontrovertible that the development of "Happiness Economics" owes a huge debt to Dick Easterlin, Professor at the University of Southern California, and the well-known Easterlin paradox (Easterlin, 1974, is surely one of the best-known book chapters in the profession). The Easterlin paradox opposed cross-section and time-series estimates of the income–happiness relationship. While, at any point in time, richer individuals are on average happier, economic growth over time yields no rise in average happiness at the country level (Sacks et al., 2010). This is actually a double paradox. Not only does the time-series elasticity flatly contradict that from cross-sections, it is also counterintuitive. If it is true that economic growth does not bring greater happiness in its wake, why is it so often considered as a key objective of public policy?

The desire to reconcile these divergent findings has been one of the main motivations of researchers using subjective well-being data over the past twenty years. The general flavor of much of the work here has been that individual well-being essentially depends on changes and comparisons more than it does on levels. As such, well-being is critically dependent on the benchmark against which people evaluate their incomes, their achievements, and all of the relative elements of their lives. Individuals evaluate their incomes against both the benchmark of what has happened to them in the past and the income of those who are in their reference group. As a result, income growth does not produce happier individuals in the long run as, first, they will adapt to their new higher living standards as their aspiration levels rise with their own income and, second, they compare their income to that of their peers, neighbors, colleagues, and family members, and their well-being depends on their relative incomes.

This argument does produce a positive cross-section elasticity: in a given country, the rich are happier than the poorer, not necessarily due to the number of dollars they have, but rather because they have more dollars than most other people. Equally, at the supranational level, those living in richer countries are happier than those living in poorer countries, not due to the benefits of wealth as such, but because of the favorable comparison with these poorer countries. The other side of the coin is that individuals in poorer countries suffer from the comparison to wealthier countries. As such, relative income concerns are not only local but also global.

Following this logic through, everything is relative and absolute levels do not matter. This view, which is in line with Kahneman and Tversky's "Prospect Theory," is arguably a rather depressing one for poor countries. If there are both local and global comparisons, then the benefits of growth will be only be felt to the extent that the country closes the gap with other countries. If there are only local comparisons, then there are no benefits of growth at all, as in the Easterlin paradox for developed countries.

To see whether this conjecture about the relativity of utility with respect to income (to use the economic jargon) holds, we need data on developing countries. To date, the vast majority of the work on income comparisons and individual well-being has appealed to data from OECD countries. However, a recent sharp increase in the availability of non-OECD data including subjective well-being information has produced a small but growing number of pieces of research looking at the correlates of individual well-being in poorer countries in Asia, Latin America, and Africa (see Clark and Senik, 2011, for a survey).

In this spirit, the current conference volume includes three chapters which offer new evidence on the relationship between income and subjective well-being in China.

The chapter by Dick Easterlin is based on Chinese time-series data of subjective well-being, and shows that average happiness has not increased there over the past two decades despite the unprecedented rate of economic growth. More precisely, well-being has followed a U-shape over time, with a trough being found around 2005. Both the Easterlin chapter and that by John Knight and Ramani Gunatilaka attribute this time-series pattern to movements over time in unemployment and social security provision, as well as rising income inequality, new urban insecurities, the uncertainty that goes hand-in-hand with economic reform, and the wide divide between the numerous rural–urban migrants and the affluent urban–*hukou* population. These findings help to explain why average happiness in China appears not to have risen, and may even have fallen, over the recent period.

China is a useful test case to see whether comparisons and adaptation should be considered a rich-country luxury, or whether they also pertain in developing countries. In this volume, Knight and Gunatilaka show that income comparisons are indeed important in China, and it is considered important to "keep up with the Zhous." Individual happiness falls as their aspirations grow, and these latter aspirations reflect what is going on in individuals' reference groups. For those who live in rural areas the reference group is most often their fellow villagers; for urban dwellers it is their fellow urban citizens; and for rural–urban migrants it is other people living in the city, both urban citizens and rural *hukou* holders.

The chapter by Clark and Senik also appeals to Chinese data. They consider a panel of individuals in Guizhou province, in which all households in a number of different villages are interviewed. The complete nature of the interviews at the village level allows household rank in the village income distribution to be determined accurately. The empirical analysis shows that the top and bottom of the income rank distribution seem to matter disproportionately in terms of subjective well-being (suggesting that it may well be a mistake to treat rank as a cardinal variable).

The ensuing discussion by Xiaobo Zhang illustrates the importance of social status in China and the reasons for this importance. In a context of considerable imbalance in the male–female ratio, parents with a son whom they wish to be married compete with each other on the market for brides. They do so by saving impressive amounts of money and then demonstrating their wealth via the housing market.

The observed phenomenon of conspicuous expenditure, in particular at the time of marriage and in official ceremonies, is part of the same pattern of behavior.

This volume, then, brings together a series of chapters which arguably attest that China is no exception when it comes to income comparisons and adaptation. This new work represents a substantial complement to existing research on these kinds of behavioral traits in developing countries (see Clark and Senik, 2011).

Should the discussion about income and happiness now definitely be closed? We do not necessarily think so. One reason for this reticence is that it is difficult to analyze long-run changes in happiness over time, as the happiness scale that is used in surveys is typically only on a bounded scale (often one to seven, or zero to ten). This leads to a potential problem of "rescaling," whereby individuals change their interpretation of the steps of the happiness scale over time as the context changes. This rescaling is a particular type of framing effect.

This problem is addressed in the chapter by Martin Ravallion, which emphasizes the methodological caveats faced by those who try to use subjective well-being assessments for policy design, in particular to generate a "social subjective poverty line." Among a number of concerns, including the choice of covariates, survey design issues, measurement error, and latent heterogeneity in personality traits and personal trade-offs, Ravallion picks out frame-of-reference effects as a key problem that is specific to such subjective satisfaction scores (as opposed to objective observable variables).

We believe that these kinds of issues do make a case for taking the results regarding long-run changes with great care, for fear of comparing what is not comparable. As it was put by Deaton (2008, p. 70): "The 'best possible life for you' is a shifting standard that will move upwards with rising living standards."

It is precisely because of these framing and rescaling effects that we started to look at the standard deviation of happiness statements. Our intuition was as follows: if individual happiness does indeed rise with development but can only be expressed on a bounded scale, and if there is no rescaling, then one should observe an increased grouping of responses at the top of the well-being scale as the country becomes richer. It turns out that we find not a grouping at the top, but a rather different change. Our chapter in this volume (Clark, Flèche, and Senik) shows that within-country happiness inequality has fallen in the majority of countries which have experienced positive income growth over the past forty years, and in particular in developed countries. This mean-preserving declining spread in happiness comes about via falls in the share of individuals who declare low and high levels of happiness. There is thus not a concentration of happiness at the top of the scale, but rather in the middle. To paraphrase Easterlin, our findings suggest that raising the incomes of all will not increase the happiness of all, but will certainly reduce its variance, and hence the risk of extreme unhappiness. Behind the veil of ignorance, lower happiness inequality would certainly be considered as attractive by risk-averse individuals.

However, our work also confirms the importance of income inequality as a determinant of life satisfaction: the rise in income inequality over the time period considered has acted to dampen this fall in happiness inequality, and in the case of the U.S. has even reversed its sign, so that happiness inequality started to rise again there in the 1990s.

Overall, this volume suggests that subjective well-being information is a useful tool to shed light on changes in welfare in developing countries. Many chapters underline the difficulty of increasing well-being, even in the presence of income growth, notably due to the importance of income comparisons and income inequality. Adaptation equally acts as a deflator in the income–happiness relationship. The research here has suggested that income comparison and adaptation are not luxuries: they are at work even in developing countries such as China. Social rank (e.g. one's rank in the income ladder of his village) is also important, creating the danger of zero-sum games.

However, there is not only bad news from the point of view of developing countries. One piece of good news is that GDP growth often seems to go hand-in-hand with lower happiness inequality. While this seemingly stylized fact is still open to interpretation, it does parallel the new objective of Chinese policy: social harmonization.

References

Clark, A.E., and Senik, C. (2011). "Will GDP Growth Increase Happiness in Developing Countries?" In R. Peccoud (Ed.), *Measure For Measure: How Well Do We Measure Development?* Paris, STIN: pp. 99–176.

Deaton, A. (2008). "Income, Health and Well-being around the World: Evidence from the Gallup World Poll." *Journal of Economic Perspectives*, **22**, 53–72.

Easterlin, R. (1974). "Does Economic Growth Improve the Human Lot?" In P.A. David and W.B. Melvin (Eds.), *Nations and Households in Economic Growth*. Palo Alto, Stanford University Press: pp. 89–125.

Sacks, D., Stevenson, B., and Wolfers, J. (2010). "Subjective Well-being, Income, Economic Development and Growth," NBER Working Paper No. 16441.

1

Life Satisfaction in the Transition from Socialism to Capitalism: Europe and China*

Richard A. Easterlin

1.1 Introduction

In theory, the transitions from centrally planned to free market economies that have been taking place in Europe and China should lead to a more efficient allocation of resources, stimulate private investment, and raise incomes. The outcome should be greater well-being. But has well-being in fact increased in the transition economies? And has the course of well-being been the same in the "big bang" transitions of central and eastern Europe and the "gradualist" transition in China (Lin 2004)? This chapter draws on several recent papers by the author, some collaborative, to address these questions (Easterlin and Plagnol 2008; Easterlin 2009; Easterlin, Morgan, Switek, and Wang 2012). It turns out that the trajectories of life satisfaction have been quite similar in Europe and China, and that well-being has not increased.

Well-being is taken here to mean subjective well-being (SWB)—that is, self-reported feelings of happiness or life satisfaction. Though not identical in concept, happiness and life satisfaction are closely related, and the terms are used here interchangeably. An example of the type of question used to gather such data is that in the World Values Survey (WVS), the principal survey used here:

* This chapter has benefited from the help of Laura Angelescu-McVey, Robson Morgan, Kelsey O'Connor, Anke Plagnol, Onnicha Sawangfa, Malgorzata Switek, and Jacqueline Smith Zweig. The University of Southern California provided financial assistance.

> All things considered, how satisfied are you with your life as a whole these days? Please use this card to help with your answer.
>
> 1 "Dissatisfied" 2 3 4 5 6 7 8 9 10 "Satisfied"

Estimates of mean life satisfaction or similar SWB measures here are the average of individuals' integer responses to questions such as this.

Until recently, economists have assumed that measures of an individual's external (observable) circumstances, especially one's income, were sufficient to assess well-being, and self-reports of subjective feelings were dismissed out of hand (Fuchs 1983, p. 14; McCloskey 1983, p. 514). The 2008 Stiglitz-Sen-Fitoussi Report, commissioned by former French President Sarkozy to propose more meaningful measures of well-being, is indicative of the sea-change that has taken place. After advocating the official collection of a variety of objective measures, the Report of the twenty-five-member Commission (including five Nobel Prize winners in economics) states:

> Research has shown that it is possible to collect meaningful and reliable data on subjective as well as objective well-being... [T]he types of questions that have proved their value within small-scale and unofficial surveys should be included in larger scale surveys undertaken by official statistical offices. (Stiglitz, Sen, and Fitoussi 2008, p. 16)

The measures used here are among those advocated in the report. I do not claim that they are the best measures of SWB, but it is surely of considerable interest to see what has been happening to people's feelings of happiness or life satisfaction when societies undergo such momentous change as has been occurring in the transitions from socialism to capitalism.

1.2 Data and Methods

The WVS has been conducted in five waves at intermittent intervals since 1982. Except for Hungary, transition countries are first included in the wave 2 surveys, done around 1989–92, near the start of most transitions. Even then, however, the number of countries covered is only thirteen, with central Asian nations totally omitted. Moreover, to obtain a comprehensive view of the life satisfaction pattern over the course of the transition it is essential to have an initial observation prior to or shortly after the start of the transition, along with one not too much later, typically near the mid-1990s. The countries satisfying these data constraints number only six: five that were part of the former Soviet Union, plus China. Of the five former members of the Soviet Union, I focus for simplicity on the largest, the Russian Federation, whose pattern is fairly representative of those found in the other four (cf. Easterlin 2009, p. 134).

The WVS data for China tend to be disproportionately urban, particularly at the earlier dates, but economic growth during the period studied was also especially focused on urban areas, and urban incomes rose markedly relative to rural (Chinese Academy of Social Sciences 2011, p. 44; Knight and Song 2005 pp. 21–2; Xu 2011, p. 214). I supplement the WVS data for China with an annual series starting in 1997 for life satisfaction in cities, collected by a leading Chinese survey organization, Horizon Research Consultancy Group (accessed 2011). The question asked (in Chinese) is: "In general, are you satisfied with your current life?" The response categories are: very satisfied, fairly satisfied, average, fairly dissatisfied, and very dissatisfied, coded here from 5 down to 1. Four other series not presented here also fit the pattern described in the next section (Easterlin, Morgan, Switek, and Wang 2012: Figure 1.1 and Table 1.2).

As a representative of central Europe, we include in our analysis East Germany (the former German Democratic Republic), for which there are annual data since June 1990—shortly before unification with West Germany—gathered in the German Socio-Economic Panel (GSOEP; Haisken-DeNew and Frick 2005). These data were made available by the German Institute for Economic Research (DIW), Berlin. This longitudinal survey contains a general satisfaction question very similar to those given above for the WVS: "How satisfied are you with your life, all things considered?" Responses are on a 0–10 integer scale.

The analysis of mean life satisfaction is supplemented by one on inequality in life satisfaction. The inequality analysis follows the procedure used by Inglehart et al. (1998). The individual responses for income and education are each arrayed from high to low and divided approximately into thirds, yielding upper, middle, and lower segments of the distribution. For each third of the population, life satisfaction is measured as the proportion responding with values of 7 to 10 on a scale from 1 (low) to 10 (high). Education is measured in terms of the highest level of education completed, except for the first survey date, when it relates to age at which education was completed. Income is based on the decile of income reported by respondents. To improve comparability with Russia and China, in this analysis I also use the WVS data for East Germany.

1.3 Results

1.3.1 *Trends in Output and Life Satisfaction*

Output growth has differed markedly between China and the European transition countries (Figure 1.1, Table 1.A1). In Europe gross domestic

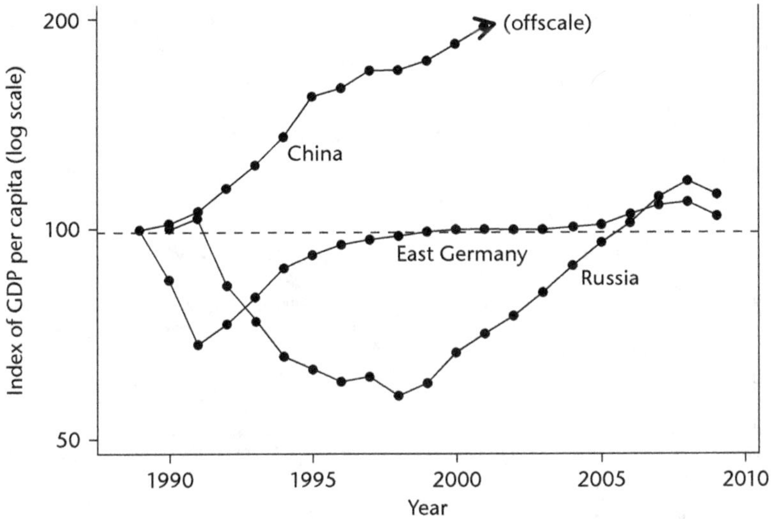

Figure 1.1. Index of real GDP per capita, specified country, c. 1990–2009

product (GDP) per capita collapsed and then recovered; in China the growth of GDP per capita over the past two decades has been the highest in worldwide records—per capita GDP and consumption have at least quadrupled. Hence there is good reason to suppose that the course of well-being might differ between China and the European countries.

In fact, the life satisfaction trajectories have been remarkably similar in Europe and China, despite the disparate output trends. The common pattern is a U-shape—a decline followed by a recovery to life satisfaction levels typically somewhat short of pre-transition values (Figure 1.2; Tables 1.A2–1.A4).

For Russia only fragmentary data are available for the pre-transition period, but as we can see from Figure 1.2, the series for Tambov, Oblast, and Belarus closely track the series for the Russian Federation in the period when they overlap. (For a more extended discussion of the pre-transition data, see Easterlin 2010, pp. 104–7.) For East Germany, the earliest observation is for 1990, but there is evidence that feelings of well-being had been declining prior to that (Noelle-Neumann 1991). To give a sense of what may have happened in East Germany prior to 1990 I have added to the figure the series for Hungary, the one transition country that was included in wave 1 of the WVS, in 1982.

The peak-to-trough declines in life satisfaction in the three countries are quite large. It is difficult to specify the precise numerical size of the declines because the initial peak value for each country is uncertain,

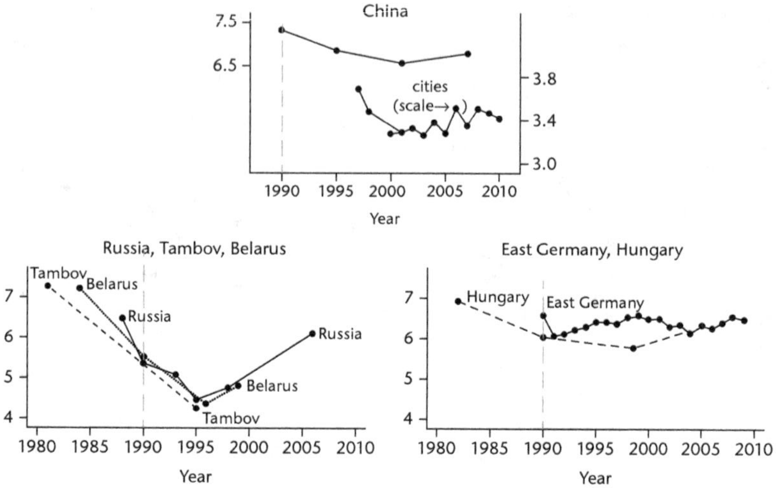

Figure 1.2. Mean life satisfaction, specified country or area, most recent 2–3 decades

and as a result the observed decline is possibly foreshortened. But Russia—the "big bang" country par excellence—clearly has a much greater decrease than the other two countries. Even for East Germany and China, however, the size of the declines observed is rare (Easterlin 2009, p. 133). For example, if we compare China's 0.76-point decline from 1990 to 2001 with the declines in the twenty-six non-transition countries for which there are WVS data for about the same period, there is only one (Turkey) that has a comparable decline (Inglehart et al. 2008; Appendix). None of the rest has a decline as large as half a point. In the case of East Germany, the decline was undoubtedly reduced by the massive public transfers from West to East Germany in the 1990s, equivalent to over 40 percent of East Germany's GDP, that especially buttressed the income situation of the lower income population (Busch 1999; Table 1.1).

The life satisfaction values under socialism suggested by Figure 1.2 are all around 7.0 or higher, only slightly below the contemporaneous numbers for most developed countries. It is noteworthy that China's 1990 life satisfaction value of 7.29 is virtually identical to the 7.26 value in 1981 in Tambov Oblast in the Soviet Union. The USSR's labor and wage policies served as a model for communist China, and this may explain the similarity. As shall be seen below, the early values of life satisfaction inequality are also quite alike in the two countries.

The 1980s values for the European countries here differ markedly from the much lower numbers reported for the European transition countries in general in the 1990s, which are usually below 6 and sometimes in the 4–5 range. These low values are frequently taken by analysts as indicative of life satisfaction under socialism, and the subsequent increase in life satisfaction from such low levels as demonstrating that the transition raised life satisfaction (Sanfey and Teksoz 2007; Guriev and Zhuravskaya 2009). The present analysis, in contrast, suggests that the 1990s values typically reflect the collapse and bottoming out of life satisfaction, and the subsequent increase a recovery to levels still short of pre-transition values.

The reason why some analysts tend to be misled is that very few countries have pre-transition observations of life satisfaction; instead, the initial readings tend to occur after the economy has collapsed. This can be illustrated by the data for Slovenia, where the first WVS (wave 2) survey was conducted in early 1992. If one simply starts with this life satisfaction observation and compares it with the trend in GDP from 1992 onward, both are upward, leading to the inference that happiness is increasing as a result of the transition to freer markets (Figure 1.3). If, however, one considers the course of GDP prior to 1992, it is clear that the 1992 life satisfaction value falls at the economy's trough, and that reported happiness at that date is unlikely to be representative of the pre-transition economic situation—which was considerably better, as is shown by the fact that GDP was about 25 percent higher in the late 1980s.

One might wonder whether the fairly high pre-transition responses on life satisfaction in Figure 1.2 might be the result of "preference falsification." This is a concept that refers to the disparity between one's private views and those expressed publicly, and was developed with particular reference to the European transition countries by Timur Kuran (1991, 1995). The idea is that for fear of reprisal, individuals in a police state might be reluctant to express to pollsters views that are unfavorable to the state. Preference falsification is most likely to occur in regard to political views, however, and it was specifically with regard to political attitudes that Kuran developed the concept. Whether individuals would feel the need for preference falsification with regard to questions about personal life circumstances is less clear. Apparently, people did publicly express feelings of discontent with personal life even in the police state era. Thus, Kuran refers to newspapers receiving "letters of complaint in abundance" and gives examples relating to economic conditions (1991, pp. 29–30), though he notes that these complaints "tended to stay within a party-defined

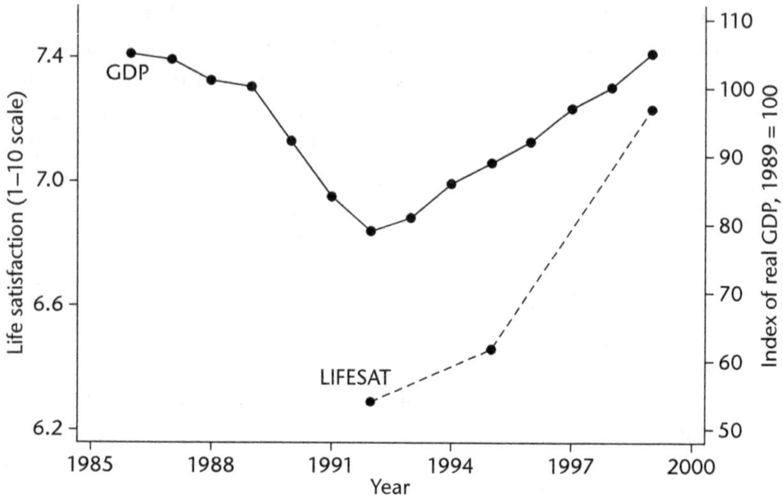

Figure 1.3. Life satisfaction, 1992–9 and index of real GDP, 1986–99, Slovenia

zone of acceptability" (1991, p. 30). He also points out that the fact that communist governments kept the results secret supports the inference that they "were not entirely flattering to them or their policies" (1991, pp. 30–1).

Indeed, the 1990 data for East Germany argue against preference falsification. Commentators on conditions in East Germany under socialism often mentioned the polluted environment and empty shelves in the markets. Consistent with such comments, when asked in 1990 to rate their satisfaction with the environment and goods availability, East Germans reported, on average, values for each only slightly above 3.0 on a 0–10 scale. Such extremely low ratings are hardly ever found, and they clearly run counter to the notion of preference falsification in responses relating to feelings about one's life circumstances.

1.3.2 *Inequality of Life Satisfaction*

In all three countries the full-period trend is toward a marked increase in inequality of life satisfaction. In China and Russia, life satisfaction is initially highly egalitarian; there is only a 3- to 5-point difference between the upper and lower thirds of the income distribution reporting life satisfaction of 7 or higher (Figure 1.4 and Table 1.A5). In East Germany the initial difference is somewhat larger, at 14 points.

By 2006–7, the difference between the highest and lowest groups increases substantially—to 29 points in China and East Germany, and 25 points in Russia. In China and East Germany life satisfaction increases slightly in the highest income tercile and decreases in the lowest, with the decline in China being quite pronounced. In Russia, the initial life satisfaction observations are considerably lower than in the other two countries, because the WVS data for Russia start in 1990, when Russia was already well into its decline in life satisfaction (Figure 1.2). Consequently, while life satisfaction increases noticeably in the highest income group, as in the other two countries, it also rises slightly in the lowest. The common pattern for the three countries is one of substantially increased disparity in life satisfaction between the upper and lower thirds of the income distribution, with the upper third improving and the lower third typically declining. A similar analysis by level of education, not presented here, confirms the results by income level.

1.3.3 *Determinants of Life Satisfaction*

The fairly high values of life satisfaction under socialism were previously pointed out. Are there any substantive reasons for crediting these pre-transition values? The answer is yes. Consider the following

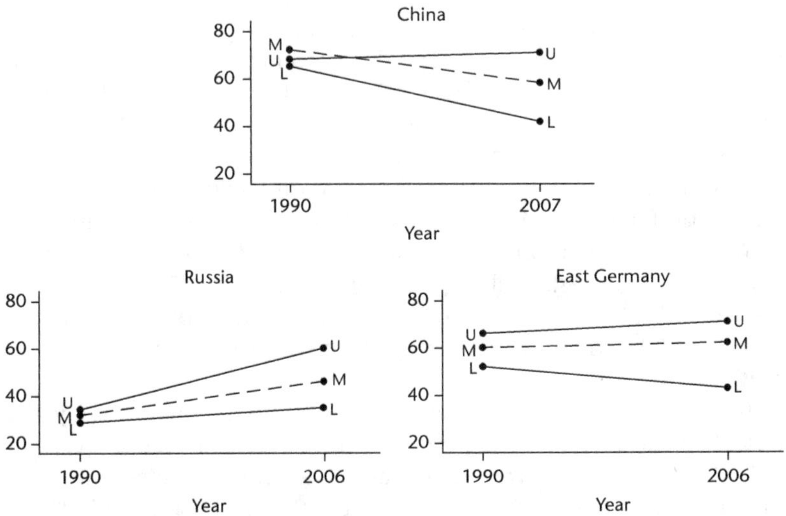

Figure 1.4. Life satisfaction of upper, middle, and lower thirds of income distribution, 1990 and 2006–7

descriptions of workers' conditions under socialism in each of the three countries:

EAST GERMANY

> Over the forty years of its existence, the DDR developed as a completely different state from the BDR. There was no unemployment, no (open) inflation, low work intensity, free medical services, and low costs for housing and public transport. (Lumley 1995, p. 29)

RUSSIA

> Before 1989, Russians lived in a country that provided economic security: unemployment was virtually unknown, pensions were guaranteed and provided a standard of living perceived to be adequate, and macroeconomic instability did not much affect the average citizen. (Brainerd and Cutler 2005, p. 125)

CHINA

> Job rights have until very recently been firmly entrenched in urban China... State-owned enterprises have... supplied extensive welfare benefits, including housing, medical services, pensions, childcare, and jobs for [grown] children... Almost all state employees, and many in the larger collectives, have thus enjoyed an "iron rice bowl"... lifetime tenure of their job and a relatively high wage in the enterprise representing a "mini welfare state." (Knight and Song, 2005, pp. 16–17)

The similarity of the descriptions of conditions in the three countries, by three different analysts, is remarkable. What they suggest, in general, is that the fairly high life satisfaction values under socialism were due to a high degree of job and income security among workers, along with an extensive social safety net.

If one accepts the fairly high pre-transition values, we are left with the question of how to explain the U-shaped pattern and the failure to recover to pre-transition levels of life satisfaction. Two developments seem principally responsible. The first is a deterioration in employment conditions and a resulting rise in workers' anxiety about the security of jobs and income. The second is the dissolution of the social safety net.

The deterioration of employment conditions is illustrated by the movement of unemployment rates in the three countries. Consistent with the quotations given above, all three countries start out with unemployment rates in the vicinity of zero (Figure 1.5 and Table 1.A6); the plot of the rates is inverted so that a downward movement indicates a worsening of employment conditions). The rates then increase

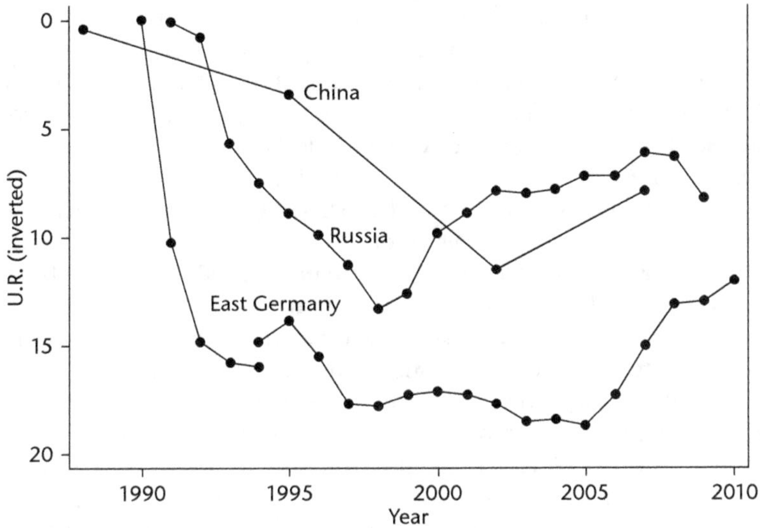

Figure 1.5. Unemployment rate (inverted), specified country, c. 1990–2010 (percentage of labor force)

to two-digit values, between 10 and 20 percent, followed by a turnaround. But the subsequent improvement is modest and the terminal values of the series are considerably higher than the initial ones. The ordering of the initial increase in unemployment rates is: East Germany, followed by Russia, and then China.

The between-country comparability of the levels of the unemployment series, especially that for China, is problematic. The change over time within each country, however, is much more reliable. In the case of China, I have chosen to use here the series with a time span about the same as that for the WVS series on life satisfaction (Knight and Xue, 2006, updated to 2007 by Knight in an email to the author). Although the observations are intermittent, the similarity in timing of the unemployment rate and life satisfaction is evident—unemployment peaks in the first part of the millennium at around the same time that life satisfaction hits bottom. Other (shorter) unemployment series also peak early in the millennium (see Cai, Park, and Zhao 2008; OECD 2010b; and the census-based series in Knight and Xue 2006).

The rise in unemployment rates is not only an index of worsening employment conditions; it is also indicative of a deteriorating social safety net, because social services were typically employer-based. Hence loss of employment meant a loss of many safety net benefits.

Among the employed, safety net benefits fell too, as employment increasingly shifted from state-owned to private firms.

There is other evidence of the dissolution of the safety net. In the case of East Germany the GSOEP surveys ask not only about life satisfaction but also about satisfaction with various aspects or "domains" of life. The responses are again indicative of the importance for life satisfaction of both employment conditions and the social safety net. Mention was previously made of the very low levels of satisfaction with the environment and goods availability among East Germans in 1990. By 2004, satisfaction with these domains had increased markedly, from not much more than 3.0 to over 6.0 (Table 1.1). Satisfaction also increased with regard to other material aspects of life, such as housing, standard of living, and household income, though much more modestly. Counteracting these improvements were negative changes in satisfaction with work, reflecting the more difficult employment conditions, and diminished satisfaction with two elements of the social safety net: health and childcare, both of which decline noticeably, despite some compensating benefits due to incorporation with the West German welfare state. The negative changes in employment conditions and the safety net offset the positive changes in material conditions, leaving overall life satisfaction essentially the same in 2004 as in 1990.

Table 1.1. Satisfaction with various life domains, East Germany, 1990 and 2004 (Scale: 0–10)

Domain	1990	2004	Change 1990 to 2004
Positive changes:			
Environment	3.11	6.47	+3.36
Goods availability	3.16	6.20	+3.04
Dwelling	6.93	7.36	+0.43
Standard of living	6.34	6.63	+0.29
Household income	5.52	5.61	+0.09
Negative changes:			
Health	6.62	6.20	−0.42
Work	7.23	6.48	−0.75
Childcare	7.54	6.48	−1.06
Overall life satisfaction	6.57	6.55	−0.02

Source: GSOEP (Haisken-DeNew and Frick 2005).

Although detailed domain satisfaction data are not available for China and Russia, it is possible to get a sense of the deterioration in the social safety net in each country from responses to the WVS question on self-reported health and satisfaction with finances. In China in 1990 there is very little difference in self-reported health between those in the upper and lowest third of the income distribution (Figure 1.6 and Tables 1.A6–1.A7). The difference in those reporting that their health is good or very good is only 4 percentage points—58 percent for the upper group and 54 percent for the lowest group. By 2007 the difference widens to 28 percentage points, with the upper income group improving in self-reported health to 72 percent and the lowest tercile dropping to 44 percent. It seems plausible that these disparate trends reflect the adverse impact on the lower income population of the increased cost of health care, resulting from the marketization of health care services. According to an OECD report on China, "Economic restructuring undermined the health care system, which became increasingly privately financed, though remaining largely publicly provided. While the population's health status was improving, a rising number of people were priced out of treatment or fell into poverty because of health care costs" (OECD 2010a, p. 19).

A similar picture is found with regard to financial satisfaction in China. An initially egalitarian situation is replaced by a highly unequal one, with financial satisfaction increasing for the upper income group and decreasing for the lowest (Figure 1.6, right panel, Table 1.A8). Although income increased absolutely for the lowest as well as the highest income group (though not as fast—see Cai, Chen, and Zhou 2010), the rise in unemployment and limited amount of unemployment

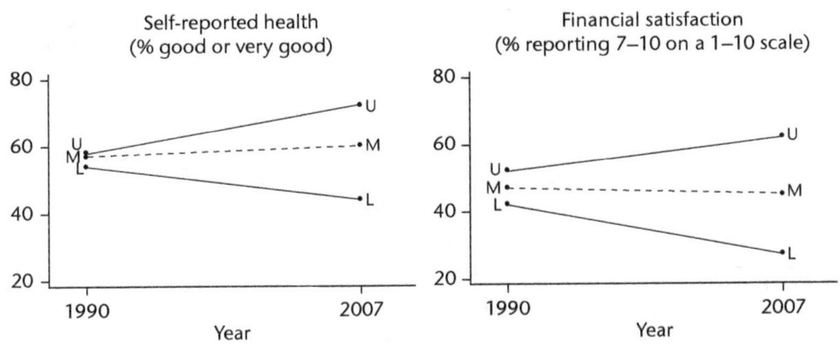

Figure 1.6. Self-reported health and financial satisfaction of upper, middle, and lower thirds of income distribution, China, 1990 and 2007

benefits available left the lowest income group with much more anxiety about their financial circumstances.

In Russia, too, inequality increases with regard to both health and financial satisfaction. There is a small difference from China in that for the lowest income group, health in Russia remains fairly flat rather than declining. As a general matter, the 1990 reports of both health and financial satisfaction in Russia are considerably lower than in China, and doubtless reflect the fact noted earlier that at that date Russia was already well into its downslide in well-being (Figure 1.7).

The picture to this point is, in general, one of marked similarity between China and Europe in the trajectories of life satisfaction and its determinants. There remains, however, the striking difference in output trends brought out by Figure 1.1. How is it possible, one may reasonably ask, for life satisfaction not to improve in China in the face of such a marked advance in per capita GDP from a very low initial level? In answer, it is pertinent to note the growing evidence of the importance of relative income comparisons and rising material aspirations in China, which tend to negate the effect of rising income (Brockmann et al. 2009; Knight and Gunatilaka 2011; Appleton and Song 2008; Tao and Chiu 2009; Oshio et al. 2011; Smyth and Nielsen 2010; and the chapter by Knight in this volume). These findings are consistent with the view common in the happiness literature that the growth in aspiration induced by rising incomes in a society undercuts the increase in life satisfaction due to rising income itself (Clark et al. 2008; Graham 2009; Easterlin 2001, 2003; Layard 2005).

Moreover, as the foregoing discussion of employment and the social safety net demonstrates, there is more to life satisfaction than material

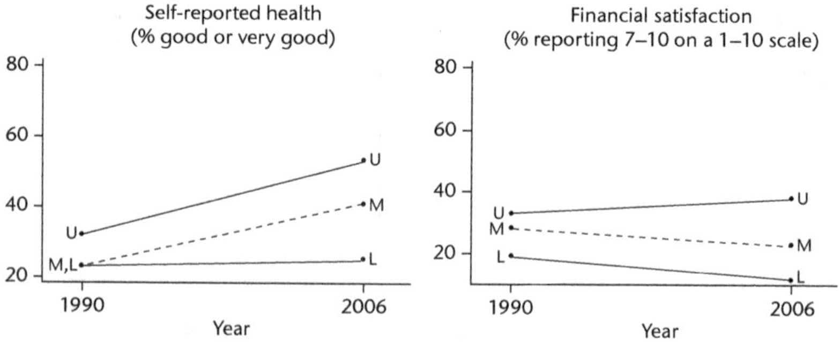

Figure 1.7. Self-reported health and financial satisfaction of upper, middle, and lower thirds of income distribution, Russia, 1990 and 2006

goods. In China, as in Europe, new concerns arose about such things as jobs and income security, the availability of health care and pensions, and provision for care of children and the elderly. The general similarity of the life satisfaction trajectories in Europe and China testifies to the overriding importance of employment and the social safety net in determining life satisfaction.

1.4 Summary and Implications

The transition from socialism to capitalism both in Europe and China has so far not raised happiness levels. The typical life satisfaction trajectory is U-shaped—a decline followed by a recovery to levels somewhat short of pre-transition numbers. Although the evidence on happiness prior to the transition is limited, it is consistent in indicating fairly high values. In the transition, the less-educated and lower-income segments of the population were hardest hit. Typically life satisfaction increased somewhat among the upper third of the population, but decreased noticeably in the lower third.

The key features determining the course of life satisfaction have been employment and safety net conditions. Under socialism workers were assured of jobs and an extensive employer-provided safety net—health care, childcare, pensions, and the like. With the transition to free markets, substantial unemployment emerged and the safety net deteriorated. Concerns rose steadily about such critical matters as finding and holding a job, reliable and affordable health care, and provision for the care of children and the elderly. The result was a decline, on average, in life satisfaction. The U-shaped movement in life satisfaction largely reflects the course of employment conditions, as proxied by unemployment rates. Starting from zero or near-zero values, unemployment rates rose to two-digit levels and then declined, though remaining above their starting point.

The transition in China differs from that in Europe in that output and incomes rose at the highest rate ever recorded, while in Europe a U-shaped movement in the economy was generally typical. It is possible that the remarkable growth in incomes in China cushioned the life satisfaction movement there, but, contrary to the expectations of many, it did not raise happiness. The fact that life satisfaction in China failed to increase noticeably along with income and output and has a U-shape similar to that found in the European transition countries is indicative of the fundamental importance of employment and the social safety net in determining the course of life satisfaction.

The similarity in the experiences of China and Europe also serves to discount the importance of political factors in determining happiness. There was wide diversity among the transition countries in political change—from a substantial increase in political and civil rights in some European countries to little or no change in China and others. Yet the deterioration in employment conditions and the dissolution of the social safety net appear everywhere to have trumped political factors in affecting SWB. As a result there are similar trajectories in life satisfaction despite diverse political circumstances. This is not to say that political conditions had no effect, but clearly employment and the safety net dominated.

The present results demonstrate the value of SWB measures such as happiness or life satisfaction as a guide to policy. Output measures lead one to focus on firms and their productivity, while happiness measures lead directly to the lives and personal concerns of individuals and bring out possible costs in terms of human suffering that are missed by GDP. Moreover, happiness and life satisfaction are concepts with which a layman can identify, unlike GDP. Both GDP and SWB have their uses, but policy makers' preoccupation with GDP has led to neglect of the individuals whose welfare is or should be the primary object of policy.

It would be a mistake to conclude from the life satisfaction experience of the transition countries that there should be a return to socialism and the gross inefficiencies of central planning. It would equally be a mistake to suppose that economic growth is unimportant as a policy objective. But what the experience of China demonstrates is that policies focused largely on economic growth are unlikely to raise happiness. Rather, the experience of both China and the European transition countries indicates that jobs—and job and income security—together with a social safety net are of critical importance to life satisfaction. It is policies directed to these ends that will raise happiness. The pursuit of such policies is easier in the context of robust economic growth. In the absence of employment and safety net policies, however, there is no assurance that economic growth in itself will increase people's feelings of well-being.

References

Appleton SM, Song L (2008) Life Satisfaction in Urban China: Components and Determinants. *World Development* 36(11): 2325–40.

Brainerd E, Cutler DM (2005) Autopsy on an Empire: Understanding Mortality in Russia and the Former Soviet Union. *Journal of Economic Perspectives* 19(1): 107–30.

Brockmann H, Delhey J, Welzel C, Yuan H (2009) The China Puzzle: Falling Happiness in a Rising Economy. *Journal of Happiness Studies* 10: 387–405.

Busch U (1999) Sozialtransfers für Ostdeutschland: Elne kritische Bilanz. *Utopie kreativ* 105: 12–26.

Cai HB, Chen YY, Zhou LA (2010) Income and Consumption Inequality in Urban China: 1992–2003. *Economic Development and Cultural Change* 58: 385–413.

Cai F, Park A, Zhao YH (2008) *China's Great Economic Transformation*, eds Brandt L, Rawki TG (Cambridge University Press, New York), pp 167–214.

Chinese Academy of Social Sciences (2011) *Blue Book of China's Society: Society of China Analysis and Forecast* (in Chinese) (Social Sciences Academic Press, China).

Clark AE, Frijters P, Shields MA (2008) Relative Income, Happiness, and Utility: An Explanation for the Easterlin Paradox and Other Puzzles. *Journal of Economic Literature* 46(1): 95–144.

Easterlin RA (2001) Income and Happiness: Towards a Unified Theory. *The Economic Journal* 111: 465–84.

Easterlin, RA (2003) Explaining Happiness. *Proceedings of the National Academy of Sciences* 100(19): 11176–83.

Easterlin RA (2009) Lost in Transition: Life Satisfaction on the Road to Capitalism. *Journal of Economic Behavior and Organization* 71: 130–45.

Easterlin RA (2010) *Happiness, Growth, and the Life Cycle* (Oxford University Press, New York).

Easterlin RA, Morgan R, Switek M, Wang F (2012) China's Life Satisfaction, 1990–2010. *Proceedings of the National Academy of Sciences*, available at: <http://www.pnas.org/content/early/2012/05/09/1205672109.abstract>.

Easterlin RA, Plagnol AC (2008) Life Satisfaction and Economic Conditions in East and West Germany Pre- and Post-Unification, *Journal of Economic Behavior and Organization* 68: 433–44.

Economic Commission for Europe (2003) *Economic Survey of Europe No.1* (United Nations, New York), available at the Federal Statistical Office of Germany: <https://www-genesis.destatis.de/genesis/online/data>.

Fuchs V (1983) *How We Live* (Harvard University Press, Cambridge).

Graham C (2009) *Happiness Around the World* (Oxford University Press, New York).

Greif A, Tabellini G (2010) Cultural and Institutional Bifurcation: China and Europe compared. *American Economic Review* 100: 135–140.

Guriev S, Zhuravskaya E (2009) (Un)Happiness in Transition. *Journal of Economic Perspectives* 23(2): 143–68.

Haisken-DeNew JP, Frick JR (2005) *Desktop Companion to the German Socio-Economic Panel* (SOEP), Version 8.0 DIW (German Institute for Economic Research, Berlin).

Horizon Research Consultancy Group (accessed 2011), available at: <http://www.horizon-china.com/>.

ILO, Labor Statistics Database, available at: <http://laborsta.ilo.org>.

Inglehart RF, Basanez M, Moreno A (1998) *Human Values and Beliefs: A Cross-Cultural Sourcebook* (University of Michigan Press, Michigan).

Inglehart RF, Peterson C, Welzel C (2008) Development, Freedom, and Rising Happiness: a Global Perspective (1981–2007). *Perspectives from Psychological Science* 3: 264–85.

Knight J, Gunatilaka R (2011) Does Economic Growth Raise Happiness in China? *Oxford Development Studies* 39(1): 1–24.

Knight J, Song L (2005) *Towards a Labour Market in China* (Oxford University Press, New York).

Knight J, Xue JJ (2006) How High Is Urban Unemployment in China? *Journal of Chinese Economic and Business Studies* 4(2): 91–107.

Kuran T (1991) Now Out of Never: The Element of Surprise in the East European Revolution of 1989, *World Politics* 44(1): 7–48.

Kuran T (1995) *Private Truths, Public Lies: The Social Consequences of Preference Falsification* (Harvard University Press, Cambridge).

Layard R (2005) *Happiness: Lessons from a New Science* (Penguin Press, New York).

Lin JY (2004) Lessons from China's Transition from a Planned to a Market Economy, *China Center for Economic Research Working Paper Series* No. E2004001.

Lumley R (1995) Labour Markets and Employment Relations in Transition in Countries of Central and Eastern Europe. *Employee Relations* 17: 24–37.

McCloskey DM (1983) The Rhetoric of Economics. *Journal of Economic Literature* 21(2): 481–517.

Noelle-Neumann E (1991) The German Revolution: The Historic Experiment of the Division and Unification of Germany as Reflected in Survey Research Findings. *International Journal of Public Opinion Research* 3: 238–59.

OECD (2010a) *China in the 2010s: Rebalancing Growth and Strengthening Social Safety Nets* (OECD, Beijing).

OECD (2010b) *OECD Economic Surveys: China, Vol. 2010/6* (OECD, Beijing).

Oshio T, Nozaki K, Kobayashi M (2011) Relative Income and Happiness in Asia: Evidence from Nationwide Surveys in China, Japan, and Korea. *Social Indicators Research* 104(3): 351–67.

Penn World Table, Version 7.0, rgdpch, available at: <http://pwt.econ.upenn.edu/php_site/pwt_index.php>.

Sanfey P, Teksoz LJ (2007) Does Transition Make You Happy? *Economics of Transition* 15: 707–31.

Smyth R, Nielsen I, Zhai QG (2010) Personal Well-being in Urban China. *Social Indicators Research* 95: 231–51.

Stiglitz JE, Sen A, and Fitoussi, J-P (2008) Report of the Commission on the Measurement of Economic Performance and Social Progress. Available at: <www.stiglitz-sen-fitoussi.fr>.

Tao HL, Chiu SY (2009) The Effects of Relative Income and Absolute Income on Happiness. *Review of Development Economics* 13(1): 164–74.

World Development Indicators, World Bank, available at: <http://data.worldbank.org/data-catalog/world-development-indicators>.

World Values Survey 2005 Official Data File, v.20081015, 2008. World Values Survey Association (www.worldvaluessurvey.org). Aggregate File Producer: ASEP/JDS, Madrid.

Xu CG (2011) The Fundamental Institutions of China's Reforms and Development. *Journal of Economic Literature* 49(4): 1076–151.

Discussion: Yann Algan

Thank you very much for this invitation. It is a great pleasure and a great honor. I am impressed to be able to comment on the work of an author who has written among the most seminal papers on happiness. As always, Richard Easterlin really focuses on the big picture, and we should always highly value this kind of approach. I will here just play the role of the boring guy who tries to go into the details, sometimes into some econometric specifications, but once again I really prefer the approach of having a big picture.

This chapter addresses a primordial question about the evolution of happiness in emerging and transition economies, by focusing on a natural experiment to look at the determinants of happiness. China is a wonderful example here for two reasons, the first being that there is a steady increase in income per capita but also some factors that are well-known drawbacks for happiness, such as social comparisons, unemployment, inequality, and a breakdown in the social safety net and social cohesion. Looking at these offsetting factors should be helpful for our understanding of the determinants of happiness. The evidence about the U-shaped evolution of happiness is very exciting and I will suggest some more evidence regarding this relationship.

Let me start with the motivating evidence. Richard has spent a lot of time showing that there might be a U-shaped relationship. I have just one or two concerns. The first is that from my perspective, just by looking at the figures, the U-shaped relationship does not seem so obvious. When I look at the WVS, the source that covers the longest period, the difference between those two points is not that large, and when I look at other surveys, like the *Pew* or *Horizon* surveys, there are a lot of discontinuities in this evolution. It would be reassuring to have more data to reach a solid conclusion about this U-shaped relationship. I am not a specialist of the happiness literature, but my suggestion would be to try to perform some statistical tests or fit some functional forms. I also have one question about the data: I wonder to what extent the WVS data is really relevant. Let me give you one example, about trust. When trust was measured in the 1990s, in the

WVS, China was one of the countries with the highest level of social trust. But Greif and Tabellini (2010) have gone back to the data, over the same time horizon, and show that trust was actually very low at that time and that the answers collected by the WVS were biased. So the extent to which we can exploit this part of the data from the WVS is an open question.

Let me now go back to the determinants of happiness: unemployment, the social safety net, and inequality. You provide a big picture with descriptive statistics about happiness and its breakdown depending on the economic background. What I would suggest is to use simple micro-regressions, looking at cross-section data from a given wave of the WVS and the coefficients associated with income per capita, national unemployment, individual unemployment, and health, and compare the weights of the different coefficients. In these regressions you can distinguish social comparisons which might undermine happiness growth over time. I think it might be worthwhile also when you go to macroeconomic evidence to control for individual characteristics, especially for age: you might find alternative explanations for the U-shaped evolution of happiness that are linked to cohort effects. At this point, it is difficult to disentangle these different effects, because we do not have any controls for them.

Going back to the determinants of the evolution of happiness, at the beginning, I thought that you wanted not only to look at the redistributive effects of this growth episode but also at social comparisons and how inequality by itself might affect happiness: in other words, it might be the case that even rich people, because they are living in a much more unequal environment, might feel much more dissatisfied. There is a large literature that has shown that inequality can affect the happiness of all social groups. In this case, instead of focusing on satisfaction with one's financial situation, I would try to look at questions on the perception of the change in inequality. The WVS includes a number of questions about whether people think that the increase in inequality is justifiable, and whether the government should actually step in to try to reduce inequality. So the concern over inequality could be measured via subjective questions. One could also use some alternative objective measures of the evolution of inequality: you refer to the Gini index, but I guess there are a lot of potential additional indicators covering the evolution of labor market institutions, especially the breakdown of permanent jobs. My last suggestion would be to exploit regional variations, especially in the WVS. You mentioned that happiness might have evolved quite differently depending on whether people live in an urban area with faster income growth or a rural area where income is stable or might even have fallen. The exploitation of this kind of regional heterogeneity in the evolution of inequality and labor market institutions might shed more light on the determinants of the evolution of happiness over time.

My last remark concerns policy recommendations. To what extent do the Chinese now want, despite the large increase in income per capita, to return to more state regulation? Some of my co-authors and I[1] have tried to look at the evolution of distrust in different institutions over the 1990s and 2000s. The way we do it is just to have an interaction term between the fact of living in a transition economy and time dummies. You could do exactly the same exercise for China, by distinguishing different regions and how happiness and social cohesion have evolved over time. What we find, with regard to the evolution of the perception of policy recommendations and whether the government should regulate business, is that if one lives in a transition economy in 2000, rather than in an OECD country, there is an increase in the demand for state regulation and in the belief that competition is harmful and the government should run business. I would be curious to learn whether this kind of pattern also applies in China.

I will conclude by wondering to what extent the evolution of happiness might be linked to a number of other changes. A lot of things went on during this period in China, especially regarding the evolution of politics, legal enforcement, and corruption. Focusing on unemployment and the social safety net is part of the answer, but I wonder whether the political and institutional environment also matters. The second question is how to differentiate between different potential explanations, especially the "Good Old Days" narrative? Older people were used to having the Socialists ruling the country, and having permanent jobs; they may have lost a lot during the transition, whereas the young generation might appreciate the new situation more, and hence report higher life satisfaction. I wonder whether it would be possible to look at the specific changes in happiness by age group.

General Discussion

Martin Ravallion expressed his worry that these surveys are largely urban and there is a gap in living standards between rural and urban

[1] Aghion P, Algan Y, Cahuc P, Shleifer A. (2010). "Regulation and Distrust." *Quarterly Journal of Economics*, 125, 1015–49.

areas, which is particularly large in China—indeed, bigger than in other developing countries—and which is fairly persistent over time. He also wondered about the future consequences of China's massive urbanization. As individuals migrate from rural to urban areas, average life satisfaction could fall in the cities, and this could happen even though average life satisfaction in the country as a whole is rising. Claudia Senik noted that it is not surprising to see life satisfaction following a U-shape over time during transition, as people experience hardship and unemployment. The question is rather whether the second end of the U is going to be higher than the first end of the U: Is it an unbalanced U or will it, as is usual, lead to a completely flat long-run trend? For certain transition countries, we have longer time series which suggest that the level of life satisfaction is higher now than it was at the beginning of transition.

Richard Easterlin answered that he was grateful for the valuable comments, both from the discussant and from other participants. A number of these are useful suggestions for further research.

The initial purpose of his chapter was to establish the nature of the change in life satisfaction in China and its presumptive causes, and the foregoing substantive comments on the chapter itself relate to the validity of the findings on each of these. Thanks to these comments he has expanded the chapter, drawing on previous work, to present a fuller comparison of the experience of both the European transition countries and China. When this is done, the commonalities are striking with regard to both the U-shaped pattern of change and its causes, the chief concerns of the discussion.

Some analysts find happiness and income rising together in the transition, and thereby conclude that the transition has resulted in higher levels of happiness. Richard Easterlin points out in the chapter that this inference is the result of the fact that the initial life satisfaction observations for a number of European transition countries occur at dates after the transition has begun and the economy has collapsed in the process of economic restructuring. The collapse of the economy is readily demonstrated by examining the course of GDP prior to the initial life satisfaction observation, as in Figure 1.3. Hence, the initial life satisfaction observations in such countries cannot be taken as representative of the state of SWB under socialism.

When one considers the experience of the few countries with evidence on the nature of life satisfaction at or before the beginning of the transition, the U-shaped movement of life satisfaction becomes clear. Also striking is the similarity in the nature of workers' employment and safety net conditions under socialism, and how for many workers—especially those of lower socioeconomic status—these conditions changed markedly for the worse in the course of the transition.

It is also evident that the question of whether the transition to freer markets has raised life satisfaction to levels higher than those under socialism is uncertain. This uncertainty about the comparative before-and-after levels of life satisfaction is true even for China, despite its remarkable growth of incomes and output from very low initial levels. This conclusion may not be to the liking of some economists, but it has a major policy implication: namely, the fundamental importance for SWB of policies directed toward full employment and the creation of a social safety net, not just raising GDP per capita.

Appendix

Table 1.A1. Index of real GDP per capita, East Germany, Russia, and China, 1989–2009

Year	East Germany	Russian Federation	China
1989	100.0		100.0
1990	84.5	100.0	101.8
1991	68.3	103.5	106.3
1992	73.3	82.9	114.3
1993	80.1	73.9	123.4
1994	87.9	65.8	135.3
1995	91.9	63.1	154.8
1996	94.9	60.7	159.1
1997	96.7	61.4	168.7
1998	97.7	57.8	168.8
1999	99.0	60.3	174.0
2000	100.0	66.7	183.7
2001	99.9	70.9	194.4
2002	100.0	75.1	216.3
2003	99.8	81.1	237.0
2004	100.8	88.6	263.5
2005	101.6	95.9	294.0
2006	104.9	102.0	330.7
2007	108.1	110.9	372.2
2008	109.5	117.2	394.2
2009	104.4	111.9	418.7

Sources: East Germany: 1989–2002. Economic Commission for Europe 2003–09. Value for 2002 extrapolated via series for all Germany in Penn World Table. Russian Federation and China: Penn World Table.

Table 1.A2. Mean life satisfaction, China 1990–2010

Year	WVS (scale 1–10)	Horizon Research (scale 1–5)
1990	7.29	
1995	6.83	
1997		3.69[a]
1998		3.48[a]
1999		3.44[a]
2000		3.27
2001	6.53	3.28[a]
2002		3.33
2003		3.26
2004		3.38
2005		3.28
2006		3.52
2007	6.76	3.35
2008		3.51
2009		3.47
2010		3.41

[a]1–4 scale, mean computed from 5, 4, 2, 1 coding.

Source: Easterlin et al. 2012, Table S1.

Table 1.A3. Mean life satisfaction, Russia, Tambov, and Belarus, specified dates

Year	Russia	Tambov	Belarus
1981		7.26	
1984			7.20
1988	6.46		
1990	5.37		5.52
1993	5.05		
1995	4.45	4.23	
1996			4.35
1998	4.74		
1999			4.81
2005	6.09		

Source: Easterlin 2010, pp. 101, 105, 109.

Table 1.A4. Mean life satisfaction, East Germany and Hungary, 1982–2009

Year	East Germany	Hungary
1982		6.93
1990	6.57	6.03
1991	6.06	
1992	6.10	
1993	6.21	
1994	6.28	
1995	6.41	
1996	6.42	
1997	6.35	
1998	6.50	5.78
1999	6.55	
2000	6.48	
2001	6.48	
2002	6.28	
2003	6.33	
2004	6.13	
2005	6.34	6.30
2006	6.26	
2007	6.39	
2008	6.54	
2009	6.47	

Source: Easterlin 2010, pp. 104, 109, 110, updated to 2009 from GSOEP (Haisken-De New and Frick 2005).

Table 1.A5. Life satisfaction of upper, middle, and lower thirds of income distribution, 1990 and 2006–7

	China		Russia		East Germany	
Income third	1990	2007	1990	2006	1990	2006
Upper	68	71	34	60	66	71
Middle	72	58	32	46	60	62
Lower	65	42	29	35	52	43

Source: 1990 Inglehart et al. 1998; 2006–7 World Values Survey 2008.

Table 1.A6. Unemployment rate, East Germany, Russia, and China, specified dates

Year	East Germany		Russian Federation		China
	ILO	Federal Stat. Office	Registered	Total	
1988					0.4
1990	0				
1991	10.3		0.1		
1992	14.8		0.8		
1993	15.8		5.7		
1994	16	14.8	7.5		
1995		13.9	8.9		3.4
1996		15.5	9.9		
1997		17.7	11.3		
1998		17.8	13.3	13.3	
1999		17.3		12.6	
2000		17.1		9.8	
2001		17.3		8.9	
2002		17.7		7.9	11.5
2003		18.5		8	
2004		18.4		7.8	
2005		18.7		7.2	
2006		17.3		7.2	
2007		15		6.1	7.9
2008		13.1		6.3	
2009		13		8.2	
2010		12			

Sources: East Germany: 1990, GSOEP (Haisken-DeNew and Frick, 2005); 1991–4, ILO, Labor Statistics Database (Registered Unemployment); 1994–2009, Federal Statistical Office of Germany. Russian Federation: ILO, Labor Statistics Database, except 2009, World Development Indicators. China: Knight and Xue, 2006, extended to 2007 via email from Knight to author.

Table 1.A7. Self-reported health of the upper, middle, and lower thirds of the income distribution, China and Russia, specified dates (percentage good or very good)

	China		Russia	
	1990	2007	1990	2007
1. Upper	58	72	32	53
2. Middle	57	60	23	41
3. Lower	54	44	23	25
(1)–(3)	4	28	9	27

Source: See Table 1.A5.

Table 1.A8. Financial satisfaction of the upper, middle, and lower thirds of the income distribution, specified dates (percentage reporting 7–10 on a 1–10 scale)

	China		Russia	
	1990	2007	1990	2007
1. Upper	52	62	33	38
2. Middle	47	45	28	23
3. Lower	42	27	19	12
(1–3)	10	35	14	26

Source: See Table 1.A5.

2

The Great Happiness Moderation: Well-being Inequality during Episodes of Income Growth*

Andrew E. Clark, Sarah Flèche, and Claudia Senik

2.1 Introduction

What should the populations of developing countries expect from income growth and development? Easterlin and various co-authors have shown that, paradoxically, average happiness does not increase over the long run during episodes of sustained growth (see Easterlin, 1995, 2003, 2005a, and 2005b, Easterlin and Angelescu, 2009 and 2010, Easterlin and Sawangfa, 2010, and Easterlin and Zimmerman, 2006). But what about the distribution of happiness? Can individuals at least count on the social harmonization of well-being?

The current chapter does not address changes in average happiness, and takes for granted the stylized fact that constitutes the Easterlin

* We thank CEPREMAP for financial support. We are grateful to participants in the PSE-CEPREMAP -DIMeco Conference on "Happiness and Economic Growth", Paris, March 9, 2012, and in particular Paul Seabright, and participants at the FUNDP Namur Economics Seminar, May 29, 2012. The BHPS data were made available through the ESRC Data Archive. The data were originally collected by the ESRC Research Centre on Micro-social Change at the University of Essex. The German data used in this chapter were made available by the German Socio-Economic Panel Study (SOEP) at the German Institute for Economic Research (DIW), Berlin: see Wagner et al. (2007). The Household, Income and Labour Dynamics in Australia (HILDA) Survey was initiated and is funded by the Australian Government Department of Families, Housing, Community Services and Indigenous Affairs (FaHCSIA), and is managed by the Melbourne Institute of Applied Economic and Social Research (Melbourne Institute). Neither the original collectors of the data nor the archives bear any responsibility for the analyses or interpretations presented here.

paradox (the flatness of happiness curves over the long run). Instead, and in contrast to most of the related literature, it appeals to the individual dimension of many of the available data sets to analyze the evolution of the distribution of happiness over time. Whereas Easterlin considered the first moment of happiness over time, we want to look here at the second moment.

From a policy point of view, the distribution of happiness across individuals is an indicator of interest, although a purely utilitarian objective would only aim to maximize total happiness. First, for risk-averse agents, happiness inequality is a bad, and behind the veil of ignorance they would certainly choose a society where happiness is more evenly distributed. Second, what egalitarian policies ultimately try to harmonize is the welfare of their citizens, not just their incomes, where the latter is just a proxy for the former. De facto, a number of authors have questioned the relevance of income inequality as measure of social inequality: Veenhoven (2005*b*), for example, advocates the measurement of inequality in longevity and happiness instead of income. Non-egalitarian governments may also try to equalize happiness because of the risk of social tension and unrest resulting from inequality in well-being. In a political economy framework, discontent theories (Tullock, 1971; Gurr, 1994) hypothesize that the expected gains from (and hence the likelihood of) rebellion are approximated by the happiness gap between the most and the least well-off. Our first objective is thus to see whether development policies bring the promise of reduced happiness gaps in this sense. Note that the variation in happiness within countries is typically twice as high as that across countries. For instance, in the World Values Survey (1981 to 2008), the average standard deviation in life satisfaction (on a ten-point scale) in a cross-section is 2.14, but only 1.01 across countries. Hence, reducing within-country inequality is a valid objective.

The second motivation for this research is to contribute to our understanding of the Easterlin paradox. There are a number of explanations of the stability of average happiness over time. The first points to the concavity of the happiness function in income, so that rising income inequality mechanically reduces the mean level of happiness (Stevenson and Wolfers, 2008*a*, 2010, 2011). There are also more "behavioral" hypotheses, proposed by Easterlin himself, among which the most prominent are social comparisons and adaptation. Finally, because happiness is rated on a bounded scale, there is potential "rescaling," in that individuals change their interpretation of the steps of the happiness scale as their income increases. All of these hypotheses are potentially consistent with a flat average happiness profile over time; however, it is not clear that they can also explain the changing distribution of happiness over time.

We here examine countries that have experienced continuous income growth over an extended period of time, between 1970 and 2010, and whose happiness profile over time is flat. We show that there is an inverse relationship over time between GDP per capita and happiness inequality. This inverse relationship also holds in cross-section correlations: across the countries in the World Values Survey (1970–2008), greater income per capita is associated with smaller standard deviations in happiness. We also focus on developed countries for which we have long annual series on happiness from surveys: Australia (HILDA), Germany (SOEP), Great Britain (BHPS), and the United States (General Social Survey). These data confirm the fall in happiness variation over time (except in more recent years in the United States). This mean-preserving declining spread of happiness comes about via a fall in both the share of individuals who declare low and high happiness scores. To paraphrase Easterlin, our findings suggest that raising the incomes of all will not increase the happiness of all, but will reduce its variance, and hence the risk of extreme unhappiness.

This harmonization in well-being is not just a mirror of the evolution in income inequality in each country: on the contrary, income inequality has risen during the period under consideration. These two opposite forces seem to coexist up to a certain point. In the United States in the 1990s, when income inequality became too large, it overcame the downward trend in happiness dispersion. In the meantime, over this period, happiness gaps between certain categories of the population (by gender, by marital status) tended to fall, as did within-group happiness inequality in general.

With respect to the various theories proposed to explain the Easterlin paradox, we find that social comparisons and simple time-dependent adaptation do not suffice to account for happiness moderation. In order to do so, it is necessary to consider more subtle concepts of adaptation (*à la* Maslow for instance) or rescaling effects. The homogenizing influence of the public good externalities of modern growth may also play a role.

2.1.1 *Existing Literature*

Some existing work has previously noted a drop in happiness inequality in developed countries over the past decade. Veenhoven (2005*b*) found, in spite of increasing income inequality, falling happiness inequality in EU countries (surveyed in the EuroBarometer) between 1973 and 2001. He also noted that the dispersion in happiness is smaller in "modern nations" than in traditional countries. Other work has documented a decline in happiness inequality in the United States and Germany from the 1970s to the 1990s, with a rebound in the 1990s. This work includes Stevenson and Wolfers (2008*b*), Ovaska and Takashima (2010), Dutta and Foster (2013) and Becchetti et al. (2011).

Stevenson and Wolfers (2008*b*) and Dutta and Foster (2013) both appeal to data from the General Social Survey in order to consider the evolution in and decomposition of happiness inequality in the United States. The former analyze the evolution of happiness inequality between 1972 and 2006. They find a 21 percent fall in happiness inequality from the 1970s to the 1990s, about one-third of which is reversed in the subsequent decade. They also decompose the evolution in happiness inequality, and show that the happiness gap between men and women has vanished and that two-thirds of the black–white happiness gap has disappeared. In parallel, education and age gaps widened between 1972 and 2006. Generally, within-group inequality declined substantially up to the 1990's, but grew thereafter. The parallel increase in income inequality is not reflected in happiness inequality. Stevenson and Wolfers suggest that "the real reason for today's lower level of happiness inequality is to be found in a pervasive decline in within-group inequality experienced by even narrowly defined demographic groups" (Stevenson and Wolfers, 2008*b*, p. S34). The role of non-pecuniary factors in shaping the well-being distribution is underlined: these include the institutional and technological changes (e.g. anti-discrimination and affirmative action, divorce laws, and birth control) that have increased the autonomy and freedom of choice of individuals, and increased opportunities for minorities. Dutta and Foster (2013) focus on the methodological aspects of measuring changing inequality in happiness, which is an ordinal variable. They apply a median-centered approach developed in a former paper and decompose happiness inequality across gender, race, and religion. Their findings are close to those of Stevenson and Wolfers, apart for their conclusion that "the progress made in the 1990s in reducing happiness inequality has been wiped out in the 2000s" (p. 6).

Becchetti et al. (2011) decompose the trend in happiness inequality in Germany (both East and West) from 1991 to 2007, using the

SOEP. They use RIF regressions[1] and decompose the variance of happiness between two periods (1991–3 and 2005–7). One of their main findings is that of no change in the coefficients: the returns to the drivers of happiness inequality do not vary over time. They also find that income inequality is not the main source of happiness inequality. Finally, they suggest that the main determinant of happiness inequality is the variance within categories of education (within variance is lower in higher education, and the weight of the higher-educated has increased over time). The common finding in this literature is the great importance of within-category variance and the lack of a relationship between income inequality and happiness inequality.

Other papers have looked at changing happiness inequality across countries, instead of over time. Ovaska and Takashima (2010) ran aggregate regressions of happiness inequality on socioeconomic controls and income distribution, as well as measures of economic and political freedom taken from the Fraser Institute and Freedom House. They identify income inequality, health inequality, and the poor quality of institutions as the main correlates of happiness inequality within countries. Ott (2010) also maps institutions to happiness inequality across a set of 131 countries in 2006.

In this chapter, we use data from the World Values Survey; the German panel (SOEP), although over a longer period than Becchetti et al. (2011); the American General Social Survey (GSS); the British Household Panel Survey (BHPS); and the Australian HILDA. We analyze the evolution of happiness inequality, defined as the standard deviation of happiness over its mean. We find, as in previous work, that changing income inequality does not predict happiness inequality. We uncover a general fall in the spread of happiness in all of the countries under consideration, although in Germany and the United States this trend breaks in the 1990s. Although Becchetti et al. (2011) document a rise in happiness inequality in Germany between 1991 and 2007, we take a longer view and obtain a different picture, whereby happiness inequality fell sharply in the 1980s and then fluctuated around a flat trend in the 1990s.

[1] Recentered Influence Function (RIF) regressions are a generalization of the Oaxaca-Blinder (Blinder, 1973, and Oaxaca, 1973) procedure to other distributional parameters beyond the mean. They allow the total change in happiness inequality to be split into the change in the distribution of happiness determinants (composition effects) and the change in the return to these determinants (coefficients). They can also detail the contribution of each determinant.

The main interest of this chapter is the distribution of happiness, not the distribution of income. A considerable number of papers have discussed the relationship between income inequality and happiness; most have discovered a negative association, although there is no consensus on the strength of this link (see Clark et al., 2008, and Senik, 2009, for surveys). Other papers in the happiness literature have documented the negative correlation between macroeconomic volatility and happiness over time (Wolfers, 2003; Di Tella et al., 2003). Finally, macroeconomists have underlined a "great moderation" in the volatility of the business cycle, starting in the 1980s (Stock and Watson, 2002; Gali and Gambetti, 2009). Although this is a different issue, macroeconomic volatility could be related to happiness inequality if income inequality is compounded by inequality in income volatility, i.e. if health, unemployment and retirement risks are concentrated in poorer households (as noted by Stevenson and Wolfers, 2008*a*).

2.2 Data and Methods

2.2.1 *A Cardinal Measure of Happiness Inequality*

We measure happiness inequality as the standard deviation in self-declared happiness by respondents in a certain country in a given year. In order to avoid any scale-dependence, we divide this by the mean value of happiness in the same country-year (the two measures are homogenous).[2] Self-declared happiness is a choice on a given scale: equality pertains when all respondents choose the same answer. Flat distributions are more unequal than those with concentration towards the top; wide flat distributions are more unequal than narrower flat ones; and multimodal distributions are more unequal than unimodal ones (see Kalmijn and Veenhoven, 2005). Standard deviation is consistent with these properties, as it captures the notion of inequality in the sense of dispersion.

Of course, calculating the standard deviation (and the mean) of happiness implies treating the variable as a continuous cardinal measure,

[2] We can refer to the general discussion by Kalmijn and Veenhoven (2005) over the adequate measure of happiness inequality. The authors conclude to the superiority of the standard deviation. They point out that the Gini index of inequality is not appropriate for happiness. Indeed, the Gini measures the share of total income that is not distributed equally, but happiness is an intensity variable, not a capacity variable: it cannot be appropriated entirely by one person or distributed flexibly amongst individuals. The same is true of Theil's index of inequality. They also discuss the drawbacks of the inter-quartile range or the proportion outside the mode.

with equidistant steps. This is incorrect, but common in the field (see van Praag, 1991, 2007; Ferrer-i-Carbonell and Frijters, 2004; van Praag and Ferrer-i-Carbonell, 2004, 2006). Van Praag (1991) has shown that respondents translate ordinal responses into a numerical scale. They may do so in a different way, but there is no reason to expect this heterogeneity to be correlated with the error term in the regression (Frey and Stutzer, 2002). Vignettes (Beegle et al., 2012) have shown that this is not correlated with happiness determinants, nor with the residual of the regressions. It has also been shown that the bias introduced by the continuity assumption is small when the scale contains a large number of categories or steps (Ferrer-i-Carbonell and Frijters, 2004), which is the case for all the data sets that we use, except the GSS (which contains only three).

Dutta and Foster (2013) criticize the treatment of ordinal happiness as cardinal as the level of inequality will depend on the chosen scale, and so will the ranking of various societies or groups in terms of happiness inequality. Deviations from the mean will not be order-preserving because the mean itself is not order-preserving under scale change. They instead propose scale-independent concepts that capture the concentration of the distribution around the median, as well as a mean-based inequality measure, which is the difference between the means in the upper and lower halves of the population.

Note that our findings are exactly identical to those in Dutta and Foster, and more generally to the papers cited previously, which use different dispersion measures. To be on the safe side, we also use the index of ordinal variation (IOV; see Berry and Mielke, 1992), a measure of polarization designed for ordinal measures, which describes the distribution of the population over a number of predetermined ordered categories and takes a value of zero when all observations fall into one category, and one in the case of extreme polarization. In order not to duplicate the tables, we just note the similarity of the two measures (the standard deviation and the IOV) for each year in each database (see Figures 2.A1–2.A2 in the Appendix).

2.2.2 *Data*

This chapter uses the five waves of the World Values Survey (WVS; 1981–2008),[3] covering 105 countries, including high-income, low-income, and transition countries (Table 2.A1). We select the time-series data that correspond to periods of positive income growth (60 countries).[4]

[3] These data sets are available at <http://worldvaluessurvey.org>.
[4] For a number of countries, we only have observations at one point in time.

Happiness measures were mostly taken from the WVS and the European Values Survey, but when happiness data was missing we include information from the ISSP and the 2002 Latinobarometer. We also analyze individual country surveys, such as the British Household Panel Survey (BHPS, 1996–2008, Table 2.A2), the German Socio-Economic Panel (SOEP, 1984–2009, Table 2.A3), the American General Social Survey (GSS, 1972–2010, Table 2.A4), and the Household, Income and Labour Dynamics in Australia survey (HILDA, 2001–2009, Table 2.A5). All figures and tables are based on weighted samples.

The Happiness and Life Satisfaction questions were administered in the same format across all these surveys but with different response scales: 1–3 in the GSS, 1–10 in the WVS, 0–10 in the SOEP and the Australian HILDA, 1–7 in the BHPS. The wording of the Life Satisfaction question in the WVS was "All things considered, how satisfied are you with your life as a whole these days?: 1 (dissatisfied)....10 (very satisfied)." In the SOEP, it was "How satisfied are you with your life, all things considered?": 0 (totally unsatisfied)... 10 (totally satisfied). The BHPS survey asked "How dissatisfied or satisfied are you with your life overall?": 1 (not satisfied at all)... 7 (completely satisfied)." The wording of the Happiness question in the GSS was "Taken all together, how would you say things are these days—would you say that you are very happy, pretty happy, or not too happy?." We do not need to harmonize these scales, as we consider the evolution of the variance of happiness over time within countries. The surveys cover representative samples of the population in participating countries, with an average sample size of 10–15,000 respondents in each wave. As is common, we select people aged between 18 and 65 years old; we also drop observations corresponding to a declared income of below $500 per year.

We use the American GSS because it is the only long-run survey containing a happiness or life satisfaction question in the United States. However, this data is not really suited to our purpose, as only three responses are possible (very happy, pretty happy, and not too happy), making the calculation of the variance problematic. However, as the evidence initially used to suggest the Easterlin paradox partly relied on American data, and because we would like to include data from the United States, we do report the results based on this data, although we consider them with some caution.

It is natural to try to relate the happiness spread to the distribution of household income within countries. Ideally, we would like to use net disposable income after tax and transfers, which is probably most closely related to (consumption and) well-being. A measure of annual net disposable combined income after receipt of public transfers (government pensions and benefits) and deduction of taxes is indeed available in the German and Australian data. This is not the case in the BHPS, where household income is measured as the sum of labor income, non-labor income, and pensions over all household members, in the previous year, but before taxes. Equally, the GSS contains a measure of "total family income," i.e. all types of income from all sources, for all members of the household, before taxes, in the previous year.

Finally, we use measures of GDP per capita taken from Heston, Summers, and Aten—the Penn World Table. We also use indicators, which are available in the World Databank, such as social expenditures, rule of law, voice and accountability, and control of corruption.[5] Voice and accountability measures the extent to which citizens are able to participate in the selection of their government, as well as freedom of expression, freedom of association, and free media. Rule of law describes the quality of contract enforcement, of the police, and of courts, as well as the likelihood of crime and violence. Control of corruption measures the extent to which public power is exercised for private gain.

2.3 Income Growth Creates a Mean-preserving Spread in Happiness

Before we turn to the relationship between income and happiness inequality over time, we briefly look at their cross-section correlation, taking the last available year for each country in the WVS. As noted in Veenhoven (2005*a*), Kalmijn and Veenhoven (2005), and Clark and Senik (2011), this cross-country analysis produces a striking result: richer countries have higher life satisfaction scores, but with lower standard deviations (Figure 2.1a). The typical relationship implies that a doubling of GDP per capita is associated with a 10 percent reduction in the spread of happiness.[6] A RIF regression[7] of the standard deviation of happiness on the log of GDP per capita, controlling for demographic variables and year fixed effects (Table 2.A7) confirms this visual impression. This negative gradient is moreover somewhat steeper in richer countries (where GDP per capita is over $8000) than in poorer countries, as illustrated in Figure 2.1b.

[5] <http://info.worldbank.org/governance/wgi/index.asp>.

[6] Figure 2.1.1 shows that the coefficient on log GDP per capita in a regression of the standard deviation over the mean is 0.049. As such, a doubling of GDP per capita changes the standard deviation by 0.049*ln(2)*mean happiness. This equals 0.23, as the mean value of happiness in the WVS is in the range of 6.7, and represents a ten percent fall in the standard deviation as this latter is in the range of 2.3.

[7] See Firpo et al. (2009) for a presentation of this method.

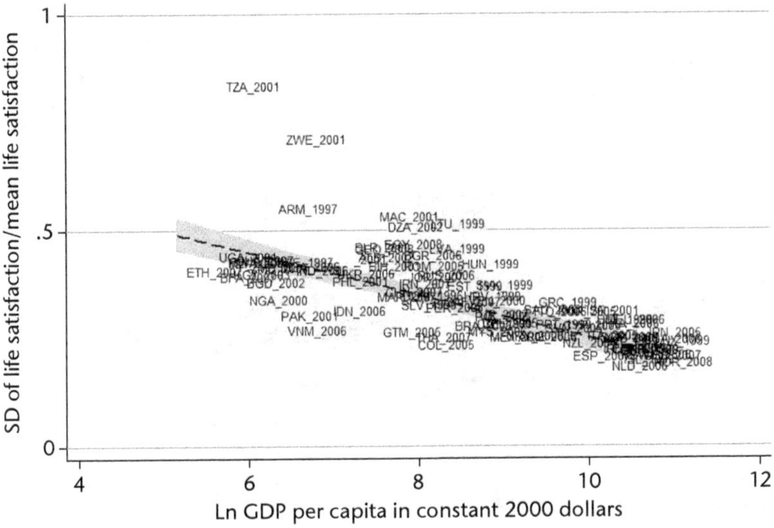

SD(Satisfaction)/mean satisfaction = –0.049** ln(GDP) + 0.74; R-squared = 0.4959

Figure 2.1a. Happiness inequality and GDP per capita, in WVS countries

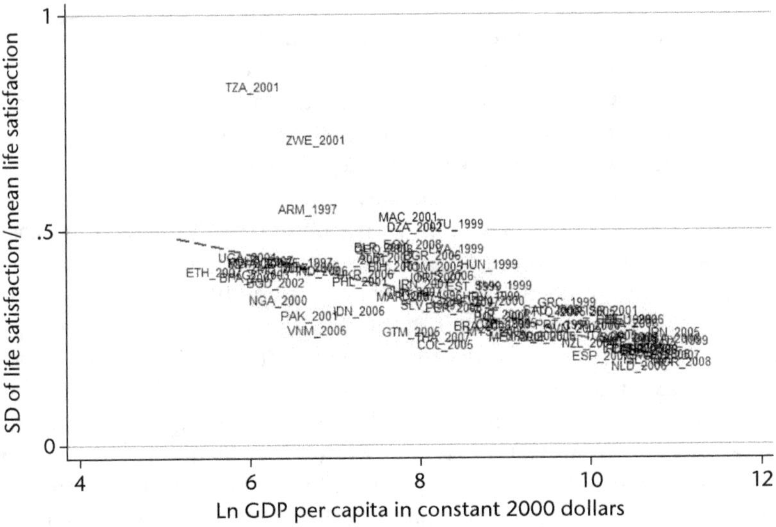

SD(Satisfaction)/mean satisfaction = –0.053** ln(GDP) + 0.78; R2 = 0.3885

SD(Satisfaction)/mean satisfaction = –0.045** ln(GDP) + 0.71; R2 = 0.2007

Figure 2.1b. Happiness inequality and GDP per capita across rich and poor countries

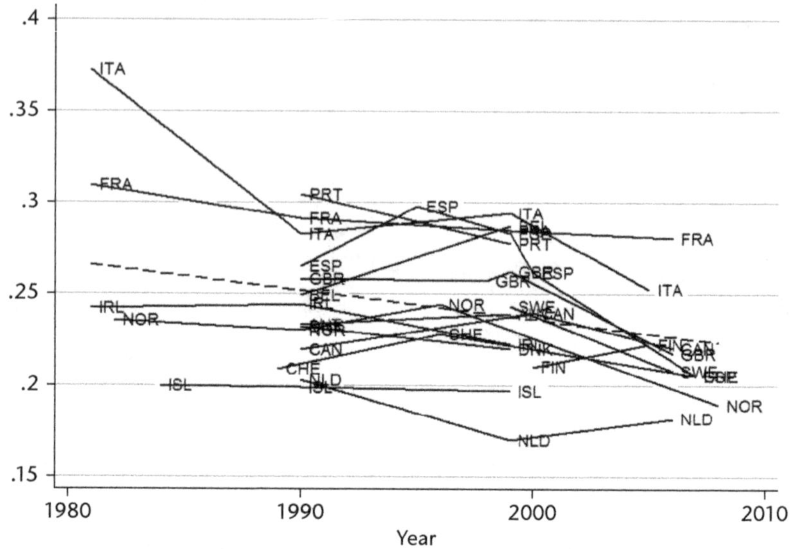

Figure 2.2. Happiness inequality over time, western countries (WVS)

2.3.1 *Time-series Evidence from the World Values Survey*

We now turn to the intertemporal relationship between GDP per capita and happiness inequality and start with the WVS, from which we retain countries that are observed at least twice, at least five years apart, and which experience strictly positive GDP growth in all of the intervening years. Figure 2.2 illustrates the downward trend in the level of happiness spread over time in western countries. Figures 2.3a and 2.3b show the change in the standard deviation in happiness over periods of at least five years of growth. Figure 2.3a illustrates the relationship between the long-run first-differences in income per capita and happiness inequality. Each point here refers to a country: the X axis corresponds to the change in GDP per capita between the two extreme dates of the growth period and the Y axis to the change in the standard deviation in happiness over the same period. The relationship is clearly negative: happiness inequality falls as per capita GDP increases over (at least five years of) time: a 10 percent increase in GDP per capita is estimated to reduce the standard deviation in happiness by 0.02 points, i.e. by about 1 percent of the typical standard deviation figure.[8] Figure 2.3b carries out the same analysis on the sub-sample of western developed countries.

[8] It will be lower by 0.043*ln(1.1)*mean happiness.

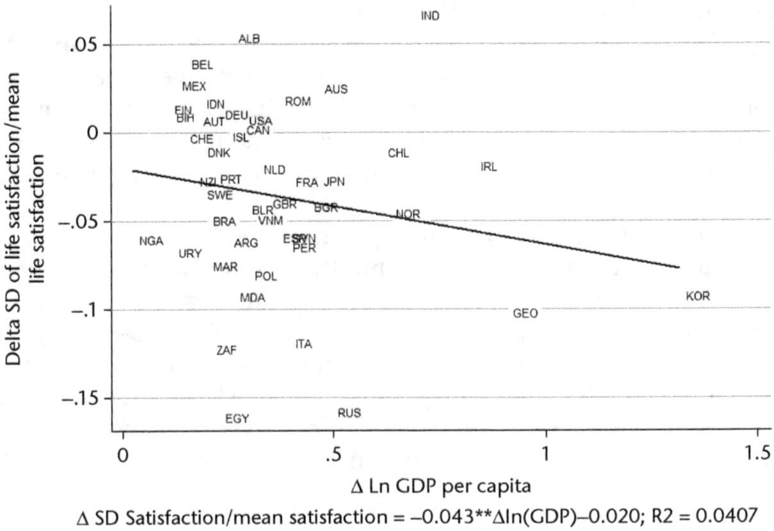

Figure 2.3a. Long-run changes in happiness inequality and GDP per capita

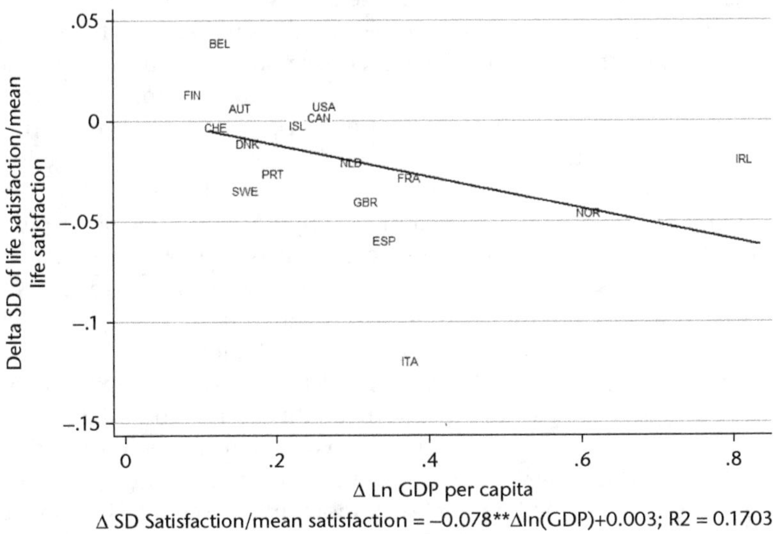

Figure 2.3b. Long-run changes in happiness inequality and GDP per capita, western countries

We run a RIF regression of the standard deviation of happiness on log GDP per capita, controlling for various demographic variables and country fixed effects. The results confirm the negative correlation between GDP per capita and the normalized standard deviation in happiness over time in WVS countries (column 1 in Table 2.A7). The estimated slope is similar to that from the regression line in Figure 2.3a.

Contrary to the relationship between average income and average happiness considered by Easterlin, there is here no contradiction between the cross-section and time-series results regarding the negative correlation between average income and happiness inequality.

The WVS shows that the fall in happiness inequality over time (at least five years) is sharper in western developed countries than in other countries. As such, we now focus on developed countries and turn to country-specific survey information.

2.3.2 *Individual Country Evidence*

Having considered the repeated cross-sections of the WVS, which contain few points in time and relatively few observations per cross-section, we now turn to country-specific surveys, which contain tens of thousands of observations each year, and are repeated almost every year. Figures 2.4 to 2.7 show two series of graphs for Great Britain, Germany, the US, and Australia. The first plots the change over time in average happiness, log GDP per capita, and average log household income (as declared in the household surveys), while the second plots the standard deviation of happiness and GDP per capita.

The average log of individual income curve, which is calculated from the surveys, is below that of GDP per capita for two reasons: first, surveys typically miss out the top incomes in a country (Atkinson et al., 2011); second, average log income will be lower than log average income if the income distribution is left-skewed. The gap between the two figures rises with income inequality. The two variables are plotted on the same graph as one of the questions in the literature is whether individual self-declared happiness is a function of log income (see Section 2.4.1). The graphs clearly show that the change in average happiness is different from that of mean log income.

Figures 2.4–2.7 are similar. We first note the Easterlin paradox: average happiness is flat over time despite income growth (either the log of the mean or the mean of the log). Second, the standard deviation in happiness falls over time. The only exceptions are Germany, where

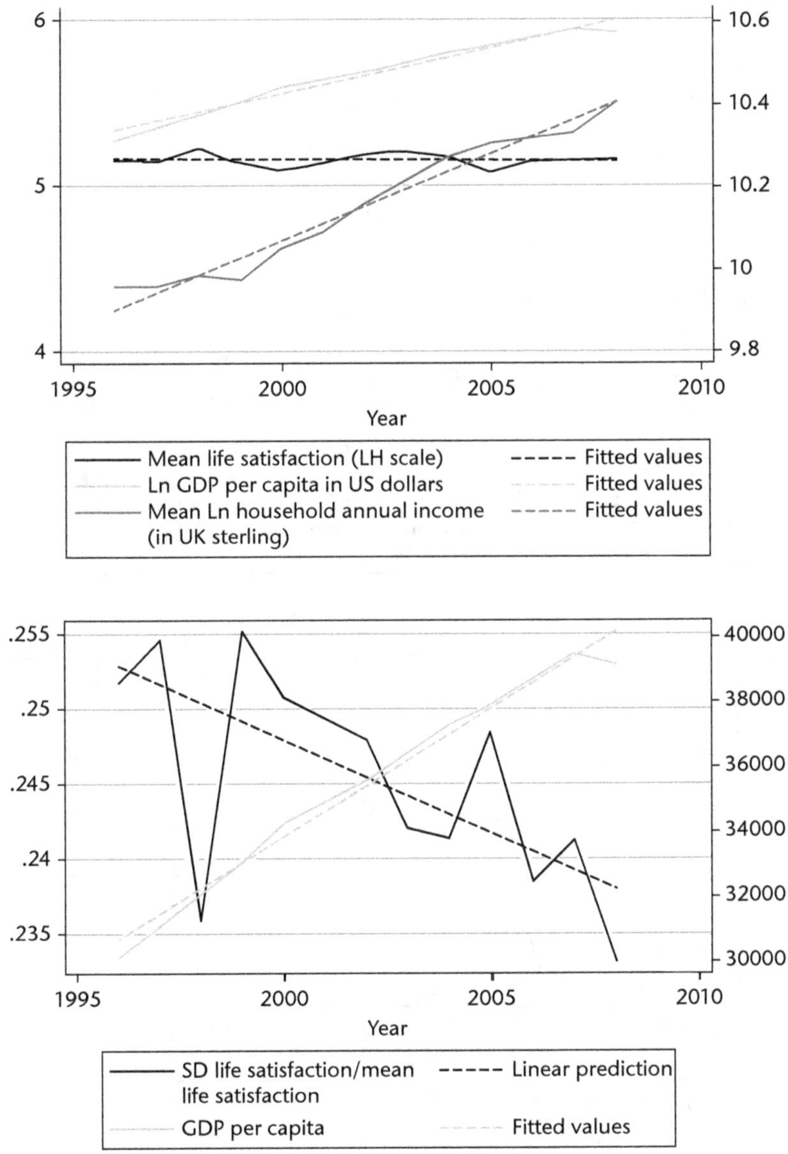

Figure 2.4. Trends in income growth, average happiness, and happiness inequality, Great Britain (BHPS)

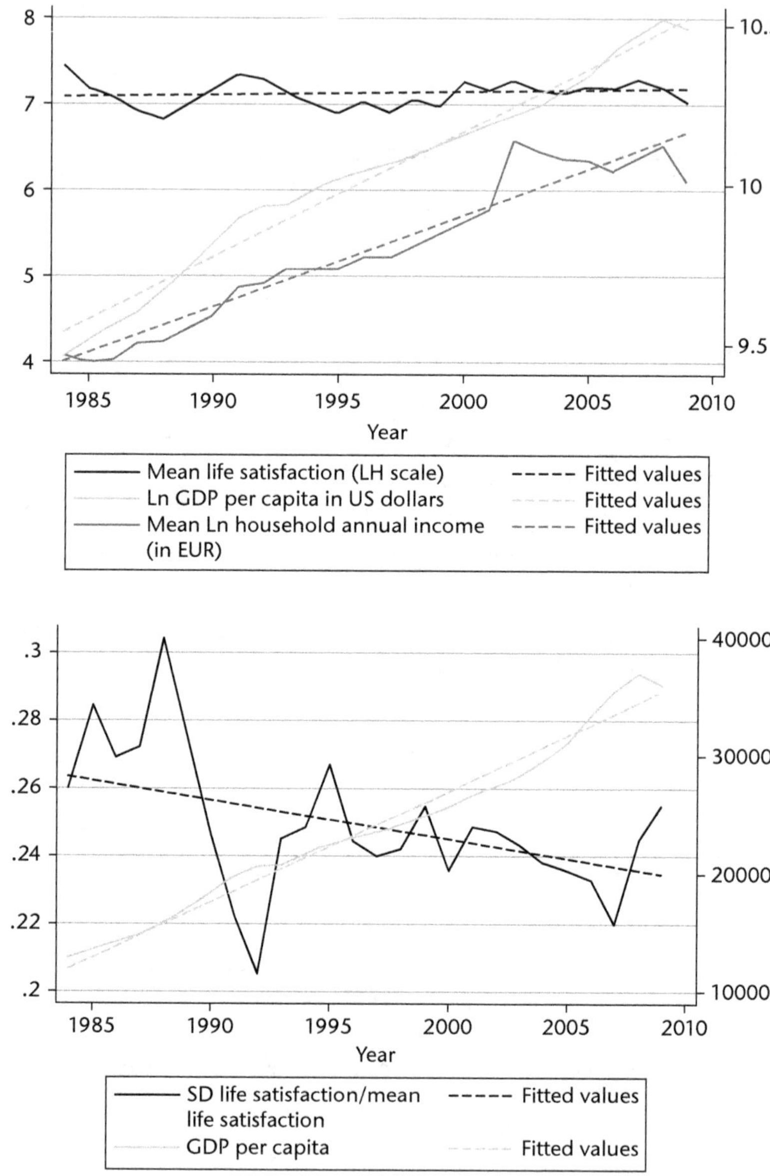

Figure 2.5. Trends in income growth, average happiness, and happiness inequality, Germany (SOEP)

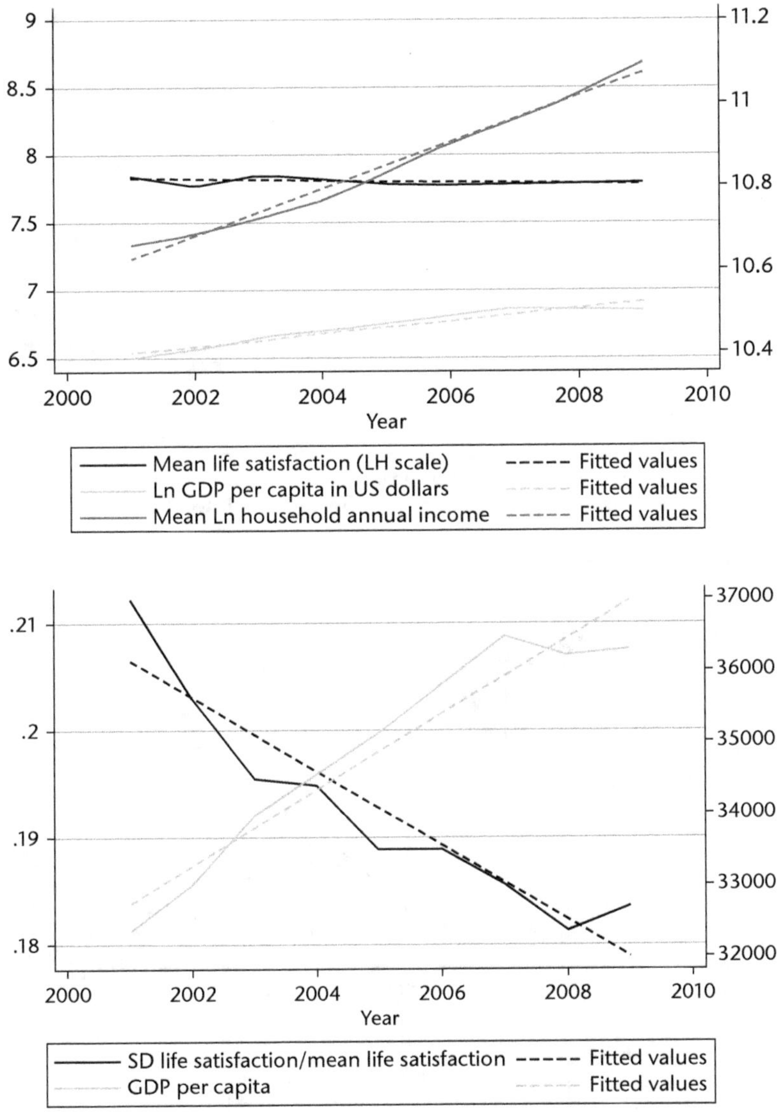

Figure 2.6. Trends in income growth, average happiness, and happiness inequality, Australia (HILDA)

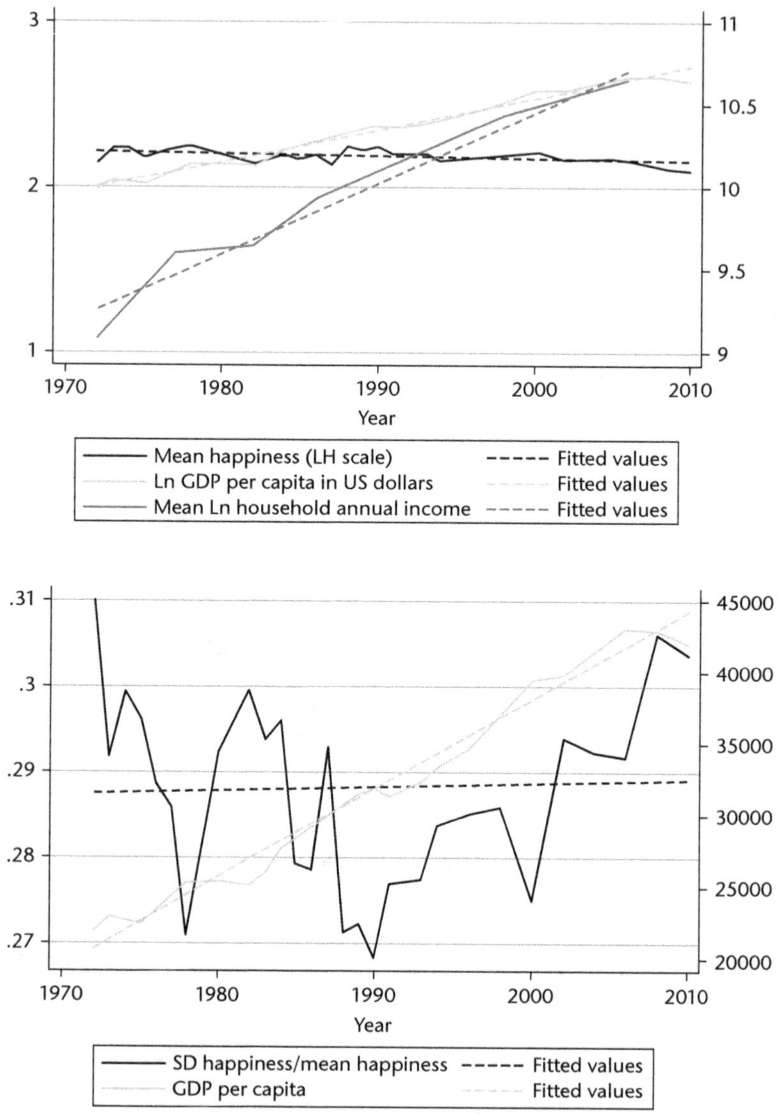

Figure 2.7. Trends in income growth, average happiness, and happiness inequality, United States (GSS)

the downward trend breaks in the 1990s, and the US, where the trend starts to rise again post-1990.

We can draw similar graphs for some of the developed countries in the WVS which meet three requirements: periods of positive income growth, information on points in time that are at least ten years apart, and a flat happiness trend. As shown in Figure 2.8, all of the countries that meet these criteria exhibit a downward trend in happiness inequality (France, Italy, Spain, the Netherlands, and Norway).

We should here underline that the negative relationship between the standard deviation in happiness and income per capita cannot be attributed to stochastic dependency or scale dependency. The latter would imply that in richer countries, where average happiness is higher, the standard deviation in happiness would also be higher. The negative correlation between average happiness and happiness dispersion should thus be interpreted as revealing an "intrinsic dependency" rather than a statistical one (in the words of Kalmijn and Veenhoven, 2005). On the other hand, Kalmijn and Veenhoven underline that on a bounded scale, maximal inequality pertains when the average value is at the middle of the scale, so that the maximum standard deviation is smaller for higher levels of average happiness. However, the actual measures of standard deviation that we obtain (in the range of 1.5–2.5) are below their maximum possible values (of around 7).

2.3.3 *Disappearing Extreme Happiness*

To fit our two stylized facts (a constant happiness trend with falling standard deviation), we expect a growing concentration of happiness over time. Figures 2.9–2.12 indeed reveal that over time the percentage declaring either very low or very high happiness shrinks, whereas the percentage in the middle rises. This is illustrated in both the histograms of self-declared happiness in the first and the last year of each survey, and by the change over time in the percentage of respondents choosing high, average, and low happiness scores. Both graphs reveal a distinct convergence to the mean over time in all of the countries under consideration.

We thus have three concomitant stylized facts for the recent period of growth, especially in developed western countries: (1) a rise in average income per capita; (2) flat average happiness; and (3) falling happiness inequality.

France

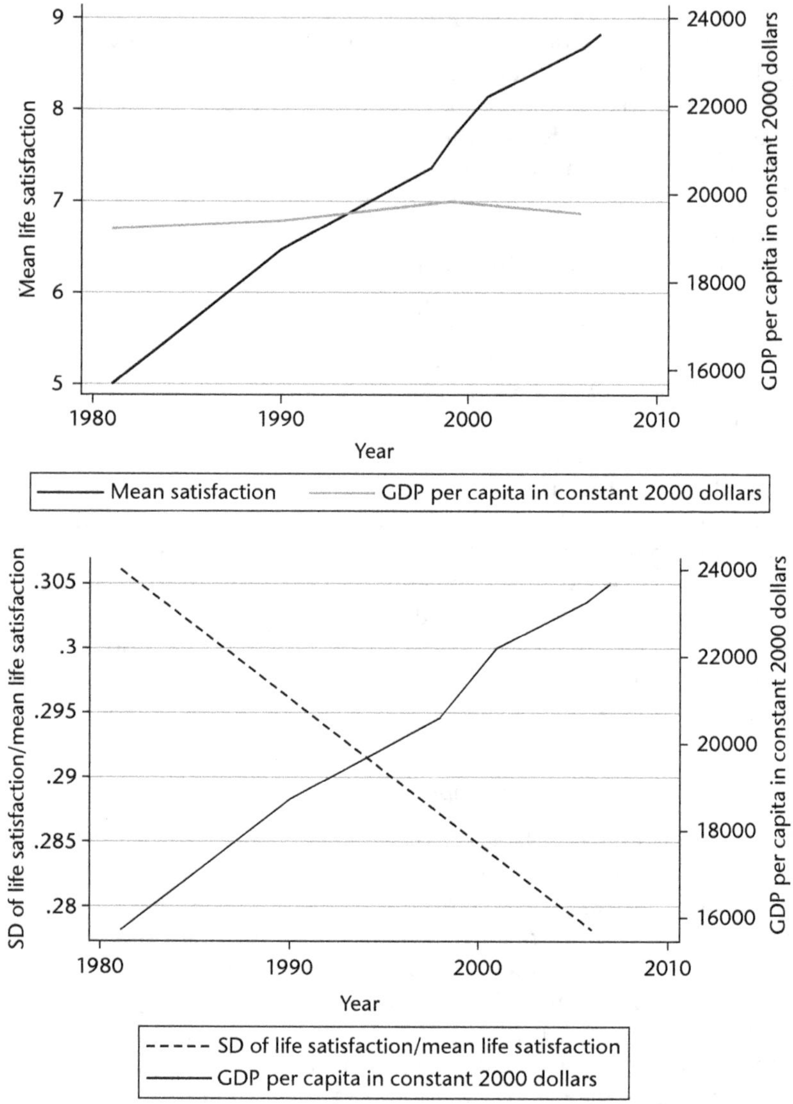

Figure 2.8. (*Continued*)

Italy

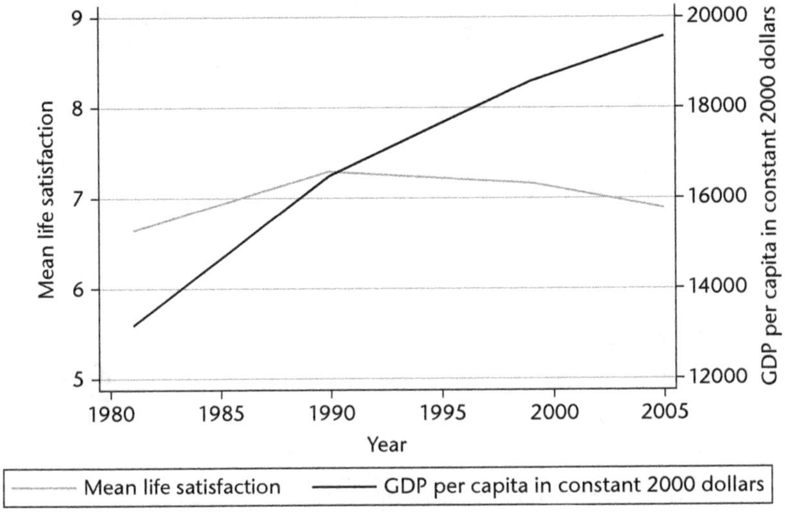

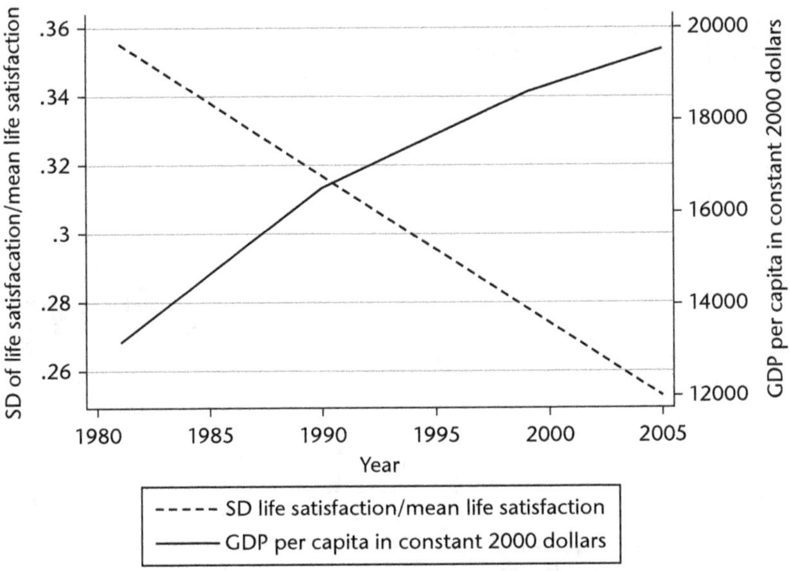

Figure 2.8. (*Continued*)

The Netherlands

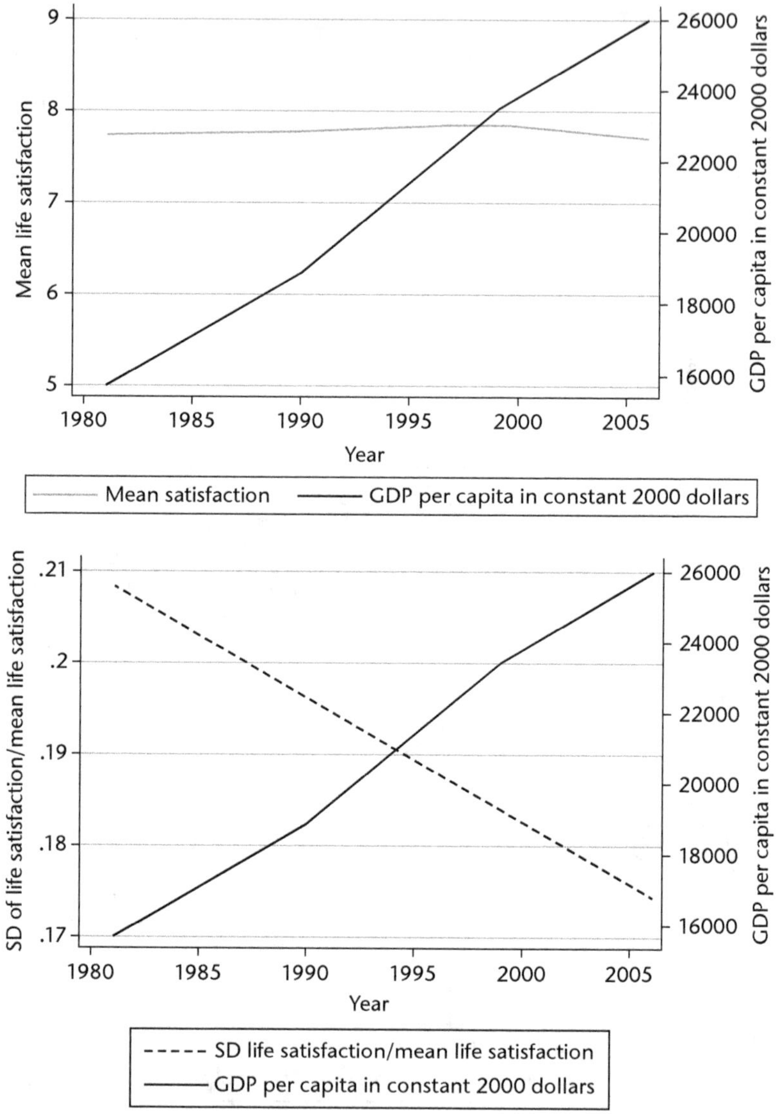

Figure 2.8. (*Continued*)

Norway

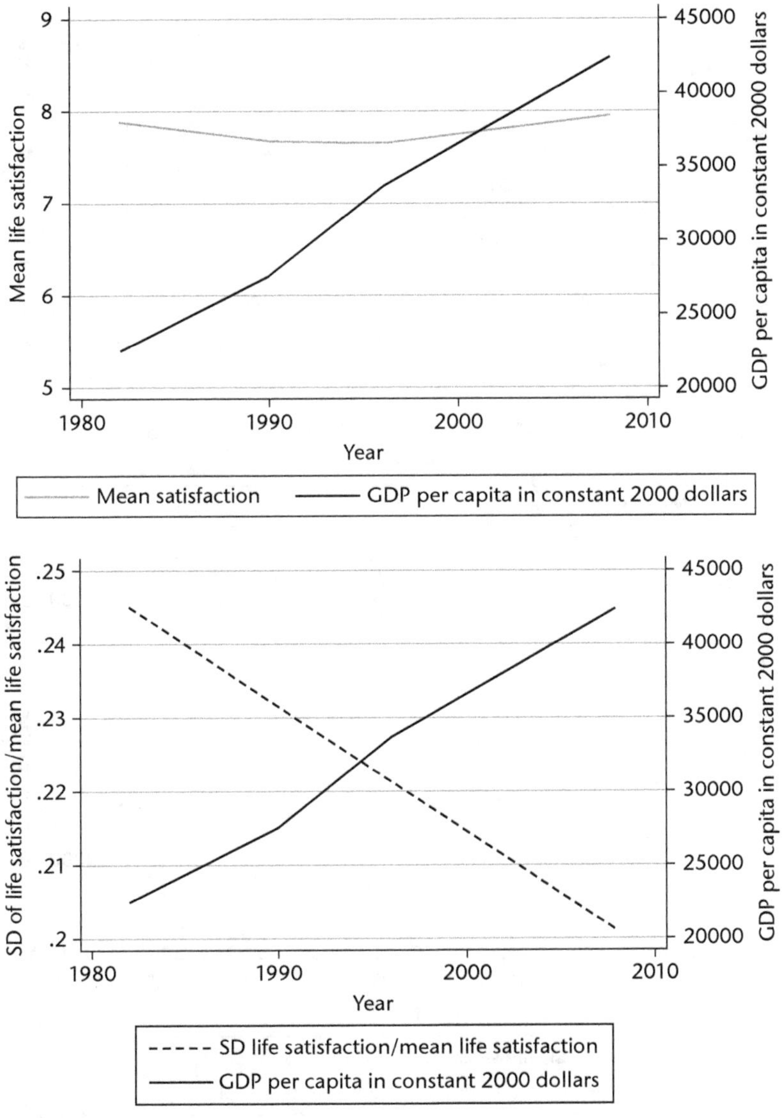

Figure 2.8. *(Continued)*

Spain

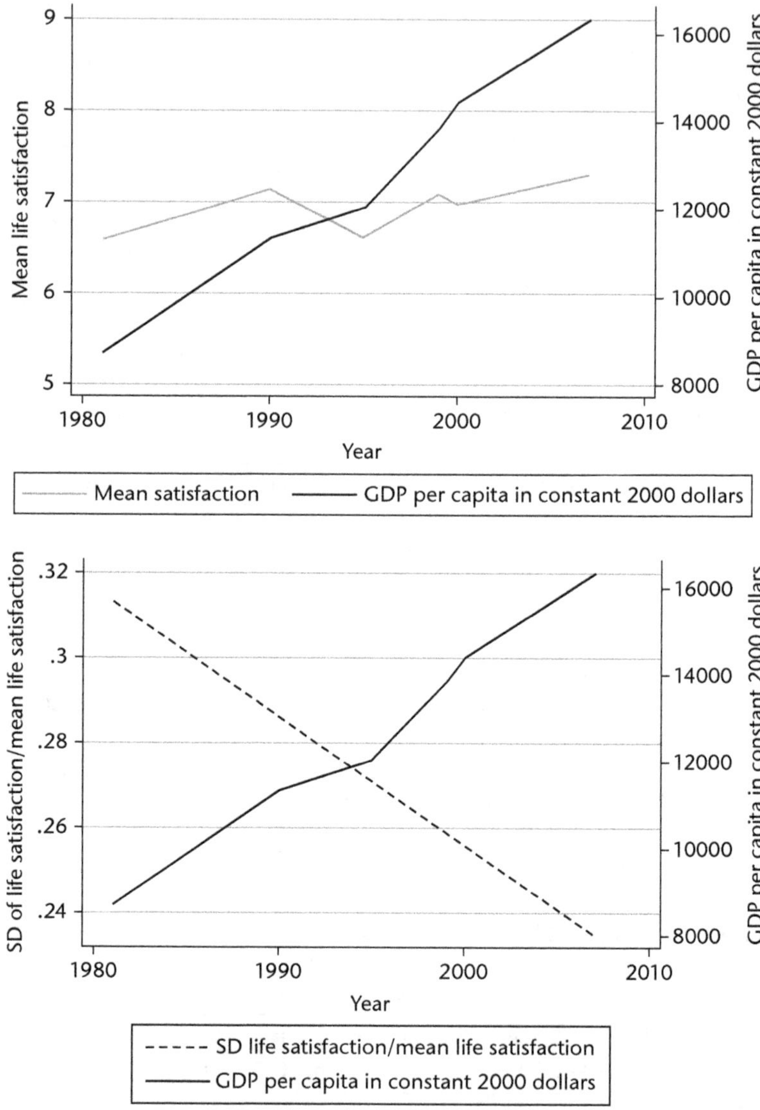

Figure 2.8. Trends in income growth, average happiness, and happiness inequality in other countries of the WVS trends

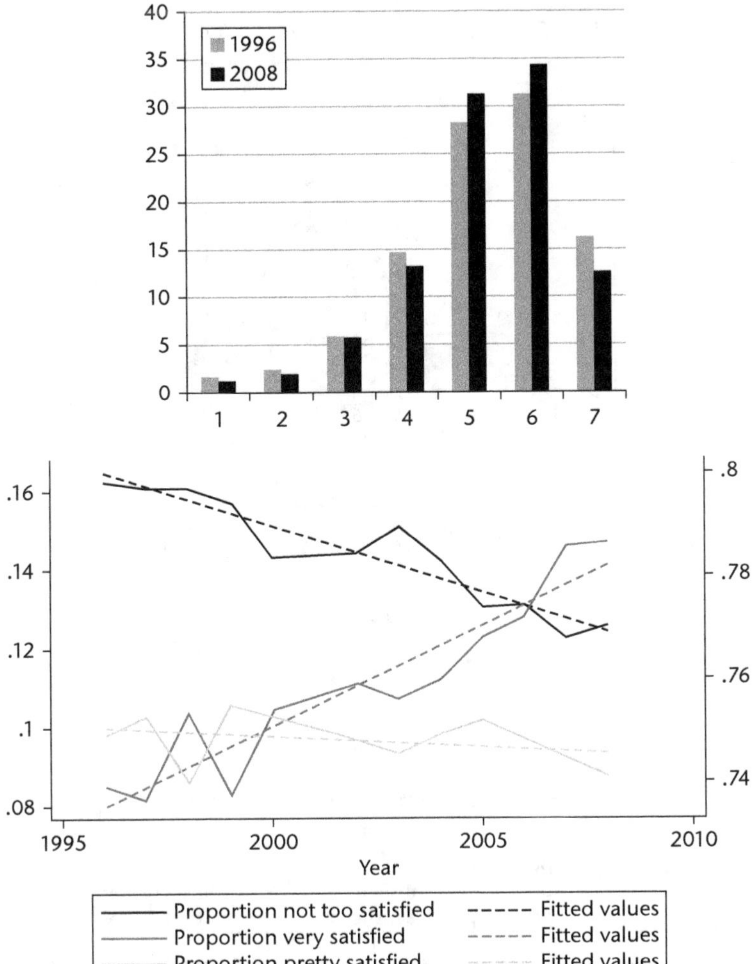

Note: Not too satisfied = 1–3; Pretty satisfied = 4–6; Very satisfied = 7.

Figure 2.9. Concentration of the happiness distribution: Great Britain (BHPS)

2.3.4 *The Role of Income Inequality*

Falling happiness inequality might be thought of as surprising, given that our time period is one of well-known rising income inequality, starting in the 1980s (Dustmann et al., 2008; Atkinson et al., 2011). If individual happiness depends on income, we should expect happiness inequality to have mirrored income inequality.

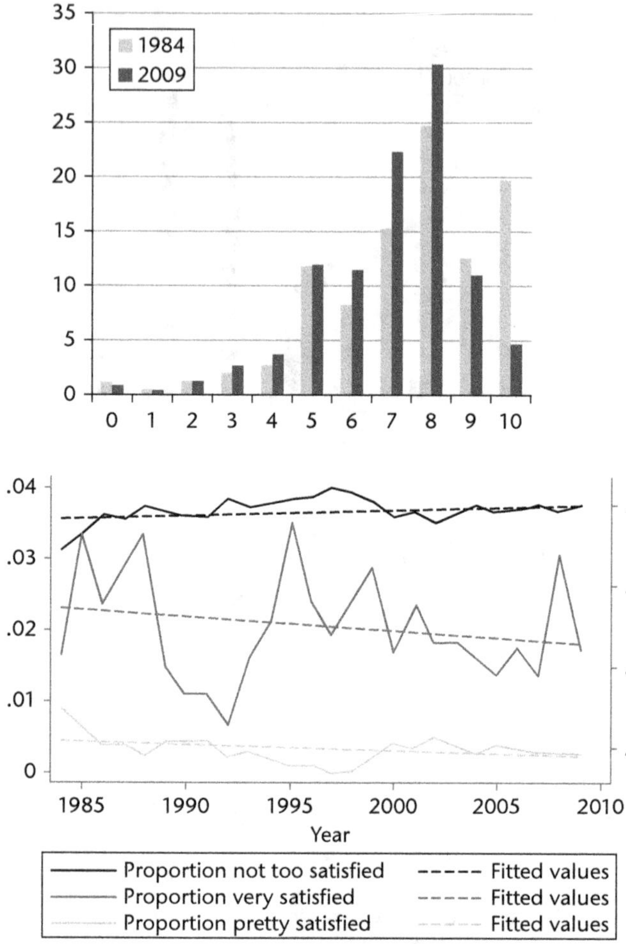

Note: Not too satisfied = 0–2; Pretty satisfied = 3–8; Very satisfied = 9–10.

Figure 2.10. Concentration of the happiness distribution: Germany (SOEP)

Figures 2.13–2.16 show the changes in the standard deviation of income and happiness in each country: income inequality follows an upward trend in all of our countries (whereas happiness inequality does not). In most countries here, the inequality in income between quintiles has risen, with the average income of the upper quintile increasing much more than that of the lower quintiles.[9] The income of

[9] See also Layard et al. (2010) for the United States.

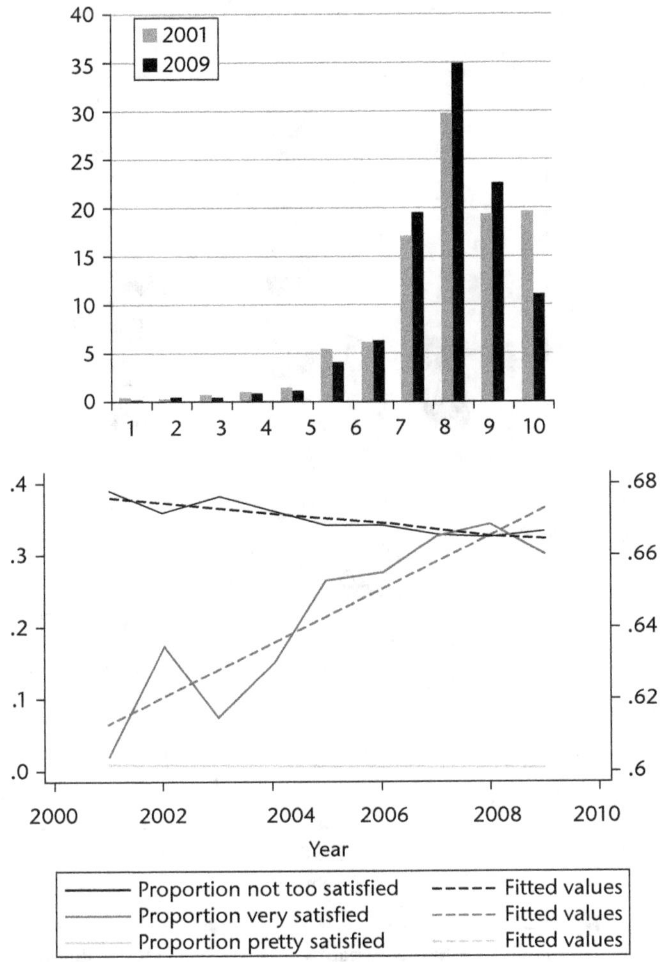

Note: Not too satisfied = 0–2; Pretty satisfied = 3–8; Very satisfied = 9–10.

Figure 2.11. Concentration of the happiness distribution: Australia (HILDA)

the bottom quintile has largely stagnated. However, when we plot the trends in happiness in the different income quintiles by country over time, we find no divergence in the happiness of the different quintiles. In the United States and Germany, between-group inequality in happiness initially fell (until 1990) but then grew again in Germany, due to the fall in the happiness of the poorest quintile. In the United States,

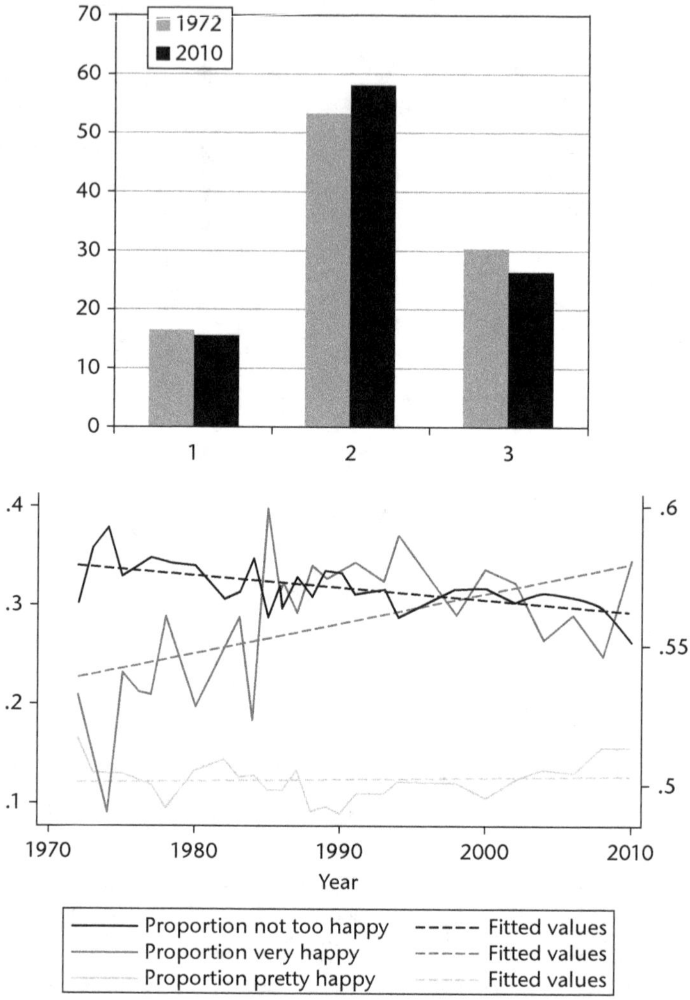

Figure 2.12. Concentration of the happiness distribution: USA (GSS)

there is a more general increasing inequality starting in the 1990s. In all of these countries, the within-quintile dispersion falls dramatically over time, although again within-group inequality increases after 1990 for the bottom quintile in Germany and the US. The general picture is hence one of increasing income inequality, which is however not matched by rising happiness inequality.

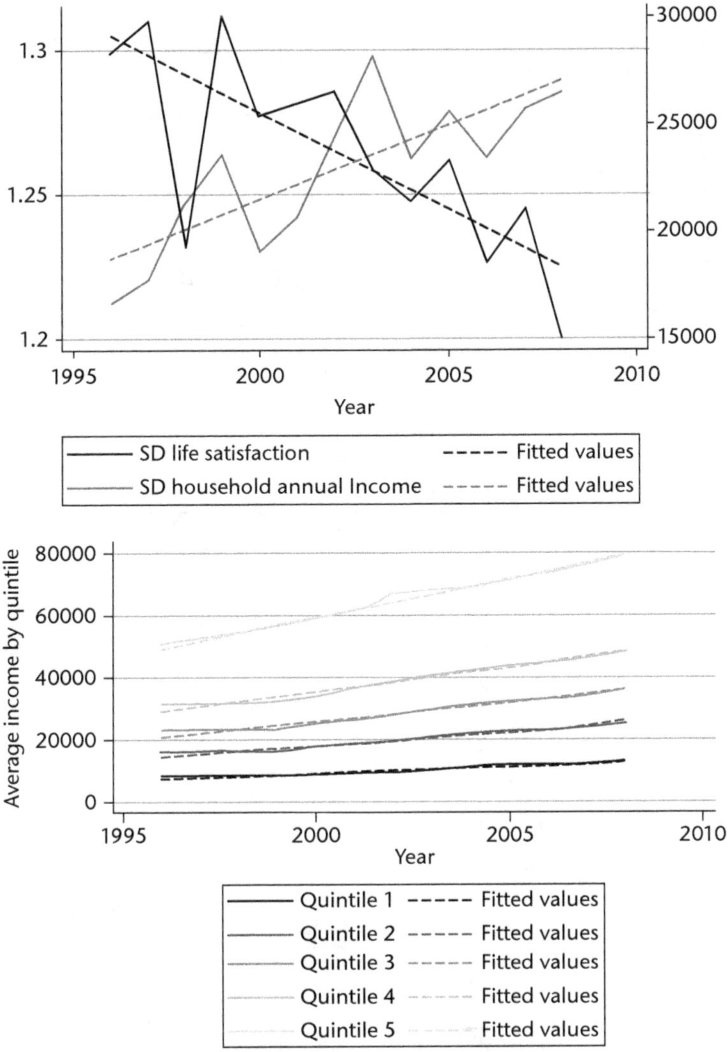

Figure 2.13. *(Continued)*

Should we then conclude that the change in happiness inequality is totally independent of income, as suggested by Stevenson and Wolfers (2008*b*), Dutta and Foster (2013), and Becchetti et al. (2011)? We answer by running a RIF regression of the standard deviation of happiness on log GDP per capita and mean log deviation (see Stevenson and Wolfers, 2010). Table 2.A3 shows that happiness

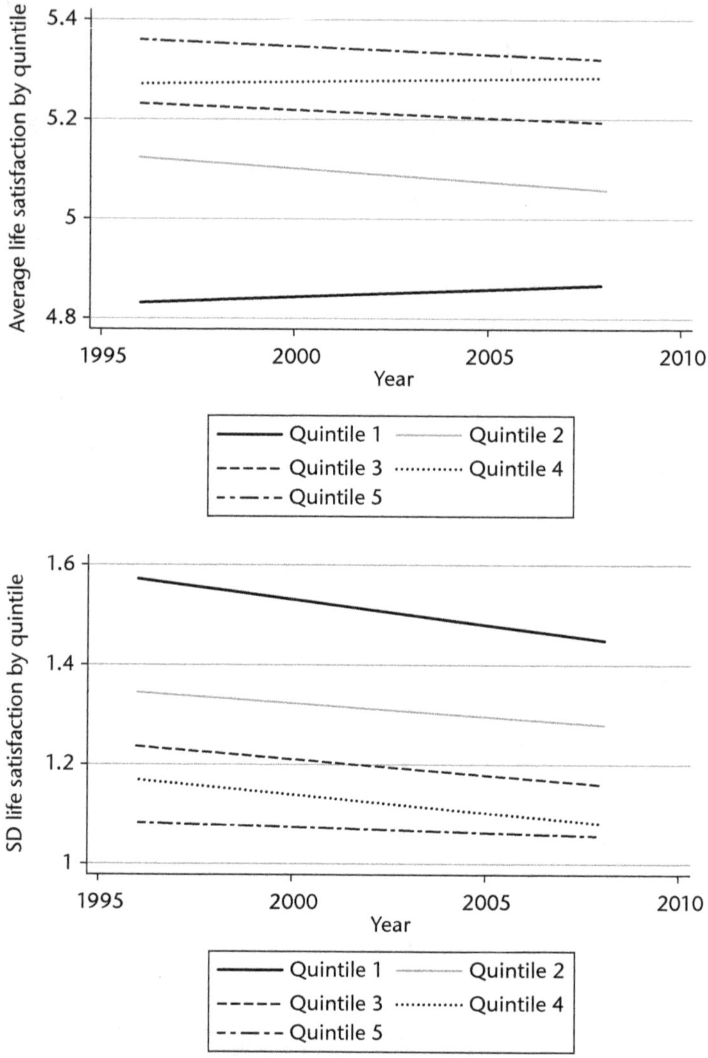

Figure 2.13. Income inequality and happiness inequality: Great Britain (BHPS)

inequality increases with the mean log deviation of income but falls with average income. This can be taken as evidence of two opposing forces, which could explain the rebound in happiness inequality at the end of the period in Germany and the United States. From the

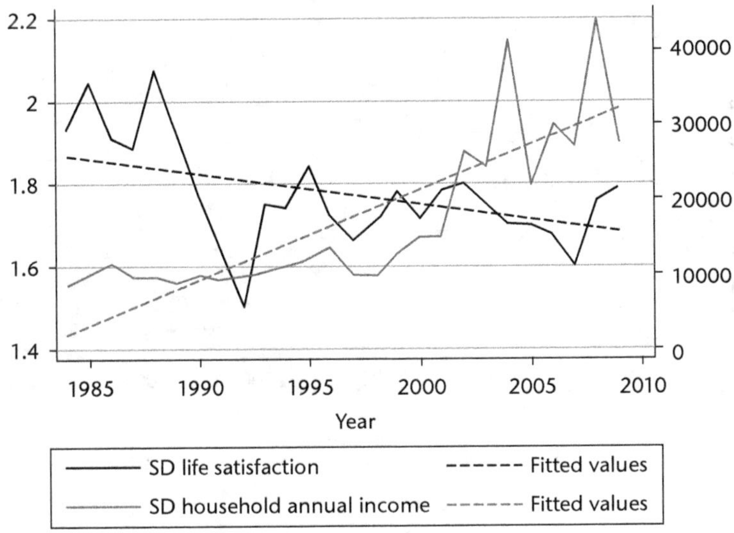

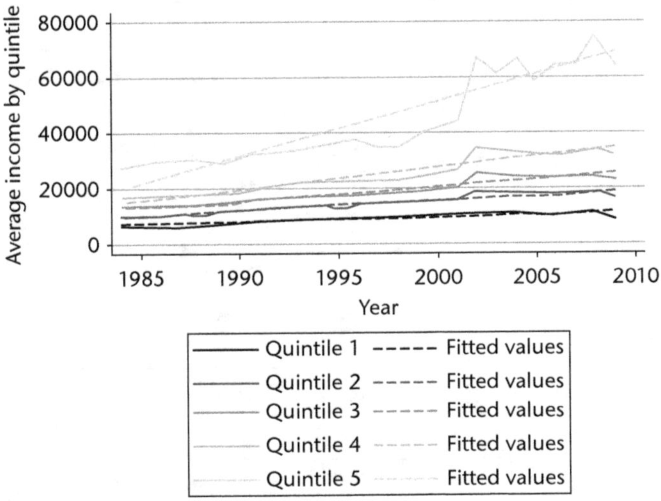

Figure 2.14. (*Continued*)

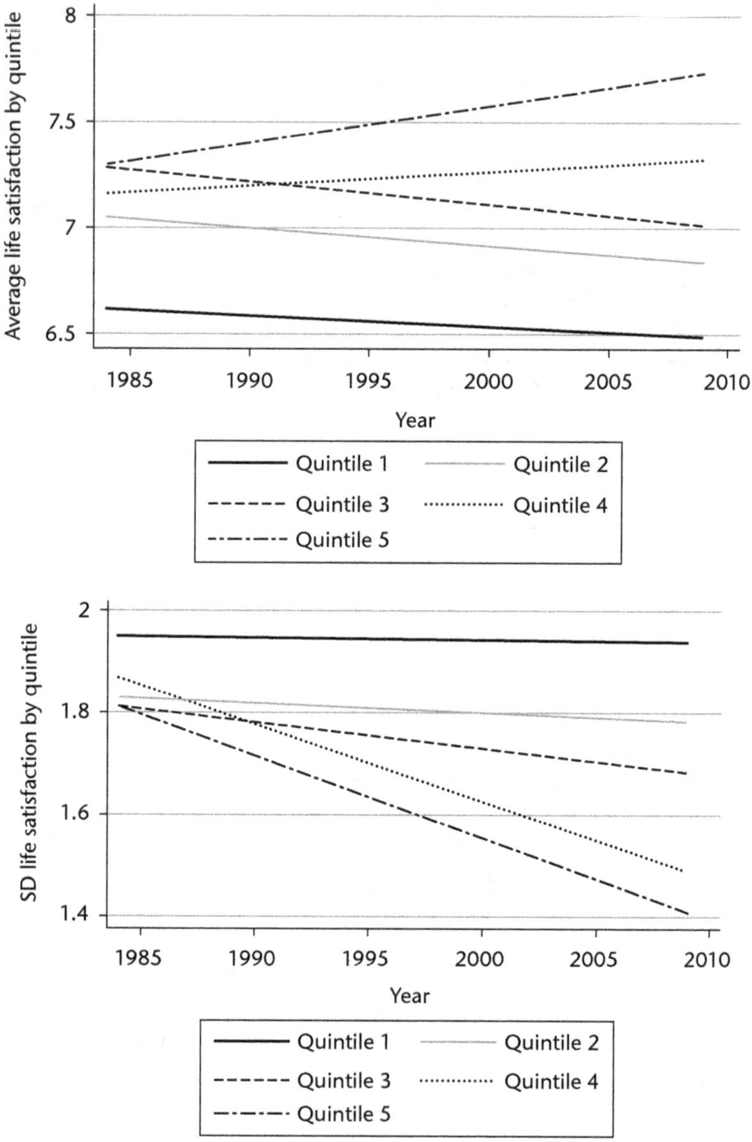

Figure 2.14. (*Continued*)

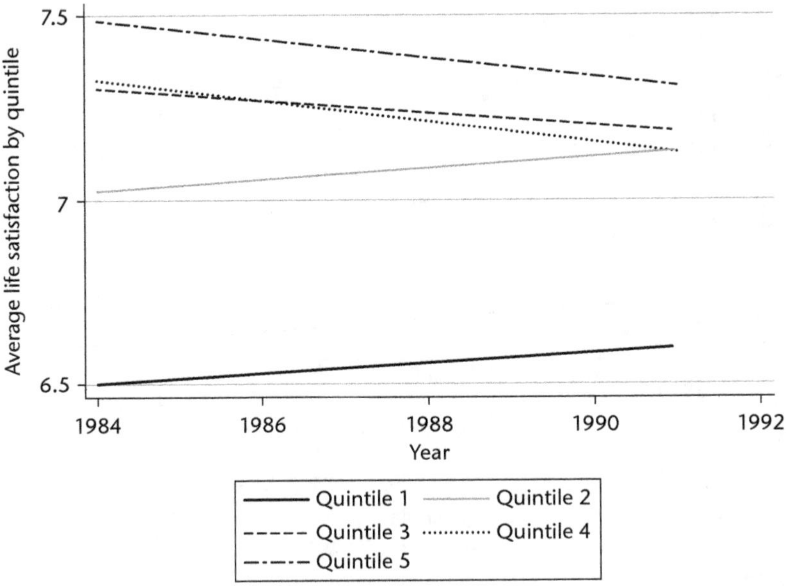

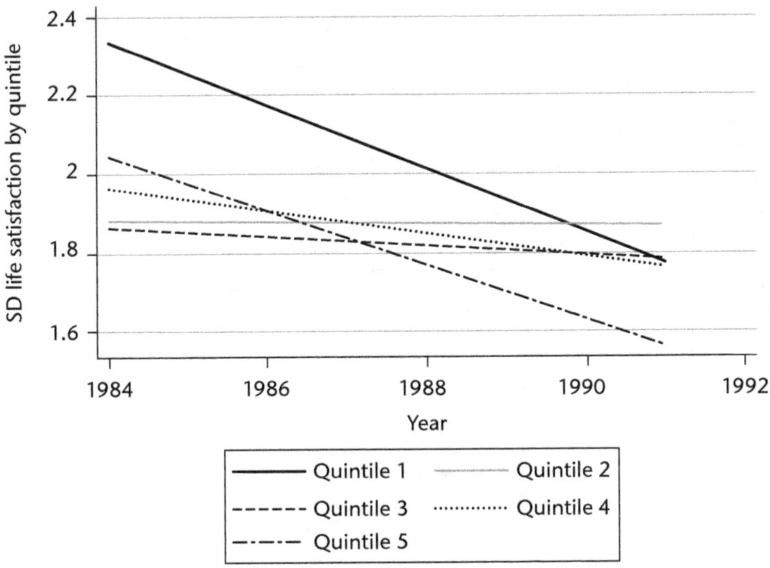

Figure 2.14. (*Continued*)

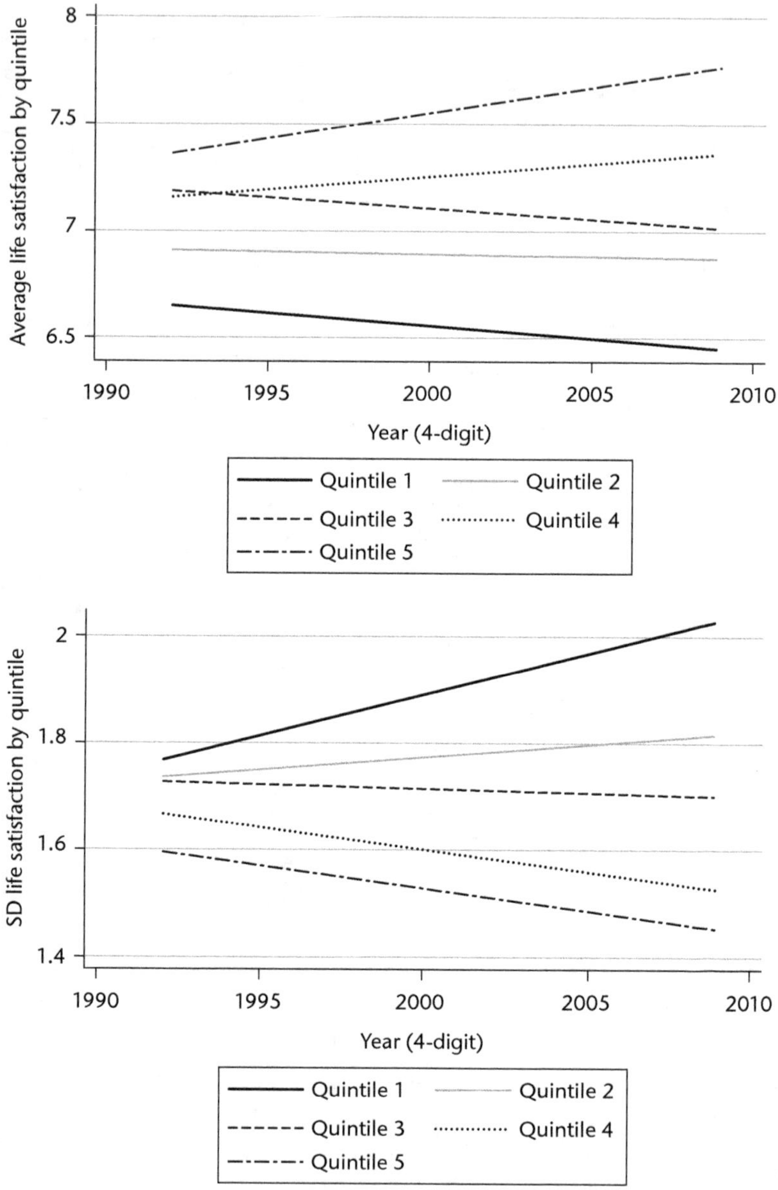

Figure 2.14. Income inequality and happiness inequality: Germany (SOEP)

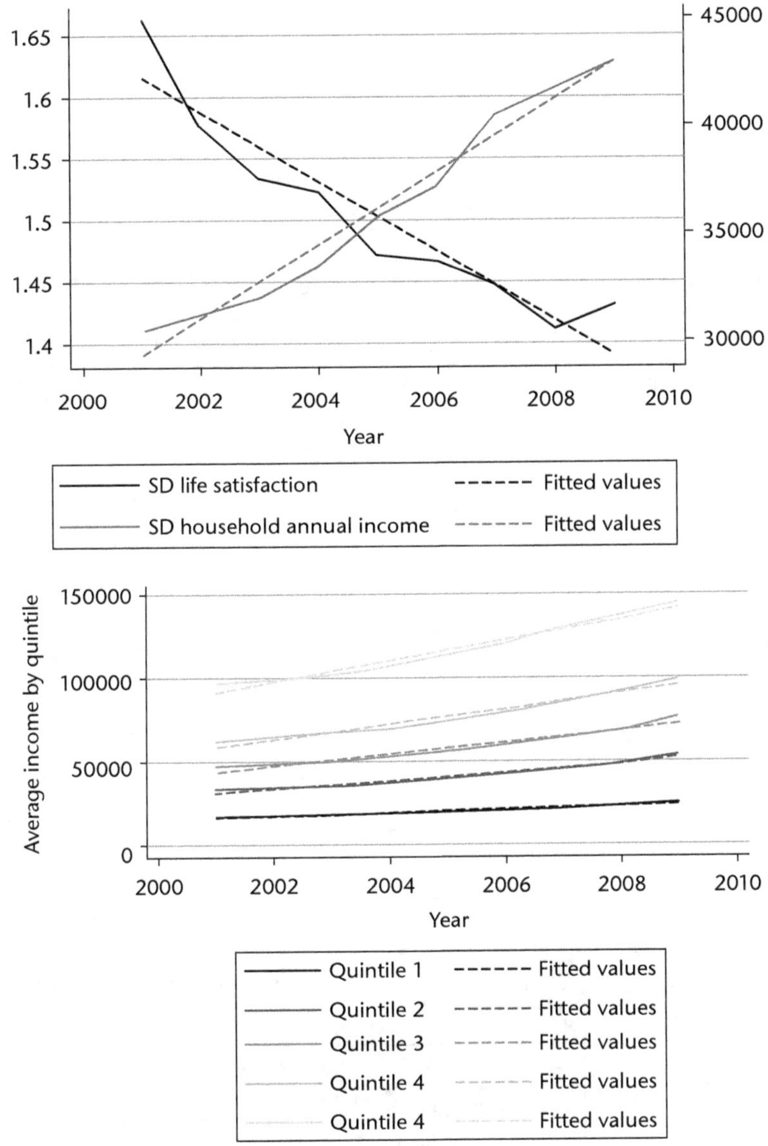

Figure 2.15. *(Continued)*

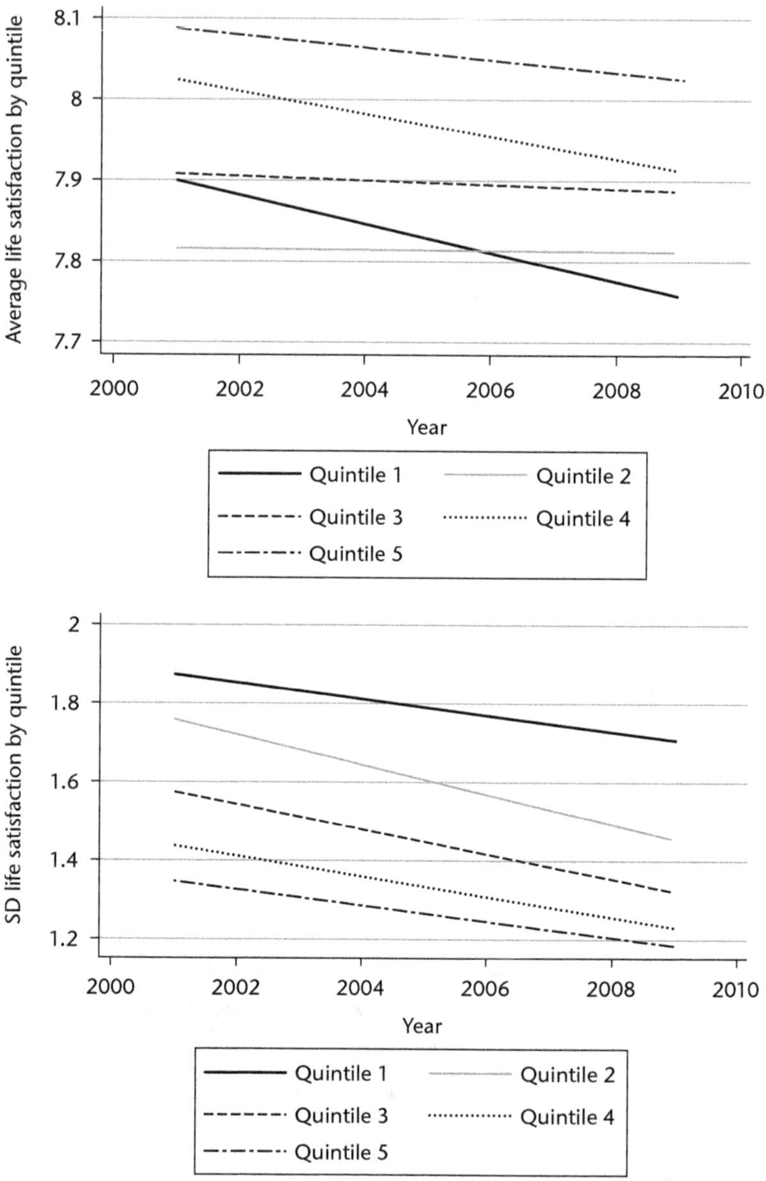

Figure 2.15. Income inequality and happiness inequality: Australia (HILDA)

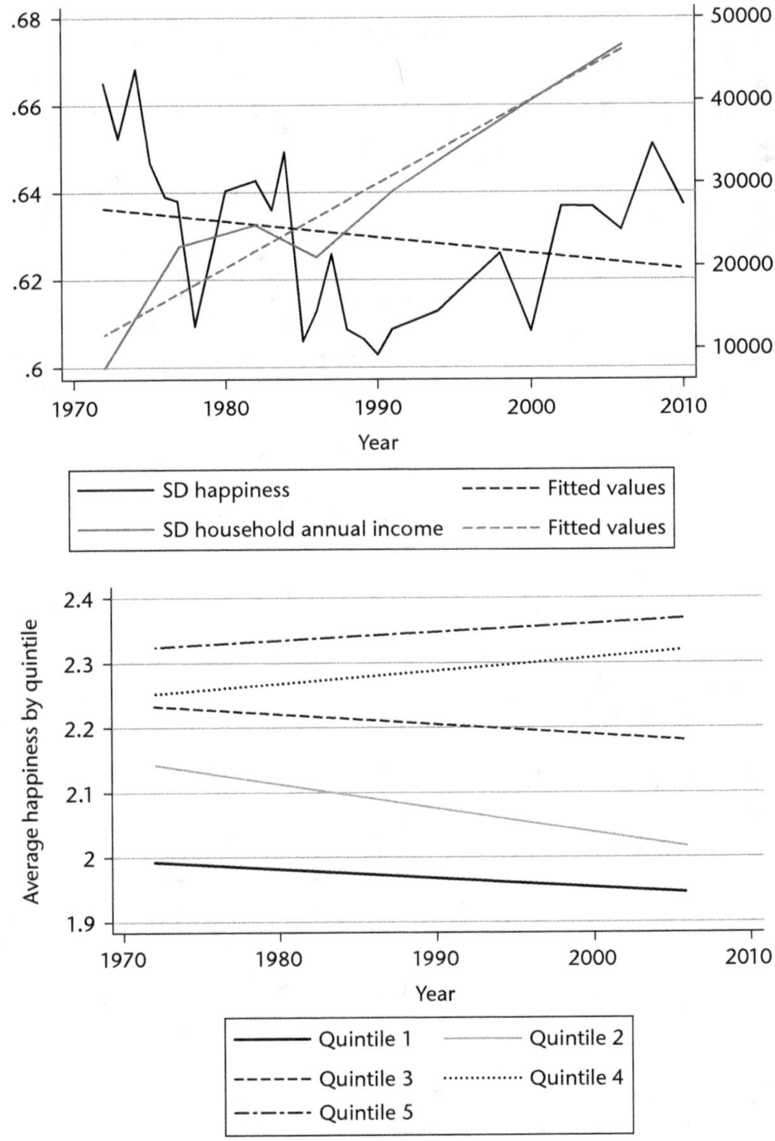

Figure 2.16. (*Continued*)

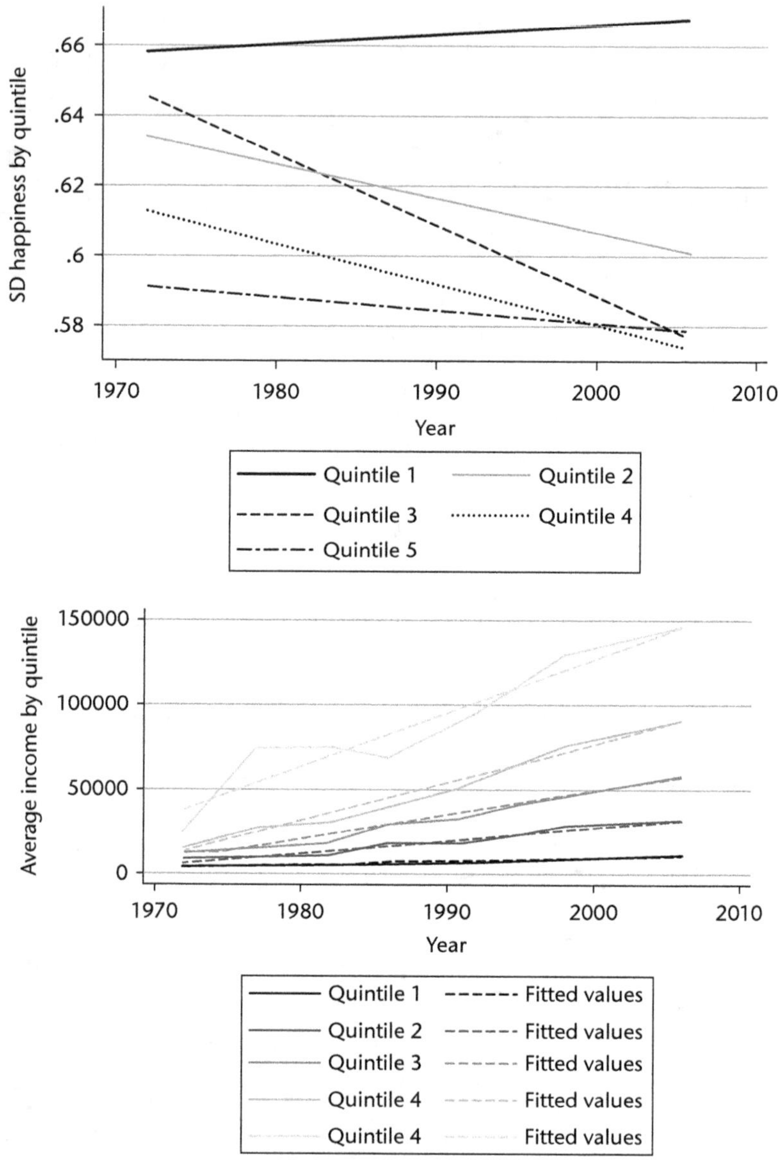

Figure 2.16. (*Continued*)

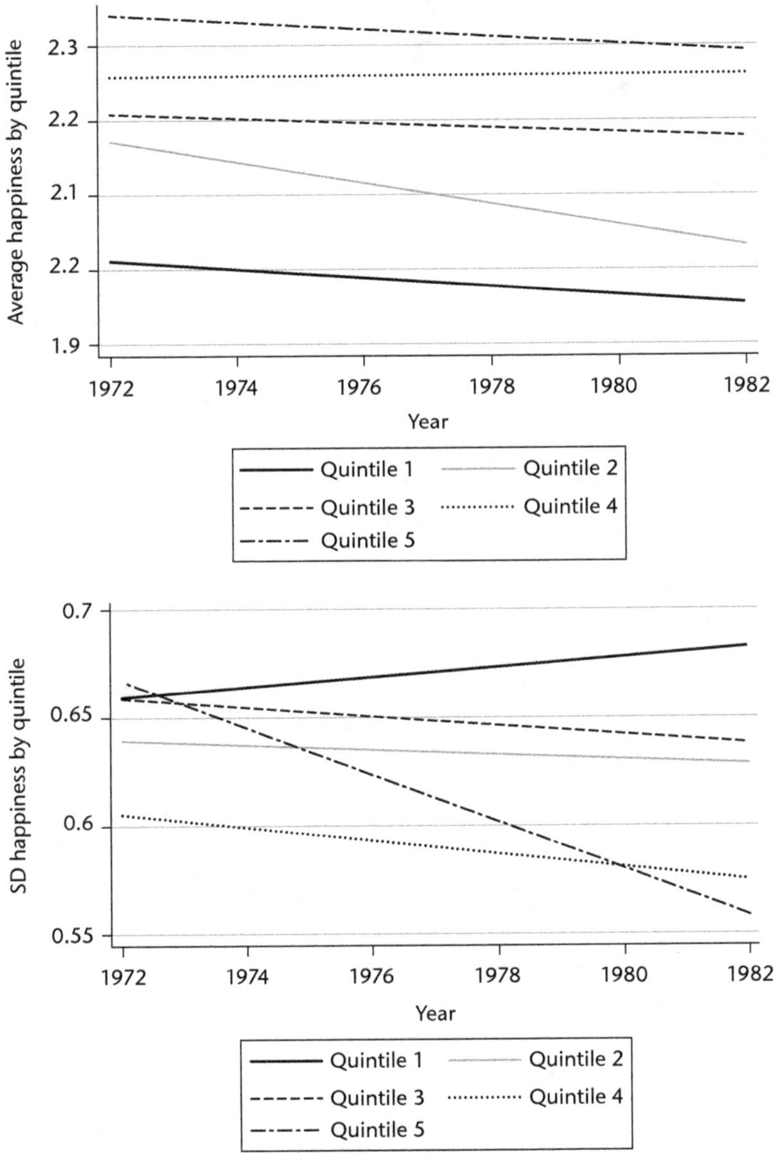

Figure 2.16. (*Continued*)

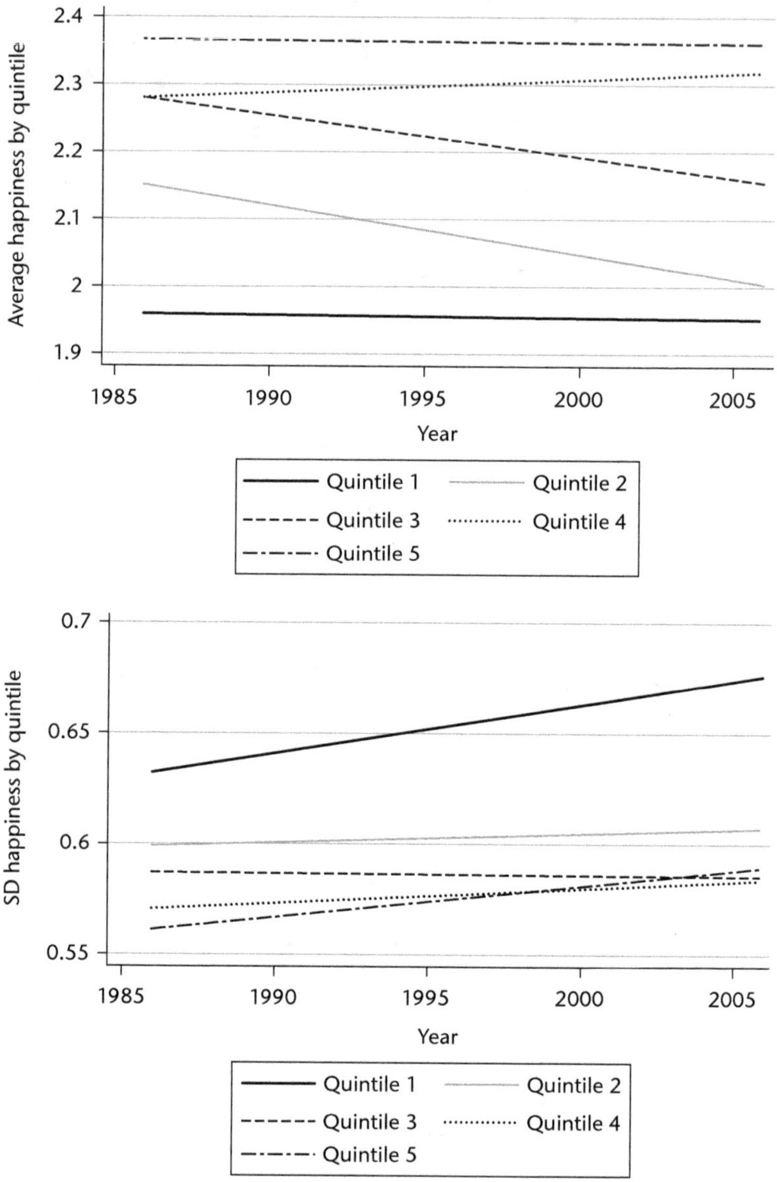

Figure 2.16. Income inequality and happiness inequality: United States (GSS)

estimated coefficients, the impact of 30 percent higher GDP per capita is counterbalanced by higher mean log deviation of 0.05 points, i.e. about 35 percent of its average value in the sample.[10]

Overall, the fall in happiness inequality over time is not driven by a parallel reduction in income inequality.[11] On the contrary, income inequality has risen in all the countries here, which acts as a countervailing force. This force is, however, not powerful enough to overcome the process of happiness equality, except in the United States towards the end of the period.

2.3.5 *Decomposing Happiness Inequality into Micro and Macro Factors*

While happiness equality over time is not driven (but rather counteracted) by income inequality, it could also reflect a composition effect, i.e. greater socio-demographic homogeneity in the population.

We here start with a visual depiction of the evolution of average happiness by socio-demographic groups, and of the dispersion of happiness by group. As shown in Appendix Figures 2.A3–2.A10, happiness gaps between groups increase by education (except in Australia) and fall by gender and marital status (before increasing in Germany and the United States after 1990). The evolution of the gaps by age group and employment status is quite different across countries. However, a common trend is that happiness inequality falls over time in all countries within age, education, gender, marital status and employment status groups, although most of this fall within groups changes sign in the United States and Germany after 1990. In sum, the general trend is that happiness dispersion within different demographic groups is declining, as uncovered by Stevenson and Wolfers (2008*a*) and Becchetti et al. (2011).

RIF estimates of the variance in happiness in each country illustrate how the composition of the population affects happiness inequality. However, Table 2.A3 shows that GDP per capita and income inequality continue to affect happiness inequality even when controlling for socio-demographic variables. As shown in Table 2.A3, this is also true in the cross-section estimates (controlling for year fixed effects).

[10] This should rise by 0.89*ln(1.3) / 4.264 = 0.05. The mean log deviation in the sample is in the region of 0.14.

[11] This may be because the impact of income inequality on happiness inequality is channeled via consumption inequality. Changes in the latter have been the object of vivid debate amongst academics. In the U.S. for instance, most authors find rising consumption inequality in the 1980s, although Krueger and Perri (2006) conclude the opposite, that consumption inequality has been flat or declining in the 1990s and has remained incomparably lower than the increase in income inequality (see Stevenson and Wolfers, 2008*b* for a review).

Lower happiness inequality does not then reflect the evolving socio-demographic composition of the population, although the within-group and between-group happiness spreads have changed over time. Even holding socio-demographic composition constant, income growth is associated with lower happiness inequality.

2.4 Interpretations

We would like to explain the following three stylized facts over time: (1) rising average income per capita; (2) stable average happiness; and (3) falling happiness inequality.

We have shown that these cannot be explained by income inequality or socio-demographic characteristics. We now consider the existing theories of the link between income and happiness to see whether they fit this pattern.

2.4.1 *Happiness as a Log Function of (Absolute) Income and Nothing Else*

Stevenson and Wolfers (henceforth S&W) have argued that the relationship—both cross-section and time-series—between income and happiness is characterized by a stable log function. Does this fit our stylized facts?

Suppose, to start, that average income growth leaves the distribution of income invariant, i.e. all incomes increase proportionally. In this case, average happiness would rise (although perhaps not spectacularly, due to concavity) and the standard deviation in happiness would remain constant (as the standard deviation is translation-invariant, and the log of a product is a sum of the logs). Hence, in order to produce the stylized facts, the distribution of income has to change. However, the only change in income distribution that would generate a mean-preserving fall in happiness inequality is a rise in the income of the poor matched by a greater fall in the income of the rich. This concentration of incomes around the median would leave average happiness constant and reduce its dispersion. However, this evolution has not been observed in any of the countries under review: it is rather the opposite that holds.

ACTUAL AND COUNTER-FACTUAL DISTRIBUTIONS OF HAPPINESS

A direct empirical test of S&W consists in asking whether the happiness function, estimated at the beginning of a period of growth, in each country correctly predicts the distribution of happiness, using the observed changes in income distribution and demographics, at the end of the period. This would be the case were individual happiness to be a stable function of individual income. However, this simulation exercise shows that the actual distribution of happiness at the end of the period is systematically different from that which is predicted. The actual distribution of happiness is always more concentrated around the mode with thinner tails of the distribution than that which is predicted (Figures 2.17–2.20). In particular, in all of the countries under consideration, were the happiness function to be stable over time, more people would be at the highest level of the happiness scale than are actually obs erved.

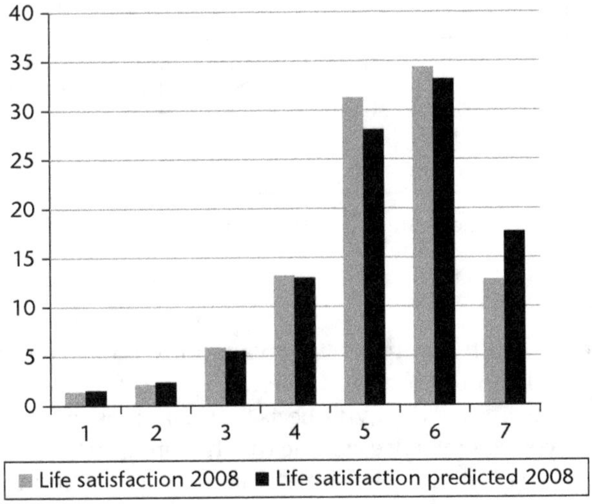

Prediction of happiness in 2008 with the demographic composition of 2008 and the happiness function of 1996

	Life satisfaction 1996	Life satisfaction 2008 predicted	Life satisfaction 2008
Average	5.23	5.47	5.24
Standard deviation	1.32	1.29	1.22

Figure 2.17. Actual and simulated distribution of happiness: Great Britain (BHPS)

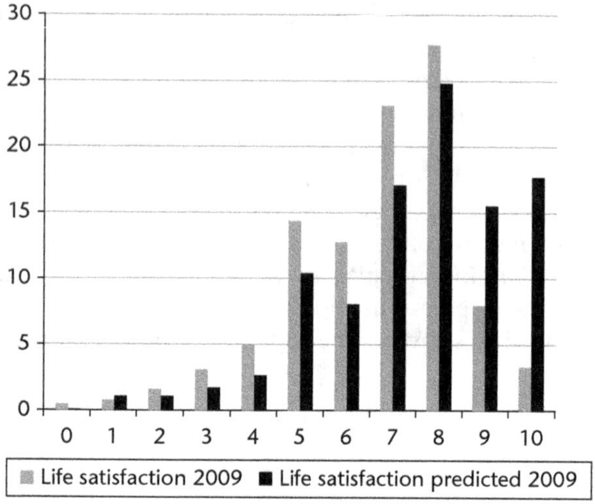

Prediction of happiness in 2009 with the happiness function estimated in 1984

	Life satisfaction 1984	Life satisfaction 2009 predicted	Life satisfaction 2009
Average	7.58	7.50	6.68
Standard deviation	1.97	2.00	1.83

Figure 2.18. Actual and simulated distribution of happiness: Germany (SOEP)

2.4.2 *Social Comparisons*

Easterlin proposed two behavioral explanations of his happiness-level paradox: social comparisons and adaptation over time. We start with social comparisons, i.e. the hypothesis that happiness is at least partly relative in income. We hence assume that happiness depends on log(y, y/y*), where y is individual income, and y* is reference income. We know, from Figures 2.13–2.16, that average income in all quintiles has increased over the period, and that the income of the top quintile has risen substantially, leading to greater income inequality, and that the standard deviation of happiness within quintiles has fallen (except in the GSS, where it increases for the bottom quintile after 1990).

Under these conditions, if everybody compares to an ever-increasing top income category, i.e. y* increases over time by a comparable amount for everybody, well-being will fall for everybody (except the richest), yielding an increase in the standard deviation in happiness.

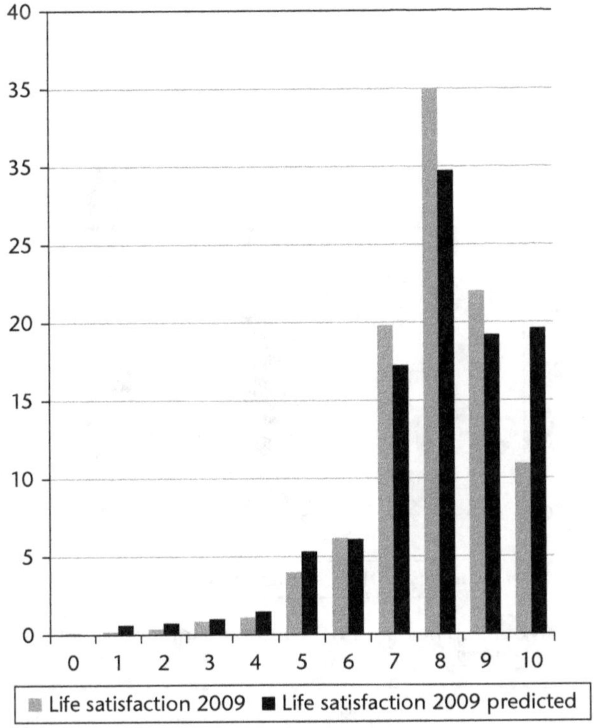

Prediction of happiness in 2009 with the happiness function estimated in 2001

	Life satisfaction 2001	Life satisfaction 2009 predicted	Life satisfaction 2009
Average	7.95	8.36	7.88
Standard deviation	1.66	1.69	1.42

Figure 2.19. Actual and simulated distribution of happiness: Australia (HILDA)

Accordingly, van Praag (2011) notes that income inequality should create an increase in happiness inequality via an envy channel. Hence, a priori, with income comparisons, rising income inequality should lead to greater happiness inequality, rather than the opposite.

There are of course, *in abstracto*, any number of configurations that could lead to a happiness concentration, but these do not correspond to the actual change in the income distribution. Suppose, for instance, that the utility is only partly relative in income, that everybody compares to average or median income, and that this latter increases whereas incomes at the

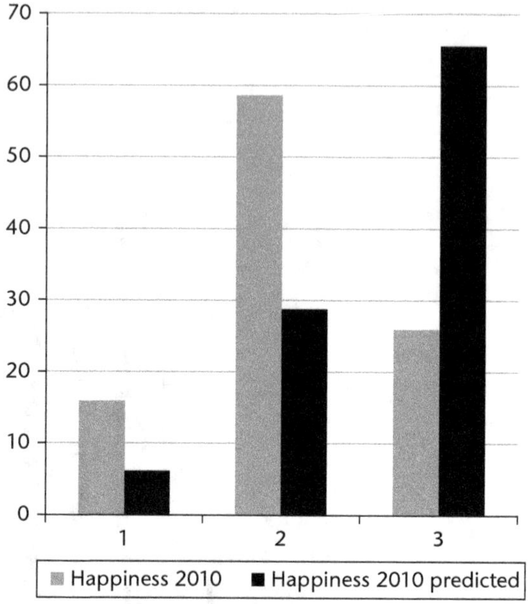

Prediction of happiness in 2010 with the happiness function estimated in 1972

	Happiness 1972	Happiness 2010 predicted	Happiness 2010
Average	2.14	2.58	2.09
Standard deviation	0.66	0.60	0.63

Figure 2.20. Actual and simulated distribution of happiness: USA (GSS)

extremes do not change: the additional happiness of the middle class will then be offset by lower happiness at the extremes. Reproducing the same reasoning "fractally," suppose that society is divided into separate groups, with comparisons within but not across groups, and that people compare to average income within each group. An analogous concentration of income within each group would then produce a similar result. Another possibility is that everybody compares to the poorest group (which itself compares to absolute poverty), and that the poorest group becomes richer over time while the incomes of all other groups remain the same: such pro-poor growth is consistent with our stylized facts.

However, empirical work seems to suggest that comparisons are mostly upward (see Clark et al., 2008 for a survey), and there is a consensus that the past three decades have not seen the enrichment of the middle class or the poorest, but rather of the richest. Our stylized facts would thus seem to require a rather subtle evolution of incomes and comparisons, whereby the richest would compare to an increasingly distant target, while the poor progressively close the gap to their target group. However, we do not observe this kind of convergence in the average happiness of the different income quintiles within each country (Figures 2.13–2.16). Overall, we do not have compelling evidence that the change in happiness results from income comparisons.

2.4.3 *Adaptation*

The second behavioral explanation of the Easterlin paradox relies on adaptation, whereby individual aspirations grow in line with material affluence. As satisfaction is argued to depend on the gap between outcomes and aspirations, it will not change if this gap is unaffected.[12]

Adaptation implies a negative effect of past income on the utility of current income.[13] Di Tella and MacCulloch (2008) and Stutzer (2004) have shown evidence of total habituation to past income levels, so that the total impact of lagged and current income is zero. It is not, however, easy to see how adaptation could generate a fall in the inequality of happiness (with a constant mean). For instance, happiness equalization would occur were adaptation to be faster at the top of the income ladder and slower at the bottom, but in this case the mean level of happiness would rise.

We now ask whether more sophisticated concepts of adaptation are consistent with the observed stylized facts regarding the first and second moments of the distribution of happiness during episodes of growth.

BLISS POINTS

Another explanation for the Easterlin paradox, which is rejected by Easterlin himself (as well as Stevenson and Wolfers, 2008*b*, and Deaton, 2008) but accepted by others, such as Layard (2005), Inglehart

[12] If adaptation is full-blown, it might be wondered why income is related to happiness at all. Easterlin (2001) hypothesizes that all children and teenagers live together at the beginning of their lives and thus make comparisons with each other and with each other's family wealth, which leads them to different happiness levels. Then, in adulthood, social groups are separated and no longer compare with each other, but remain on their specific satisfaction path.

[13] Another type of adaptation is that of changing aspirations, not because of one's own past experience, but from other people's standard of living, a concept that is close to comparisons (see Section 2.4.2).

(1997), Inglehart et al. (2008), Di Tella et al. (2010), and, more recently, Proto and Rustichini (2012), is that the positive gradient in happiness disappears after a certain bliss point,[14] located at around $10–15,000 per annum (Layard, 2005; Frey and Stutzer, 2002), or at $26–33,000 (Proto and Rustichini, 2012). The hypothesis of a satiation point is a particular case of adaptation, as it postulates complete adaptation above a certain income threshold.

Although the idea of a satiation point is controversial, we should see whether it can explain the stylized facts analyzed in this chapter. We believe that it cannot. If only the rich become richer (but no happier, because they are beyond the bliss point), this will not reduce happiness inequality. If all incomes increase and progressively reach the bliss point beyond which income ceases to yield happiness, then average happiness would rise until everybody reaches the bliss point; the same holds if only the poor become richer.

MASLOW AND POSTMODERN VALUES

Another more sophisticated version of adaptation is the evolution of needs and aspirations *à la* Maslow. Maslow (1943) proposed a model of the stages of development of human needs, motivations or aspirations. The most basic needs are (1) physiological needs (air, food, drink, shelter, warmth, sex, and sleep) and (2) safety needs (protection, security, order, law, stability, and limits); then come more elaborate needs such as (3) belongingness and love (family, affection, relationships, and work group), (4) esteem (achievement, status, responsibility, and reputation), and (5) self-actualization (personal growth and fulfillment). The first two types of needs create physiological distress in the case of deficiency and physiological bliss when they are fulfilled, whereas the three subsequent needs are "meta-motivations" of a superior kind. Maslow suggests that the most basic level of needs must be met before the individual desires (or focuses their motivation on) the secondary or higher-level needs, although the five types of needs may overlap. Maslow's theory can be translated into the framework of economics by suggesting that subjective well-being depends on the multidimensional gap between needs and attainments, but with the weights attached to each dimension depending on the context and level of affluence. As individuals fulfill their basic needs, they take them for granted, and reduce the importance attached to this dimension. They then start

[14] One question is of course whether this bliss point would not increase with the country's level of affluence. For instance, Proto and Rustichini (2012) calculate that the level of this threshold is around $26,000–$30,000 for all countries in the World Values Survey, but between $30,000 and $33,000 for EU countries.

attaching more importance to the other dimensions, for which the gap between needs and outcomes remains considerable. Maslow thus implies a "preference drift" (van Praag, 1971) not only in the dimension of income, but also in a number of other life dimensions.

One important point is that the three higher needs may be more difficult to fulfill than the two basic needs. This recalls the distinction between survival and living. It would seem uncontroversial that being happy about the meaning of one's life is less straightforward than being happy to survive. Inglehart (1997, pp. 64–5) illustrates this opposition between survival and modern societies:

> the transition from a society of starvation to a society of security brings a dramatic increase in subjective well-being. But we find a threshold at which economic growth no longer seems to increase subjective well-being significantly. This may be linked with the fact that, at this level, starvation is no longer a real concern for most people. Survival begins to be taken for granted [...] At low levels of economic development, even modest economic gains bring a high return in terms of caloric intake, clothing, shelter, medical care and ultimately in life expectancy itself.... But once a society has reached a certain threshold of development... non-economic aspects of life become increasingly important.

Inglehart (2010) proposes an explanation : "Economic development increases people's sense of existential security, leading them to shift their emphasis from survival values towards self-expression values and free choice. . . . Emphasis on freedom increases with rising economic security" (p. 353).

This theory implies that, as societies develop, the share of the population fulfilling their basic needs increases, and that still facing survival risks shrinks. However, as long as there remains some precariousness in society, the poor may feel happy to escape it, and their aspirations may reflect a mix of material and non-material needs. This would explain why average happiness does not increase while the percentage at the extreme happiness levels falls (individuals are more difficult to satisfy, but the poor are happy to escape material distress).

A recent paper by Proto and Rustichini (2012) suggests that neurotic individuals at the top of the income scale are driving the Easterlin paradox, because of their particular tendency to adapt. Even absent this assumption (about neuroticism), it is likely that growth and technological progress increase the possibilities and aspirations of the wealthiest. At the same time, development brings extended access to basic goods (corresponding to basic needs 1 and 2). Modern growth is typically associated with a better general level of education and health, greater life expectancy at birth, less child mortality, more public infrastructure, and the extension of a social welfare system that provides insurance against the major risks of life (illness, unemployment, and retirement). It is thus possible that the share of the population that feels totally deprived (the bottom of the scale) and totally satisfied (the top of the scale) both shrink. This is consistent with what we observe in the data.

RESCALING

Adaptation of needs *à la* Maslow is difficult to distinguish from another phenomenon: that of rescaling. Rescaling is a type of adaptation that does not concern latent satisfaction, i.e. the relationship between income and the actual level of happiness, but rather the relationship between latent happiness and self-declared happiness. The fact that happiness is very often measured on a bounded scale leads us to suspect that the meaning of the scale is context-dependent, i.e. the interpretation given to each step of the scale changes with the general context. Quoting Deaton (2008, p. 70): "The 'best possible life for you' is a shifting standard that will move upwards with rising living standards." The intuition is that, as the world of opportunities changes, people also change their understanding of what maximum possible happiness represents (that associated with the tenth rung of the happiness ladder), and the worst possible situation (the lowest rung of the ladder), and more generally of what the steps of the happiness ladder mean. But this does not necessarily mean that they are less happy with what they have (which would be classic adaptation). The notion of the satisfaction treadmill, as opposed to the hedonic treadmill, captures this idea (Frederick and Loewenstein, 1999; Frederick, 2007).

One scenario that would fit our stylized facts is that people "rescale" more at the top of the ladder than at the bottom, because their world of opportunities expands more than that of the less wealthy. This would create convergence whereby the self-declared happiness of the poor would rise whereas that of the rich would not.

In sum, even if it is difficult to disentangle adaptation from rescaling, and even if both are reminiscent of Maslow's theory of needs, these theories predict that adaptation is stronger at the top of the social scale, which is consistent with the decreasing spread of happiness over time.

2.4.4 *Social Equality and Social Expenditure*

A last channel yielding the stylized facts is that from the externalities of economic growth and modernization. In many western countries, economic development has been accompanied by the creation and extension of a welfare system, which *stricto sensu* consists of social insurance against major life risks (health, unemployment, and retirement insurance) and the provision of social transfers, but more generally brings improvements in the realm of education, health, life expectancy, child mortality, etc. Along these lines, Table 2.A3 shows that the share of social spending in national GDP reduces the variance in happiness in WVS countries.

But modern growth comes along with other types of benefits: material public goods such as infrastructure for transportation and communication, but also non-material public goods, such as reduced violence and crime, the benefit of living in a country where people are more educated, greater freedom of choice in private life, political freedom, transparency and pluralism, better governance, etc. Some authors, e.g. Ott (2005), underline the negative correlation of measures of the quality of institutions and governance (including democracy, freedom, and government effectiveness), as well as gender-empowerment measures, with happiness inequality. Veenhoven (2005*b*) attributes the fall in happiness inequality in EU countries in 1973–2001 to the hypothesis that any inequality in resources has been more than compensated by greater equality in personal capabilities. Ovaska and Takashima (2010) regress happiness inequality on socioeconomic controls and income distribution, as well as economic and political freedom measures taken from the Fraser Institute and Freedom House. Their country-level regressions show that the standard deviation in national happiness across WVS countries falls with the different indices of political freedom.

All of these political, economic, and social changes can be seen as public goods, i.e. amenities accessible to all of a country's inhabitants (although they may marginally differently benefit different population groups). It is straightforward that the increased provision of public goods will reduce the happiness spread across the population.[15] This extension of the positive externalities of modern growth cannot, however, explain why average happiness should be flat over time. Hence, this hypothesis alone cannot explain our stylized facts; it has to be considered together with adaptation or rescaling.

2.5 Conclusions

In spite of the great U-turn (Veenhoven, 2005*b*) that saw income inequality rise in western countries in the 1980s, happiness inequality is

[15] Technically, the extension of the sphere of public goods is equivalent to increasing every citizen's consumption by a similar positive amount. If happiness is a log function of consumption, this will naturally reduce the dispersion of happiness across individuals.

falling in modern societies. We have provided international evidence of this evolution using information from the WVS and country-specific surveys from Australia, Great Britain, Germany, and the United States. The decline in the spread of happiness comes as a second-moment complement to the first-moment Easterlin paradox (the stability of average happiness over long periods of income growth). Taken together, these two stylized facts are difficult to explain under the hypothesis that individual happiness is a stable concave function of income. More behavioral hypotheses, such as income comparisons and simple adaptation over time also seem to be insufficient. However, Maslow-style adaptation and rescaling are both consistent with these changes. The extension of public amenities brought about by modern growth may well also have contributed to this homogeneity of happiness in modern nations.

The interpretation we offer of the new "augmented" Easterlin paradox brings a less pessimistic vision of development. If raising the income of all may not raise the happiness of all, it will at least reduce the gaps between them, provided that income inequality is not too large. Although the current state of data availability makes it easier to establish this new conjecture about the concentration of happiness for developed countries, this perspective is more promising for developing countries, as it allows the benefits of modern growth and a robust welfare system to accrue to all concerned.

References

Atkinson, T., Piketty, T., and Saez, E. (2011). "Top Incomes in the Long Run of History," *Journal of Economic Literature*, 49, 3–71.

Becchetti L., Massari, R., and Naticchioni P. (2011). "The Drivers of Happiness Inequality. Suggestions for Promoting Social Cohesion," Università di Cassino, Dipartimento di Scienze Economiche, WP No. 6/2011.

Beegle, K., Himelein, K., and Ravallion, M. (2012). "Frame-of-reference Bias in Subjective Welfare Regressions," *Journal of Economic Behavior and Organization*, 81, 556–70.

Berry, K.J. and Mielke, P.W., Jr. (1992), "Assessment of Variation in Ordinal Data," *Perceptual and Motor Skills*, 74, 63–6.

Blinder, A.S. (1973). "Wage Discrimination: Reduced Form and Structural Estimates," *Journal of Human Resources*, 8, 436–55.

Clark, A.E., Frijters, P., and Shields, M. (2008). "Relative Income, Happiness and Utility: An Explanation for the Easterlin Paradox and Other Puzzles," *Journal of Economic Literature*, 46, 95–144.

Clark, A.E. and Senik, C. (2011). "Will GDP Growth Increase Happiness in Developing Countries?" In R. Peccoud (Ed.), *Measure For Measure: How Well Do We Measure Development?* Paris, STIN: 99–176.

Deaton, A. (2008). "Income, Health and Well-being around the World: Evidence from the Gallup World Poll," *Journal of Economic Perspectives,* 22, 53–72.

Di Tella, R., Haisken-De New, J., and MacCulloch, R. (2010). "Happiness Adaptation to Income and to Status in an Individual Panel," *Journal of Economic Behavior & Organization,* 76, 834–52.

Di Tella, R. and MacCulloch, R. (2008). "Gross National Happiness as an Answer to the Easterlin Paradox?" *Journal of Development Economics,* 86, 22–42.

Di Tella, R., MacCulloch, R., and Oswald, A. (2003). "The Macroeconomics of Happiness," *Review of Economics and Statistics,* 85, 809–27.

Dustmann, C., Ludsteck, J., and Schönberg, U. (2008). "Revisiting the German Wage Structure," *Quarterly Journal of Economics,* 124, 843–81.

Dutta, I., and Foster, J. (2013). "Inequality of Happiness in the US: 1972–2010," *Review of Income and Wealth,* 59, 393–415.

Easterlin, R. (1974). "Does Economic Growth Improve the Human Lot?" In P.A. David and W.B. Melvin (Eds.), *Nations and Households in Economic Growth.* Palo Alto, Stanford University Press: 89–125.

Easterlin, R. (1995). "Will Raising the Incomes of All Increase the Happiness of All?" *Journal of Economic Behavior and Organization,* 27, 35–47.

Easterlin, R. (2001). "Income and Happiness: Towards a Unified Theory." *Economic Journal,* 111, 465–84.

Easterlin, R. (2003). "Explaining Happiness," *Proceedings of the National Academy of Science,* 100, 11176–83.

Easterlin, R. (2005*a*). "Diminishing Marginal Utility of Income? Caveat Emptor," *Social Indicators Research* 70, 243–55.

Easterlin, R. (2005*b*). "Feeding the Illusion of Growth and Happiness: A Reply to Hagerty and Veenhoven," *Social Indicators Research,* 74, 429–43.

Easterlin, R. and Angelescu, L. (2009). "Happiness and Growth the World Over: Time Series Evidence on the Happiness–Income Paradox," IZA Discussion Paper No. 4060.

Easterlin, R. and Angelescu, L. (2010). "Modern Economic Growth: Cross-sectional and Time-series Evidence." In Kenneth C. Land (Ed.), *Handbook of Social Indicators and Quality of Life Research.* New York and London: Springer, 113–36.

Easterlin, R. and Sawangfa, O. (2010). "Happiness and Growth: Does the Cross-section Predict Time Trends? Evidence from Developing Countries." In E. Diener, J. Helliwell, and D. Kahneman (Eds.) *International Differences in Well-Being.* New York: Oxford University Press, pp. 162–212.

Easterlin, R. and Zimmermann, A. (2006). "Life Satisfaction and Economic Outcomes in Germany in Pre and Post Unification." IZA Discussion Paper No. 2494.

Easterlin, R. and Zimmermann, A. (2009). "Lost in Transition: Life Satisfaction on the Road to Capitalism," *Journal of Economic Behavior and Organization,* 71, 130–45.

Ferrer-i-Carbonell, A., and Frijters, P. (2004). "How Important Is Methodology for the Estimates of the Determinants of Happiness?" *Economic Journal,* 114, 641–59.

Firpo, S., Fortin, N., and Lemieux, T. (2009). "Unconditional Quantile Regressions," *Econometrica*, 77, 953–73.

Frederick, S. (2007). "Hedonic Treadmill." *H-Baumeister (Encyc)-45348.qxd.* 419–20.

Frederick, S. and Loewenstein, G. (1999). "Hedonic Adaptation." In D. Kahneman, E. Diener, and N. Schwarz (Eds.), *Well-being: The Foundations of Hedonic Psychology.* New York: Russell Sage Foundation, pp. 302–29.

Frey, B.S. and Stutzer, A. (2002). "What Can Economists Learn from Happiness Research?" *Journal of Economic Literature,* 40, 402–35.

Galí, J. and Gambetti, L. (2009). "On the Sources of the Great Moderation," *American Economic Journal: Macroeconomics*, 1, 26–57.

Gurr, T.R. (1994). "Peoples against States: Ethnopolitical Conflict and the Changing World System," *International Studies Quarterly*, 38, 347–77.

Heston, A., Summers, R., and Aten, B. (2011). Penn World Table Version 7.0, Center for International Comparisons of Production, Income and Prices at the University of Pennsylvania, May 2011.

Inglehart, R. (1997). *Modernization and Post-Modernization: Cultural, Economic and Political Change in 43 Societies.* Princeton, NJ: Princeton University Press.

Inglehart, R. (2010). "Faith and Freedom: Traditional and Modern Ways to Happiness." In E. Diener, J.F. Helliwell, and D. Kahneman (Eds.), *International Differences in Well-Being.* New York: Oxford University Press, pp. 351–97.

Inglehart, R., Foa, R., Peterson, C., and Welzel, C. (2008). "Development, Freedom, and Rising Happiness: A Global Perspective (1981–2007)," *Perspectives on Psychological Science*, 3, 264–85.

Kalmijn, W. and Veenhoven, R. (2005). "Measuring Inequality of Happiness in Nations: In Search for Proper Statistics," *Journal of Happiness Studies*, 6, 357–96.

Krueger, D. and Perri, F. (2006). "Does Income Inequality Lead to Consumption Inequality?" *Review of Economic Studies*, 73, 163–93.

Layard, R. (2005). *Happiness: Lessons from a New Science.* London: Penguin.

Layard, R., Mayraz, G., and Nickell S., (2010). "Does Relative Income Matter? Are the Critics Right?" In E. Diener, J.F. Helliwell, and D. Kahneman (Eds.), *International Differences in Well-Being.* New York: Oxford University Press, pp. 139–65.

Maslow, A. (1943). "A Theory of Human Motivation," *Psychological Review*, 50, 370–96.

Oaxaca, R. (1973). "Male–Female Wage Differentials in Urban Labor Markets," *International Economic Review*, 14, 693–709.

Ott, J. (2005). "Level and Inequality of Happiness in Nations: Does Greater Happiness of a Greater Number Imply Greater Inequality of Happiness?" *Journal of Happiness Studies*, 6 (Special issue: "Inequality of Happiness in Nations"), 387–420.

Ott, J. (2010). "Greater Happiness for a Greater Number: Some Non-controversial Options for Governments," *Journal of Happiness Studies*, 11, 631–47.

Ovaska, T. and Takashima, R. (2010). "Does a Rising Tide Lift All the Boats? Explaining the National Inequality of Happiness," *Journal of Economic Issues*, 44, 205–24.

Polity IV Project: Political Regime Characteristics and Transitions, 1800–2009. Monty G. Marshall, Director Monty G. Marshall and Keith Jaggers, Principal Investigators, Center for Systemic Peace and Colorado State University; Ted Robert Gurr, Founder, University of Maryland, <http://www.systemicpeace.org/polity/polity4.htm>.

Proto, E. and Rustichini, A. (2012). "Life Satisfaction, Household Income and Personality Traits." The Warwick Economics Research Paper Series (TWERPS) 988, University of Warwick, Department of Economics.

Senik, C. (2009). "Income Distribution and Subjective Well-being," in OECD, *Subjective Well-being and Social Policy*.

Stevenson, B. and Wolfers, J. (2008*a*), "Economic Growth and Subjective Well-being: Reassessing the Easterlin Paradox," *Brookings Papers on Economic Activity*, Spring.

Stevenson, B. and Wolfers, J. (2008*b*). "Happiness Inequality in the United States," *Journal of Legal Studies*, 37, 533–79.

Stevenson, B. and Wolfers, J. (2010). "Inequality and Subjective Well-being," mimeo.

Stevenson, B. and Wolfers, J. (2011). "Trust in Public Institutions over the Business Cycle," NBER Working Paper 16891.

Stock, J. and Watson, M. (2002). "Has the Business Cycle Changed and Why?" *NBER Macroeconomics Annual*, 17, 159–230.

Stutzer, A. (2004). "The Role of Income Aspirations in Individual Happiness," *Journal of Economic Behavior and Organization*, 54, 89–109.

Tullock G. (1971). "The Paradox of Revolution," *Public Choice*, 11, 89–100.

Van Praag, B.M. (1971). "The Welfare Function of Income in Belgium: An Empirical Investigation," *European Economic Review*, 2, 337–69.

Van Praag, B.M. (1991). "Ordinal and Cardinal Utility," *Journal of Econometrics*, 50, 69–89.

Van Praag, B.M. (2007). "Perspectives from the Happiness Literature and the Role of New Instruments for Policy Analysis," *CESifo Economic Studies*, 53, 42–68.

Van Praag, B. (2011). "Well-being Inequality and Reference Groups: An Agenda for New Research," *Journal of Economic Inequality*, 9, 11–127.

Van Praag, B.M. and Ferrer-i-Carbonell, A. (2006). "An Almost Integration-free Approach to Ordered Response Models," Tinbergen Institute Discussion Paper 06-047/3.

Veenhoven, R. (2005*a*). "Return of Inequality in Modern Society? Test by Dispersion of Life-Satisfaction Across Time and Nations," *Journal of Happiness Studies*, 6, 457–87.

Veenhoven, R. (2005*b*). "Inequality of Happiness in Nations," *Journal of Happiness Studies*, 6, 351–5.

Wagner, G., Frick, J., and Schupp, J. (2007). "The German Socio-Economic Panel Study (SOEP)—Scope, Evolution and Enhancements," *Schmollers Jahrbuch*, 127, 139–69.

Wolfers, J. (2003). "Is Business Cycle Volatility Costly? Evidence from Surveys of Subjective Well-being," *International Finance*, 6, 1–26.

Discussion: Paul Seabright

Thank you very much. I am immensely happy to discuss this fascinating chapter. Having a job for which you are paid to come and talk about interesting scientific findings in a group of really delightful colleagues, especially when somebody else has done all the hard work, seems to me one of the ingredients of a very satisfying life.

In discussing this chapter I shall broadly accept that the findings are as the authors claim them to be. There is a clear reduction in the variance of reported happiness at a time when measures of income show increasing variance. This stylized fact looks broadly incompatible with most theories that make happiness a concave function of income, even relative income. I would like to draw attention to one statistical puzzle. Then I shall suggest a hypothesis to explain the findings, which is quite close to the rescaling hypothesis.

The statistical puzzle is this: as Claudia told us, the reduction in the variance in the distribution comes about via a transfer of probability mass from the extreme points to the interior. Something she didn't draw our attention to is that in the only three countries for which we have scales with multiple interior points, those points that gain mass from the extremes are substantially to the right of the distribution. In Great Britain it is points 5 and 6 in a scale out of 7. In Germany, it is points 6, 7, and 8 out of 10. In Australia it is 7, 8, and 9 out of 10. So quite a lot of people who were formerly reporting low scores are now reporting median scores, and any decline is really confined to people at the very top end. Now, you could reasonably react that anybody who reports their life as being the best it could possibly be is illustrating a significant lack of imagination. Changes in the proportions of people who report the very best outcomes may reflect a different way of thinking about the possibilities that our life could take. This may be hard to compare against the welfare implications of the very broad-based shift we see in these data from the bottom points to the upper middle of the distribution.

I'd like to suggest a version of the rescaling interpretation. The happiness that people report is a function of their actual states of well-being, plus three things: first, the state of their own self-understanding; second, various norms and conventions about reporting their own feelings; and third, strategic and signaling motivations. Changes in reported happiness over time could come from changes in their actual state of well-being, but it could also come from changes in one of those three elements.

Contrast this with a commonly held but very misleading method for happiness—which is the temperature of your bath water. How is the temperature of your bath? 10 means "perfect"; 9 means "a tiny adjustment please"; 8 means "please open the cold/hot tap a few more seconds," and so on... Reporting the temperature of your bath water reflects clear subjective sensations. You're not likely to make mistakes about how you feel; you don't even have to think very much about it, and there are no strategic motives for misrepresentation (outside of James Bond movies, at least).

Answering the question "All things considered, how satisfied are you with your life these days?" involves a very different psychological process. First, it demands reflection, it consumes cognitive resources, and it improves with training. Second, it is strategic. It is part of an implicit negotiation with others. I have a pretty good life, but if I made the mistake of telling my colleagues I had a perfect life, there would be a dramatic increase in the number of committees I would be put on and the number of extra demands on my time and energy. It would be insane to report my life satisfaction as a 10 out of 10.

Then there are subjective norms and conventions, which powerfully affect what is considered reasonable to report. Think first about the process of ageing. Most people in this room know that getting old sucks—but you don't talk about it, because you don't want to be boring. There is a very strong convention against complaining about the general shared process of ageing. But this is a convention that under conceivable circumstances might change. Imagine a medical innovation, which prolongs people's vigorously youthful life from 30 to the age of 60, but which is extremely expensive, and therefore available only for a minority of the population. If that were to happen, I predict, it would become legitimate to complain about how horrible it is to get older, because this process would be avoidable in principle but some people would be condemned to it by poverty.

Second, there are conventions that are gender-related. This graph, from the famous Stevenson and Wolfers study,[16] demonstrates that women in

[16] Stevenson, B., and Wolfers, J. (2009). "The Paradox of Declining Female Happiness." NBER Working Paper No. 14969.

the United States have become less happy over the past thirty-five years. The result is driven essentially by a decline in the proportion of women reporting themselves as very happy. Now, you don't have to believe that *Mad Men* is a historical document to be aware that very different conventions were in place about what women, especially married women, were allowed to say about the quality of their family life in the 1950s and 1960s, compared to what it was legitimate to say in the 1990s and 2000s.

What does this mean for ways of explaining the great happiness moderation? We need to explain why individuals are less likely to report life satisfaction at the extremes of the distribution. What I want to suggest is the following: over time, there has been an increase in the range of personal experience among each person's reference group. Part of this is due to improving education. People have a greater identification with the extremes of human fortune, and a growing ability to see that they are not themselves at the extremes. Part of it is due to the fact that individuals are typically in touch with a much wider range of former friends and colleagues than their parents' generation were, and are aware of a wider range of things that have happened to them. And both of these phenomena are reinforced by greater media exposure and improved communications in general. This makes people less likely to be at the extremes of the distribution than they might be, for any given level of subjective satisfaction with their lives. Not until we can explore more carefully the gap between how people feel and what they think it reasonable to report can we properly interpret the findings of this fascinating chapter, and of the wider literature of which it forms a part.

General Discussion

Daniel Cohen emphasized that Claudia Senik had said two things: one is that residual happiness inequality has fallen and the second that residual income has increased. It seems that it is the percentage of the happiest people which has declined. If this comes from residual unhappiness among the happiest people then it is not related to income. Therefore, almost logically, what this means is that the people who were more optimistic for unobservable reasons have become less so over the years: is that right? Claudia Senik agreed but suggested that people may also have developed higher aspirations. For instance, in a globalized world, they might start comparing not to the top executives in their own country, but to the top executives in the whole world. Richard Easterlin suggested that what is happening might depend on labor market circumstances. People at the top might be feeling less secure about their jobs and incomes and more vulnerable about unemployment: that would explain the shift downward. And people at the bottom receive benefits from the social safety net that enable them to escape the negative consequences of unemployment. Any different effect by labor market status would be worth investigating. On Maslow, Richard Easterlin said that he was not aware of any evidence that people actually do go through this scale. Social comparisons exist in poor as well as rich societies. Otherwise, China would exhibit increasing life satisfaction, from physiological to security to social. But this has not happened because social comparisons have been there all the time. He therefore feels very uncomfortable with Maslow. John Knight noted that it would be interesting to measure the amount of stress that people feel. It is possible that there has been an increasing correlation between income and stress, as both the rewards and the responsibilities of top jobs have grown. High-income earners might be more stressed than in the past and this could be more important than is normally recognized. Claudia Senik welcomed these additional interpretations. It is indeed a critical research question to know whether individuals have higher aspirations; whether they are deceived by modern growth because they are under greater stress, or now feel more insecure about their high positions. Her view of Maslow's theory sees it just as a more sophisticated—multidimensional—version of adaptation. The idea is that you don't only adapt to your income, but that, in a way, the weights attached to the different arguments of your utility function change with your level of affluence. This is totally consistent with the average level of happiness remaining constant. People's aspirations change, not only in terms of income but also in other domains, and this leaves average happiness constant over time. Daniel Cohen underlined that anthropologists, starting with Marshall Sahlins, say the poorest societies are those that are at the top of the Maslow pyramid. It doesn't take riches to start thinking about the purpose of life. Richard Easterlin insisted that it is hard to avoid social comparisons. Claudia Senik emphasized she is not claiming that social comparisons are not there; rather, her point is that it is difficult to explain the stylized facts that she has uncovered on the basis of social comparisons: this is because comparisons would drive happiness inequality upwards rather than downwards.

Appendix

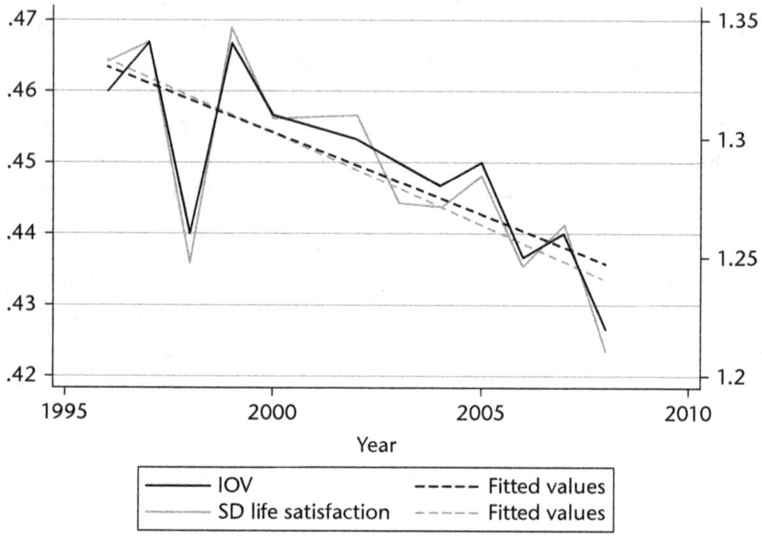

Figure 2.A1. Comparison: Index of Ordinal Variation (IOV) and standard deviation

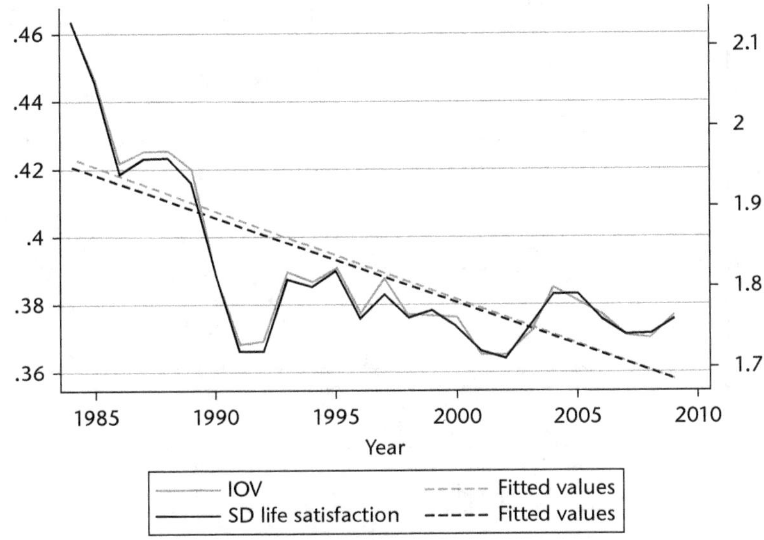

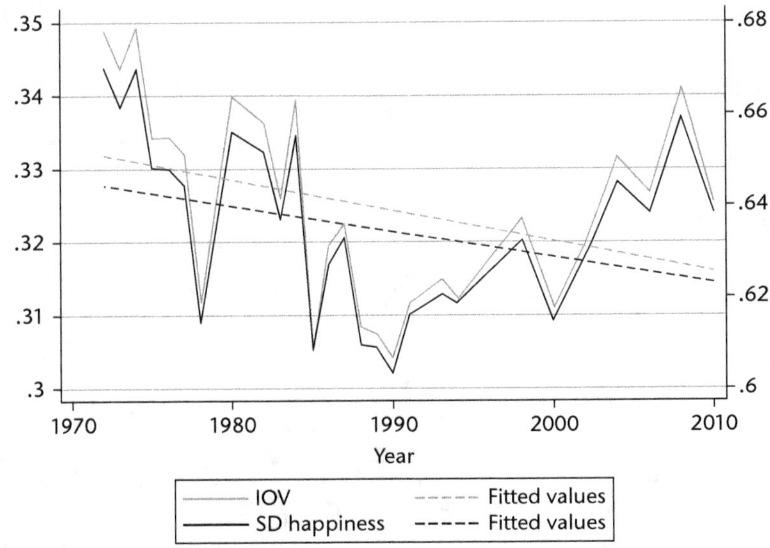

Figure 2.A1. *(Continued)*

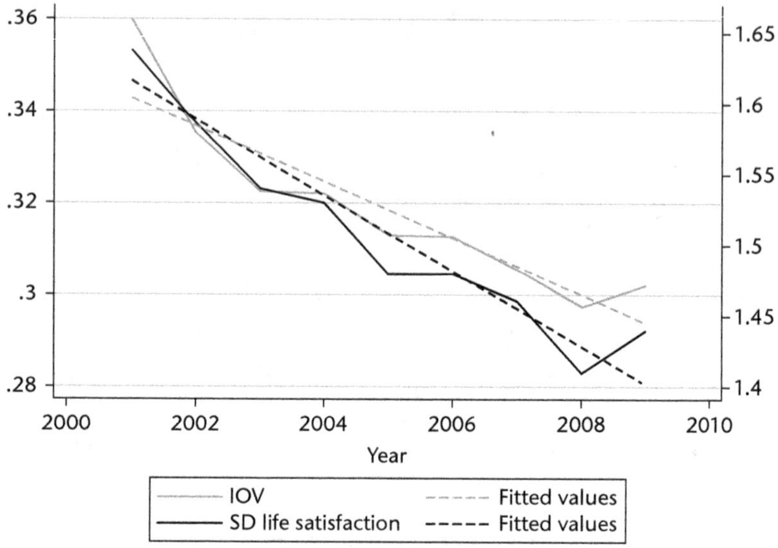

Figure 2.A1. (*Continued*)

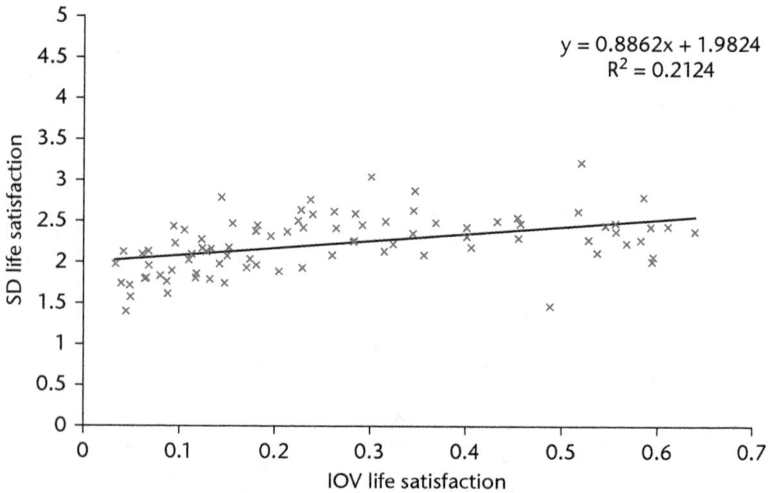

Figure 2.A2. Joint distribution of IOV and standard deviation of life satisfaction

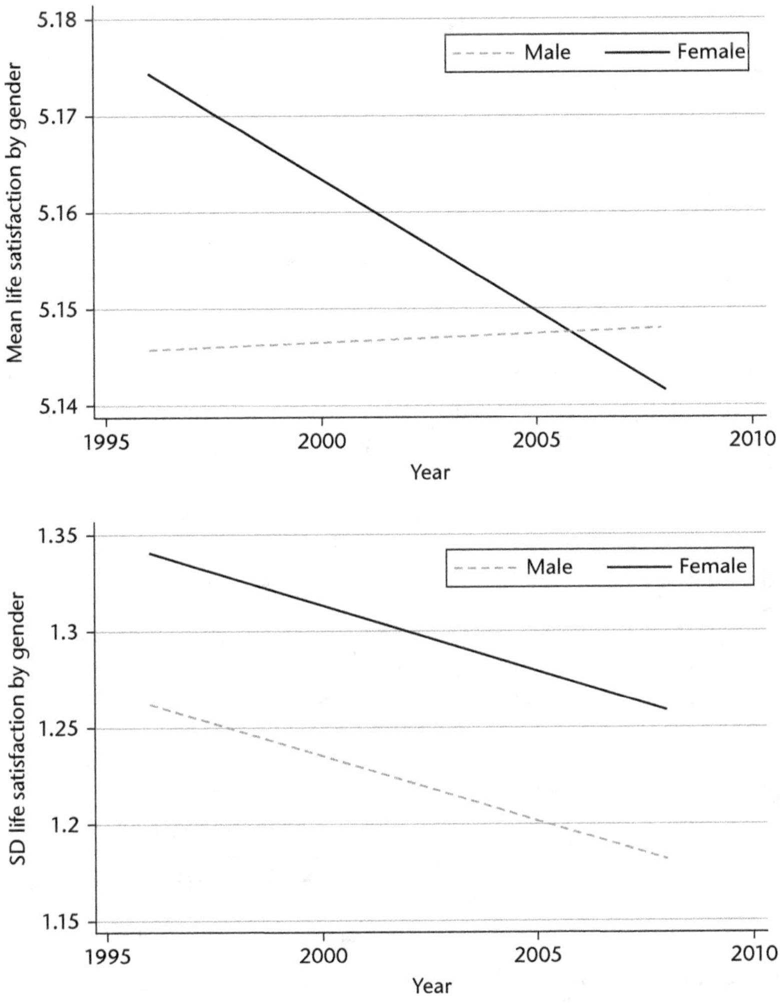

Figure 2.A3. (*Continued*)

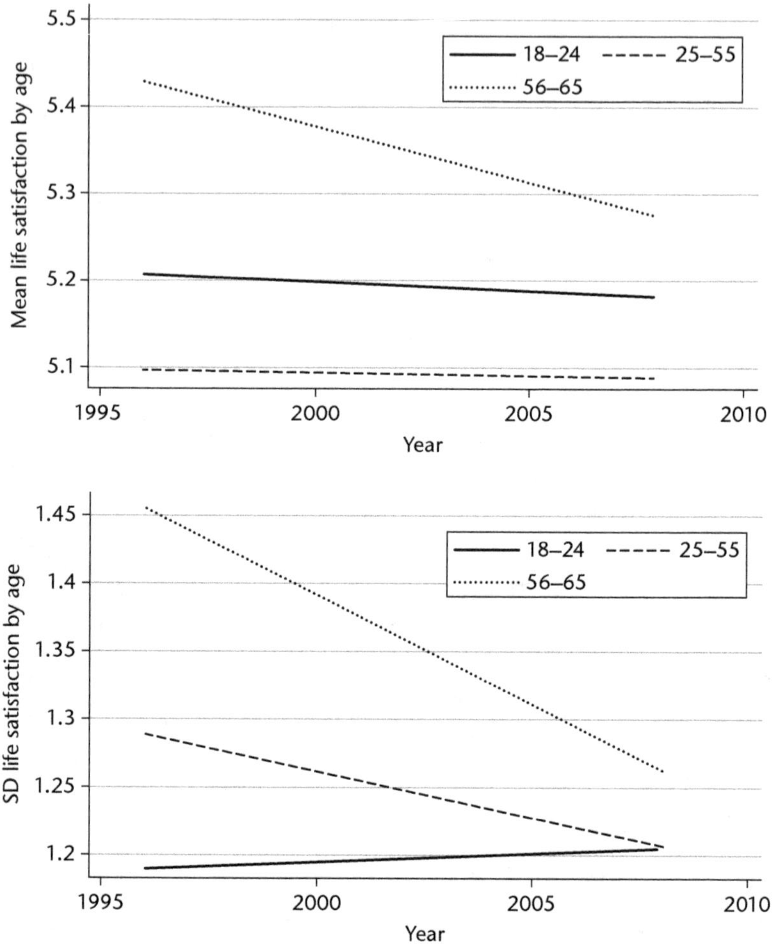

Figure 2.A3. *(Continued)*

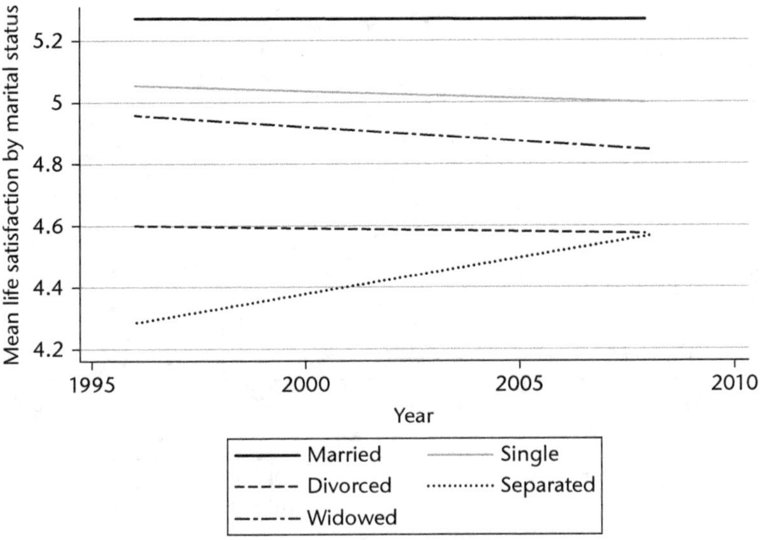

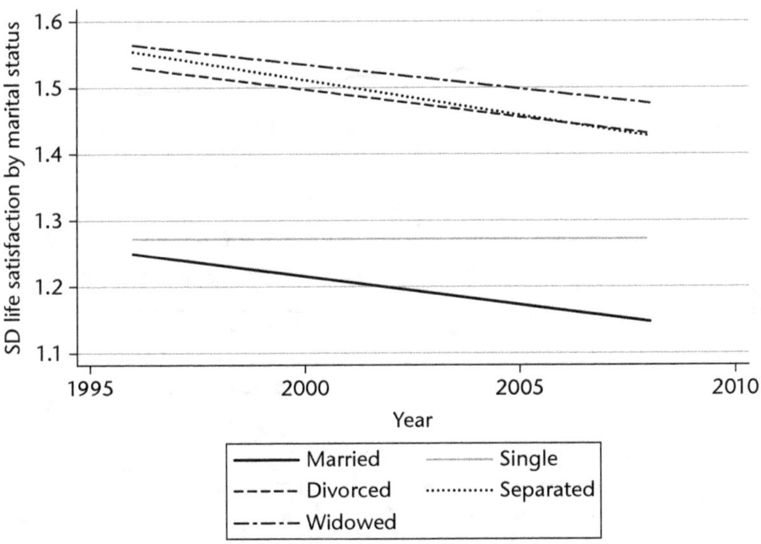

Figure 2.A3. (*Continued*)

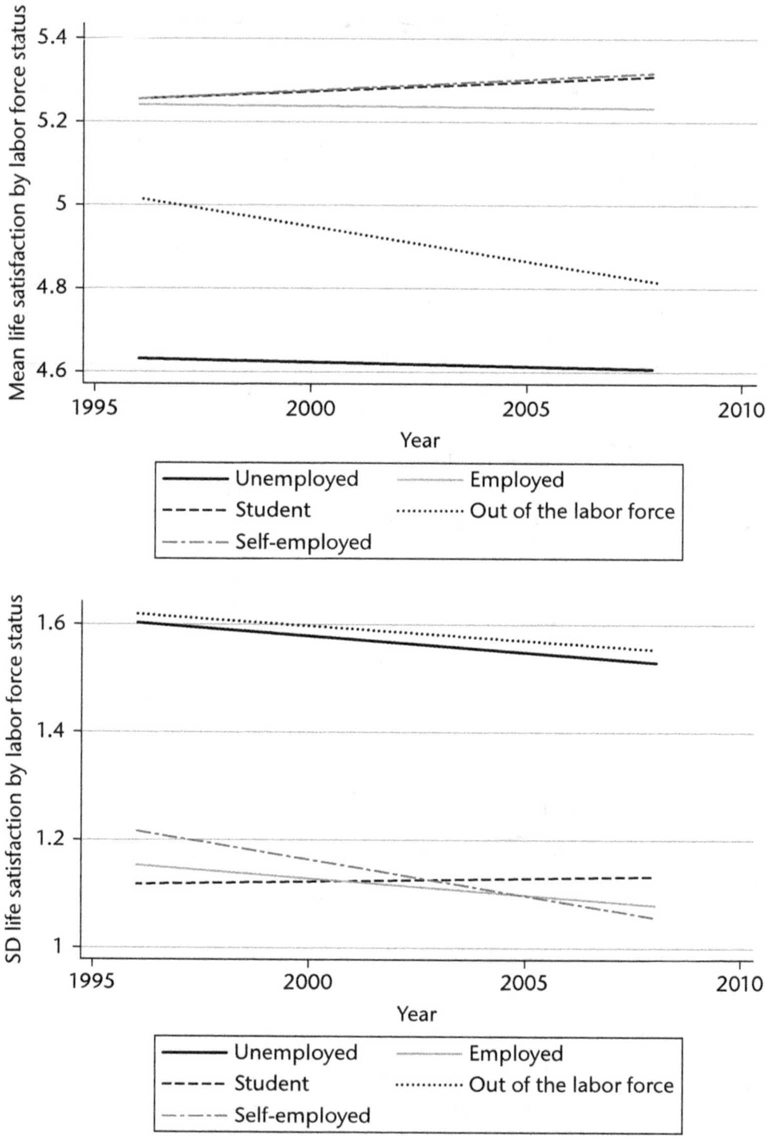

Figure 2.A3. *(Continued)*

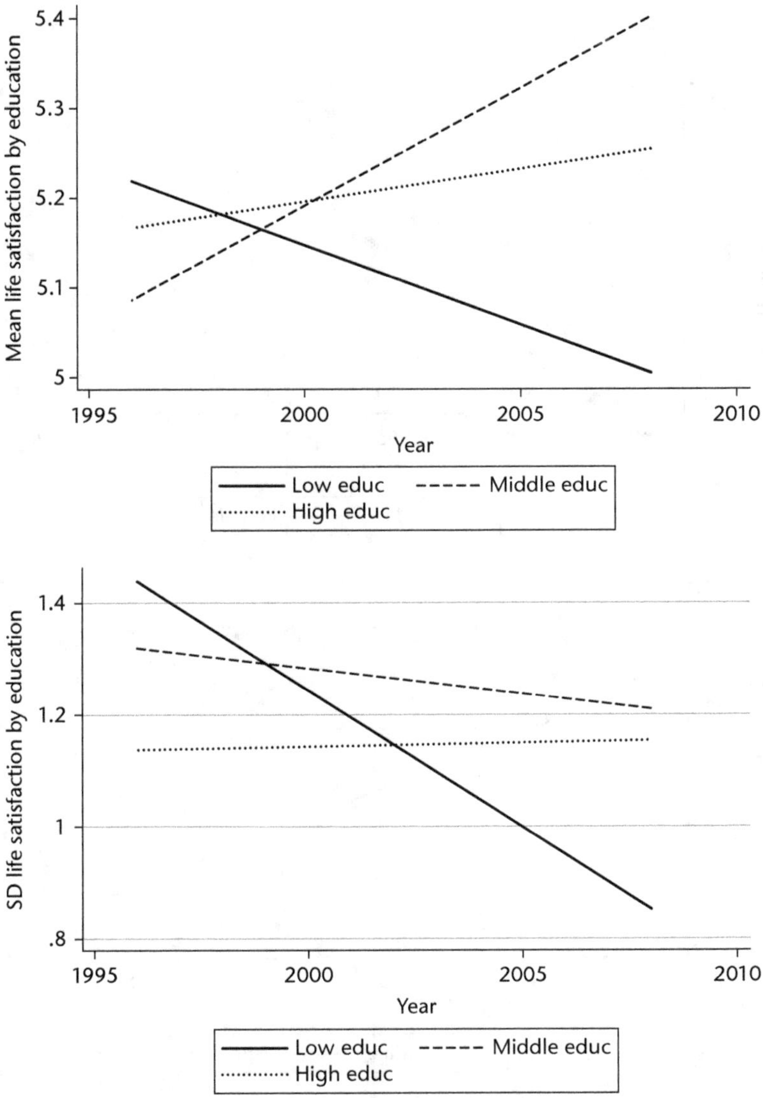

Figure 2.A3. Variance decomposition by demographic groups: BHPS

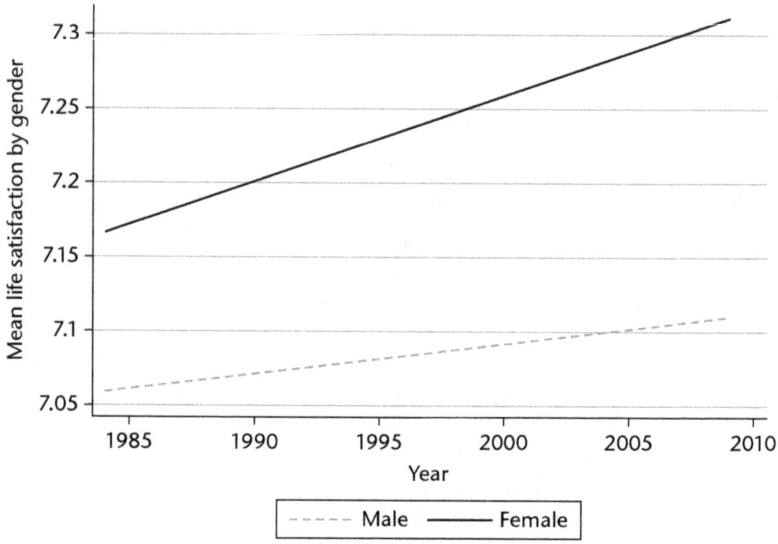

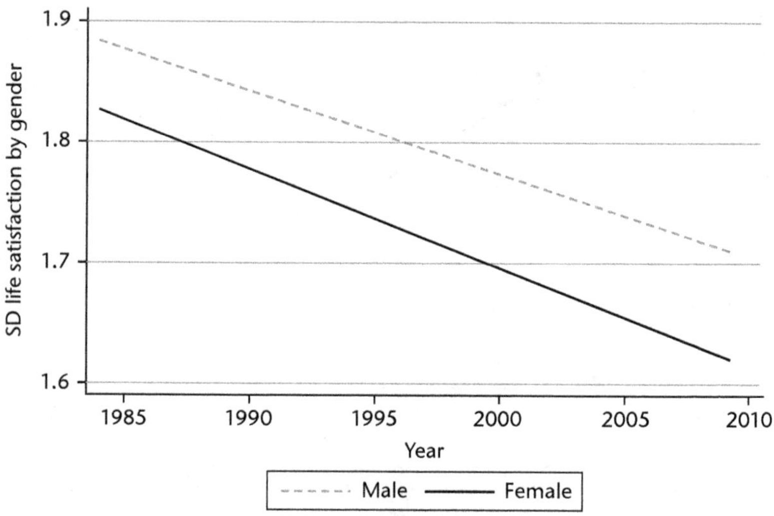

Figure 2.A4. (*Continued*)

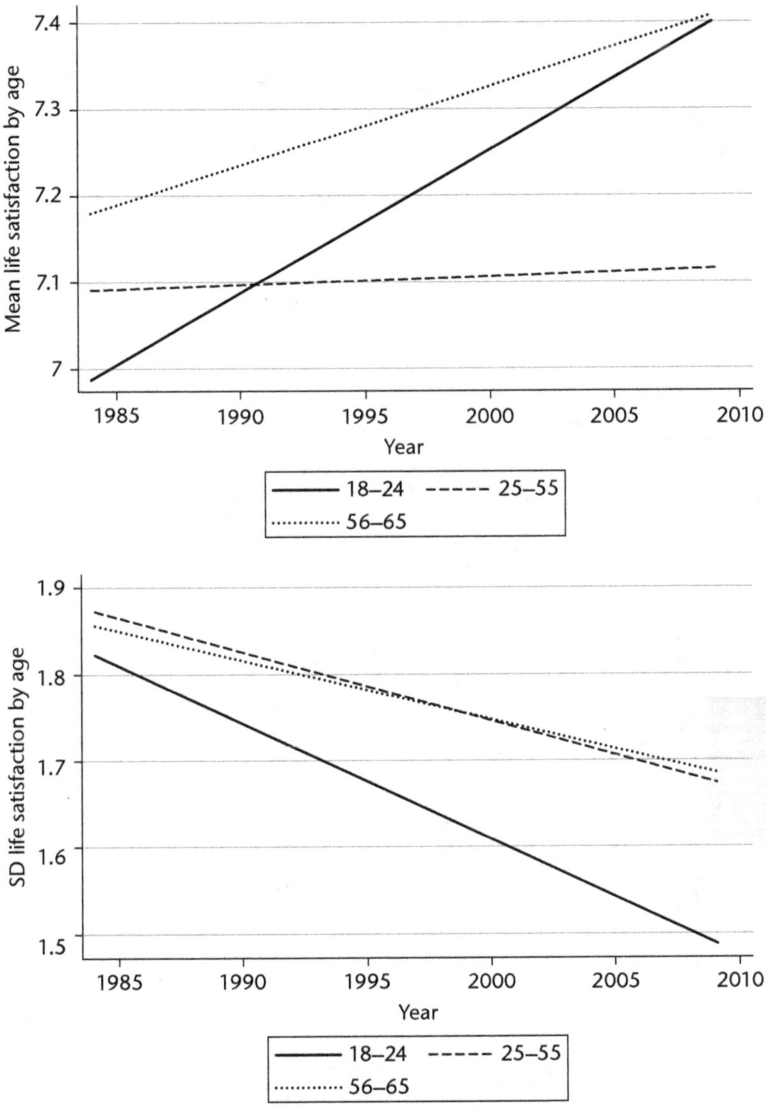

Figure 2.A4. (*Continued*)

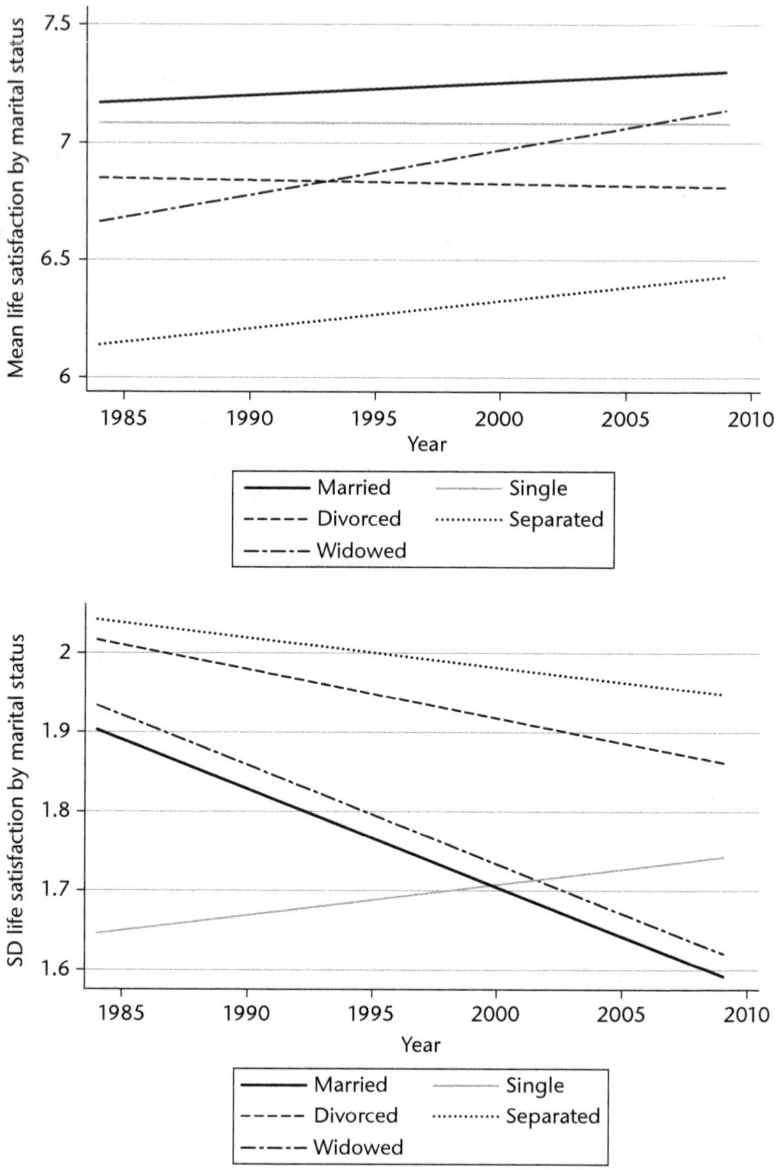

Figure 2.A4. (*Continued*)

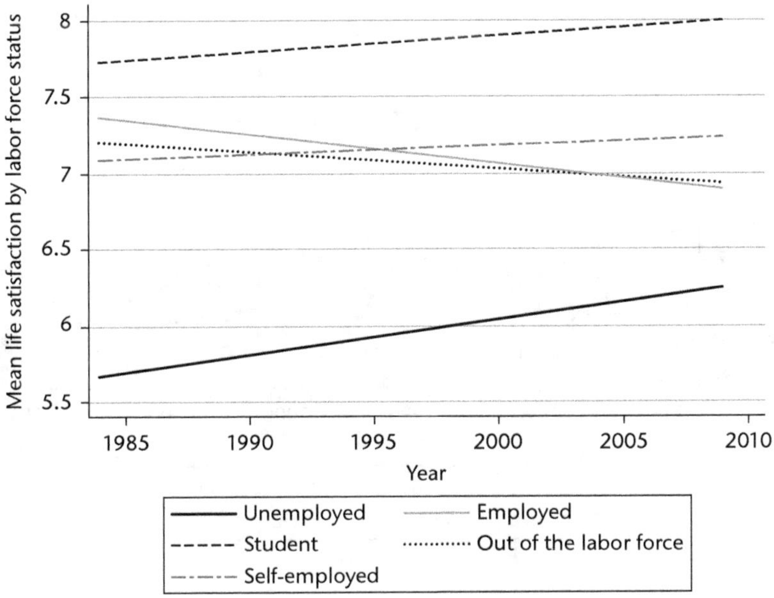

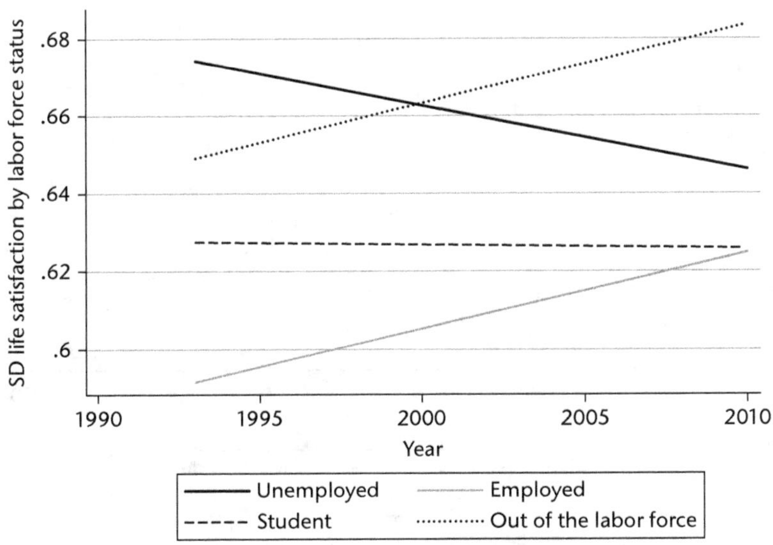

Figure 2.A4. (*Continued*)

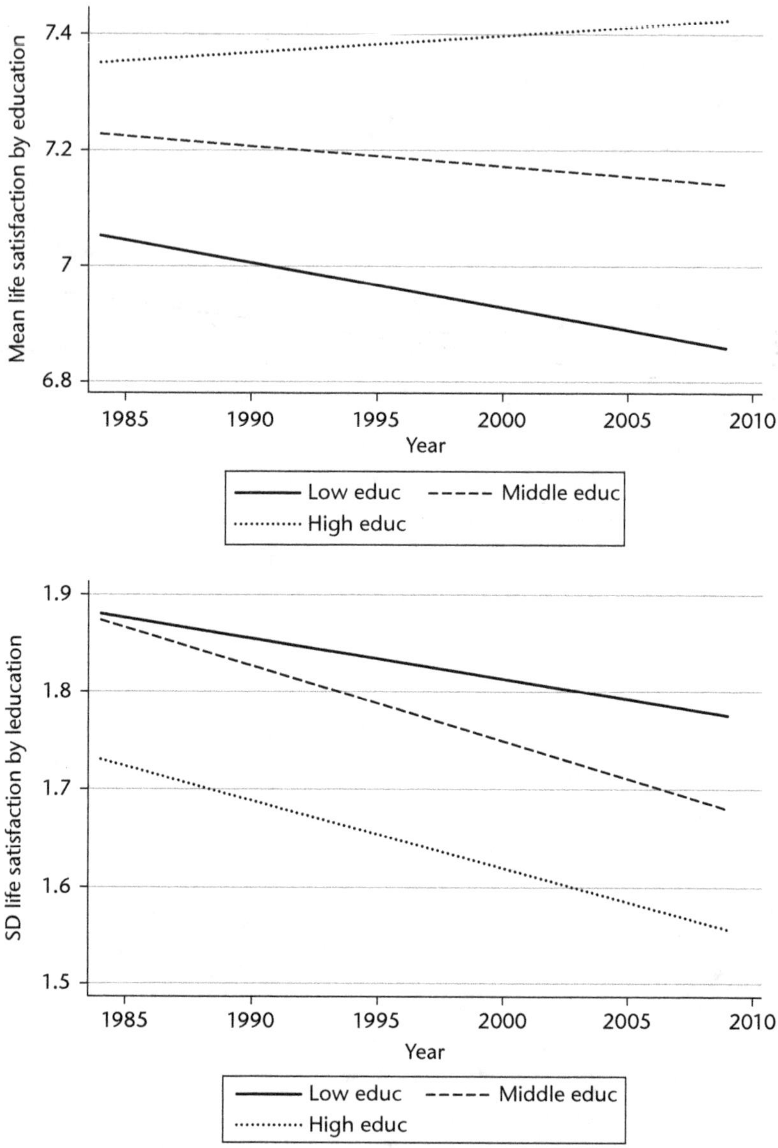

Figure 2.A4. Variance decomposition by demographic groups: SOEP

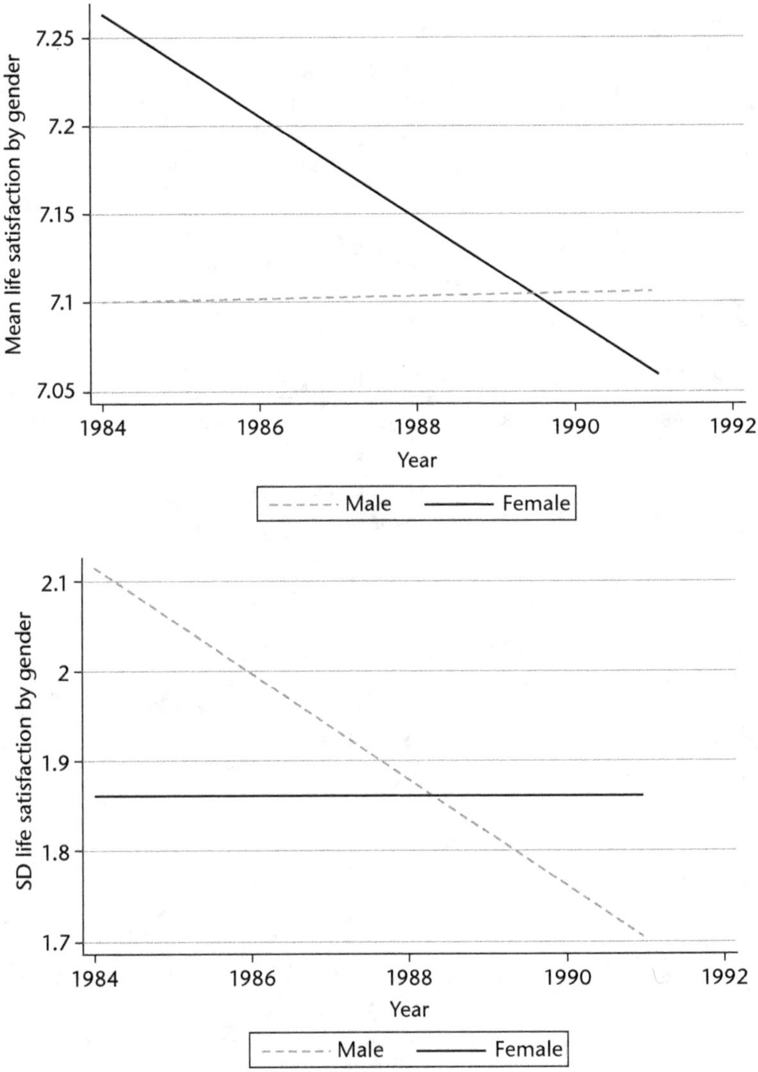

Figure 2.A5. (*Continued*)

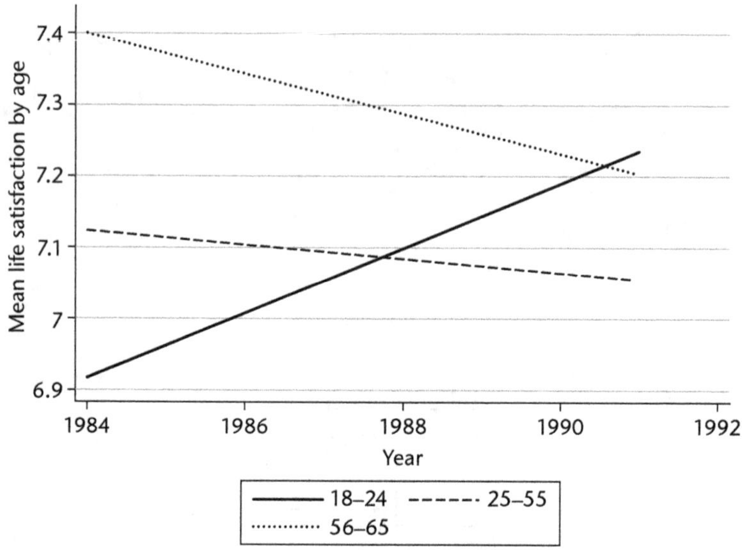

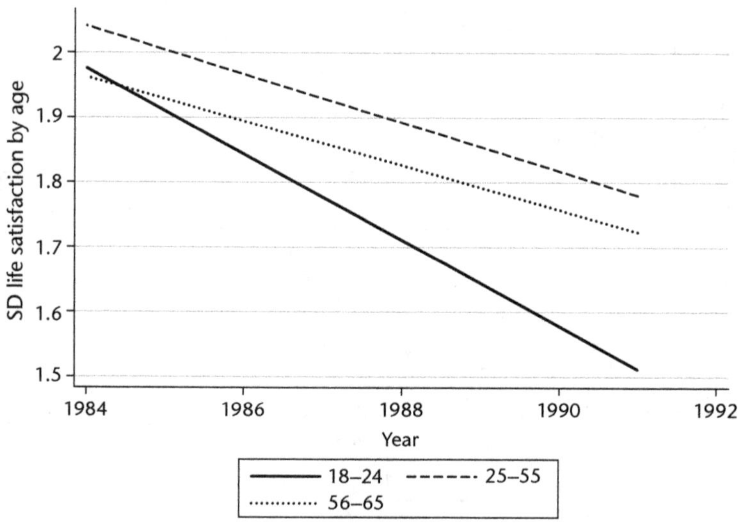

Figure 2.A5. (*Continued*)

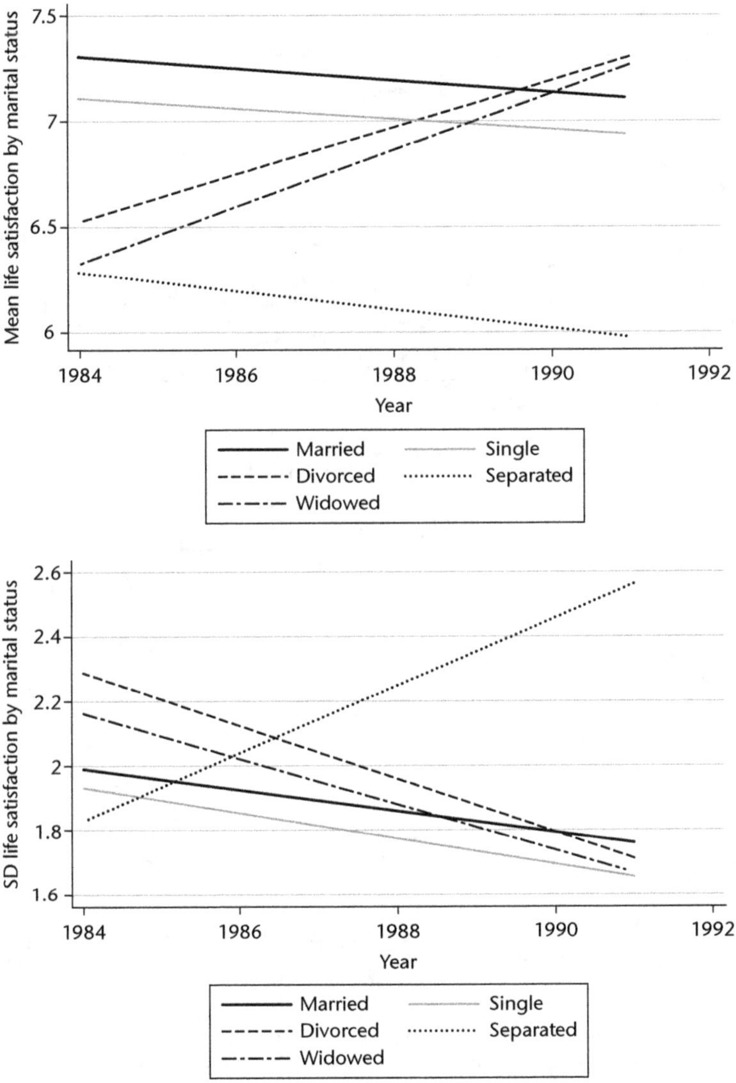

Figure 2.A5. (*Continued*)

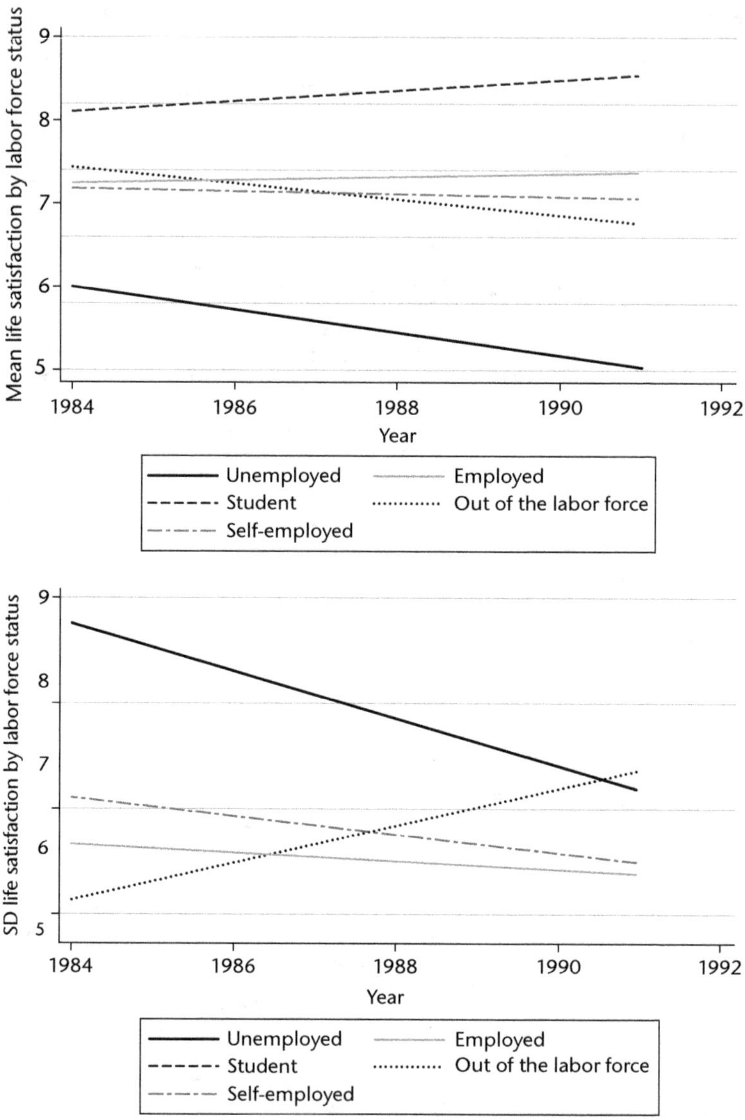

Figure 2.A5. (*Continued*)

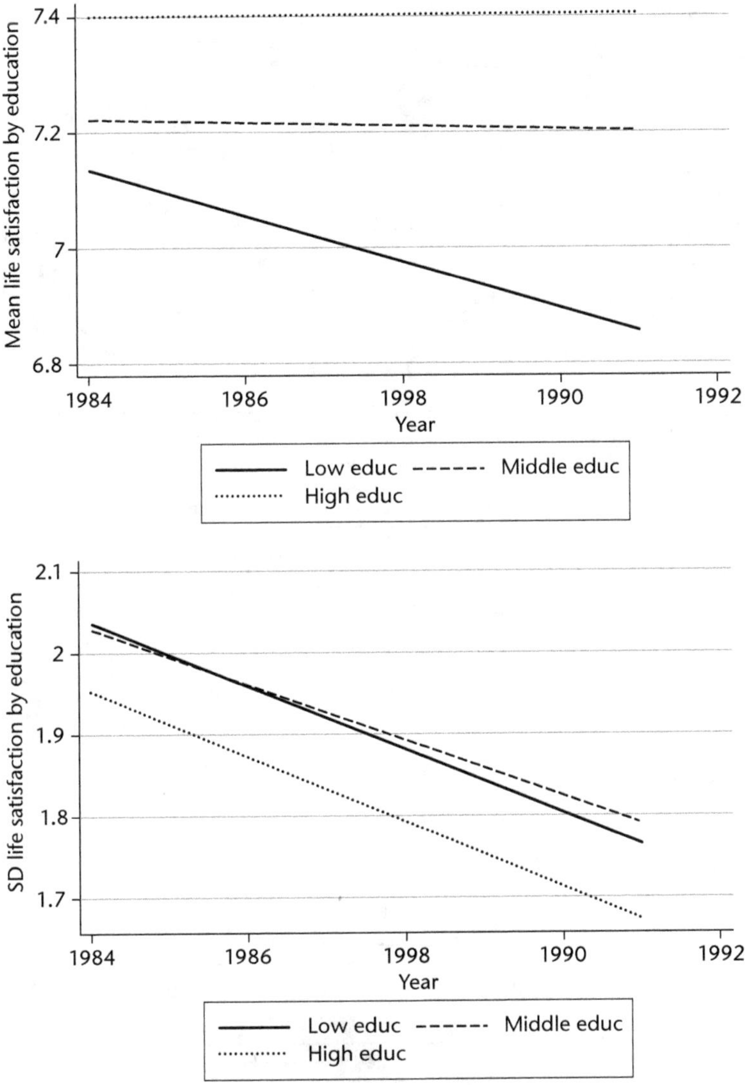

Figure 2.A5. Variance decomposition by demographic groups: SOEP (1984–90)

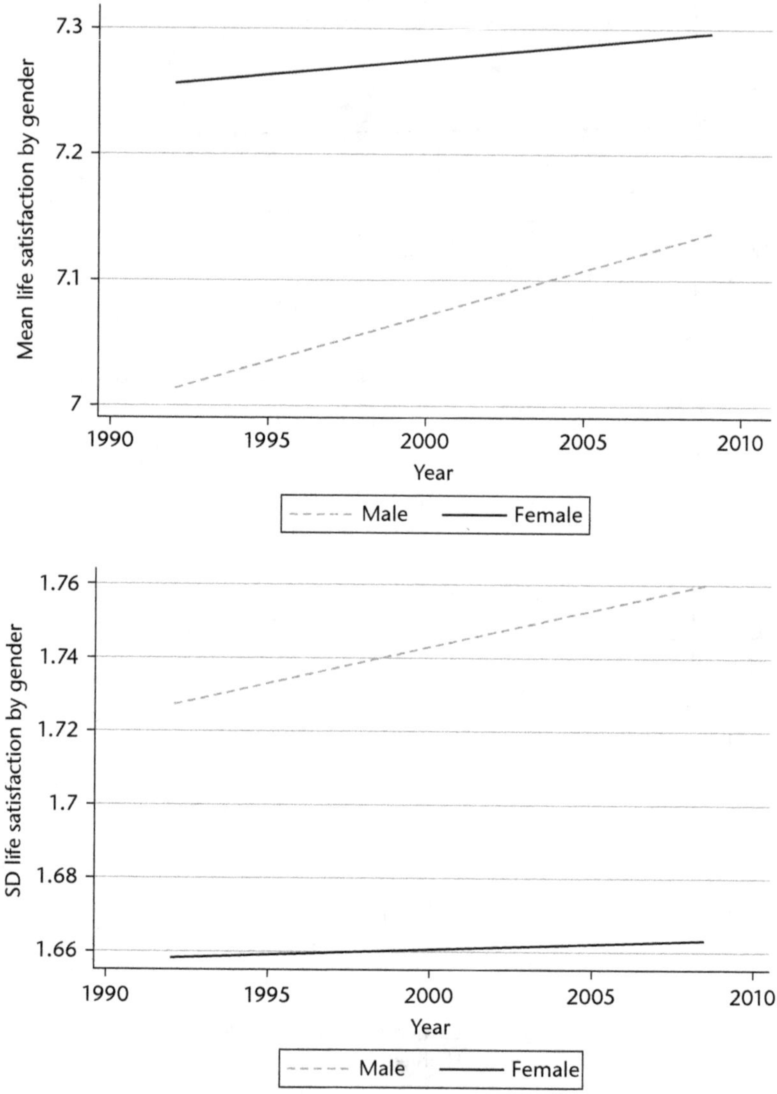

Figure 2.A6. (*Continued*)

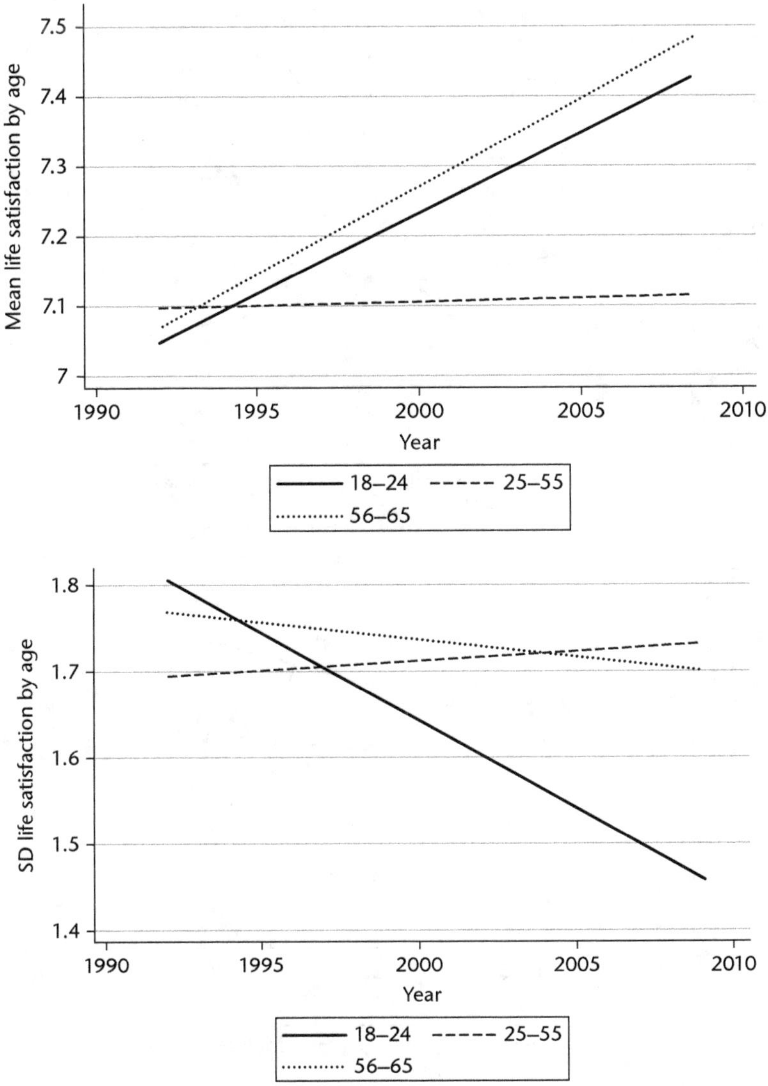

Figure 2.A6. (*Continued*)

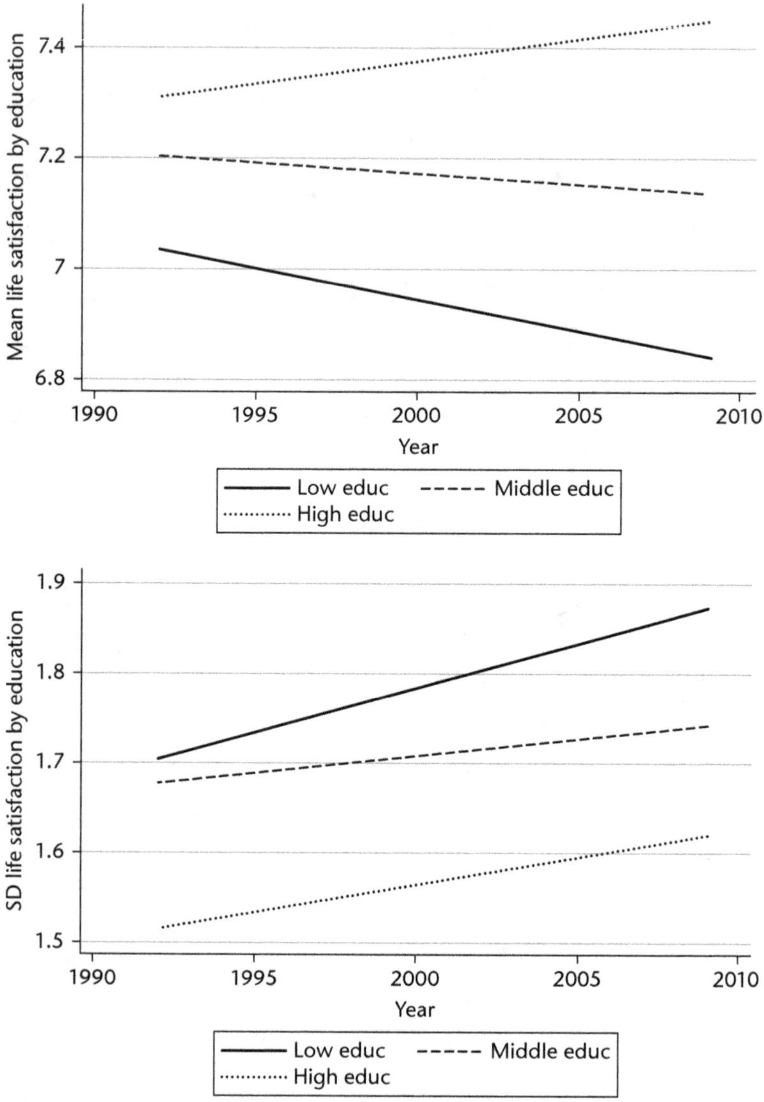

Figure 2.A6. (*Continued*)

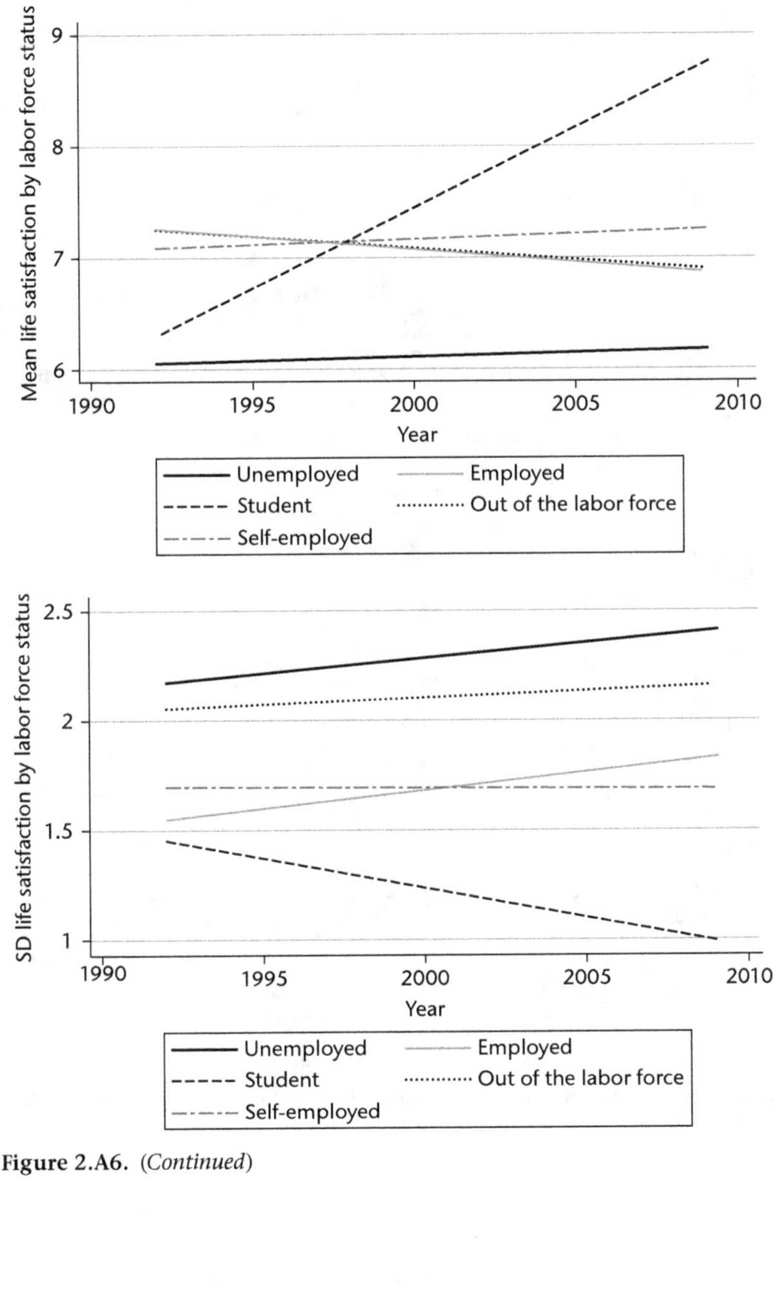

Figure 2.A6. (*Continued*)

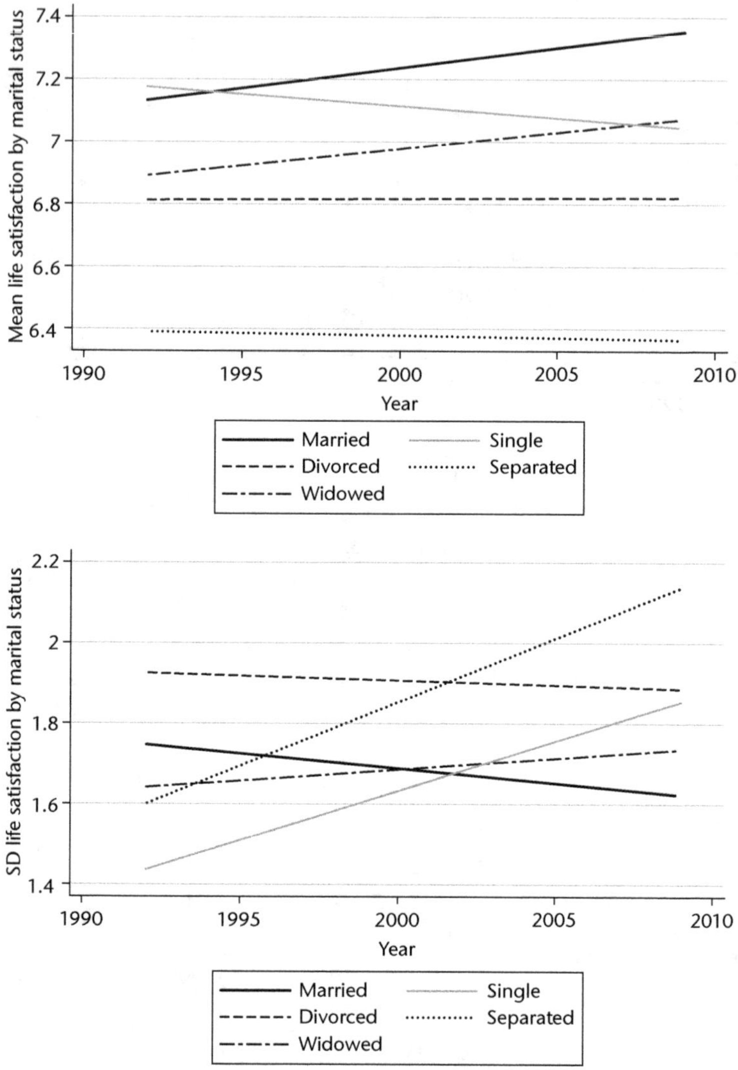

Figure 2.A6. Variance decomposition by demographic groups: SOEP (1992–2010)

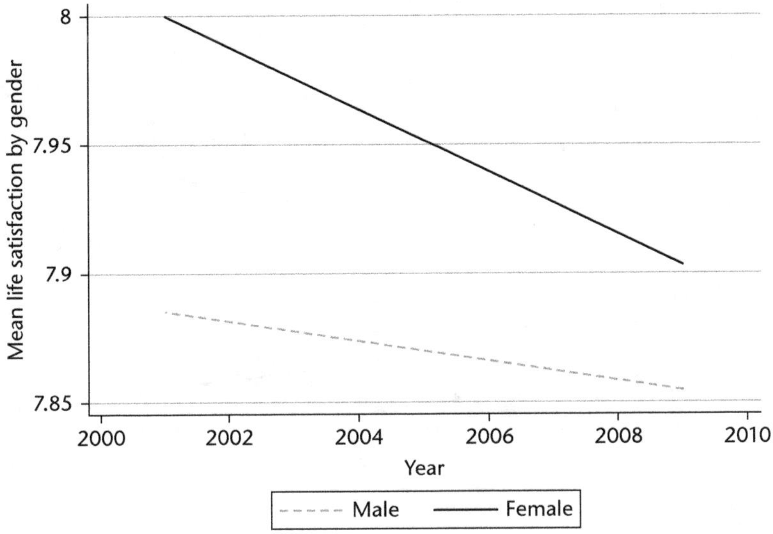

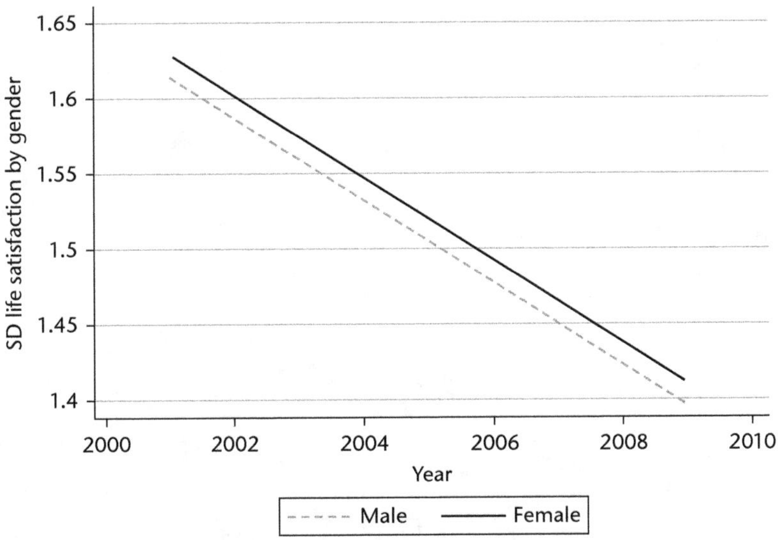

Figure 2.A7. (*Continued*)

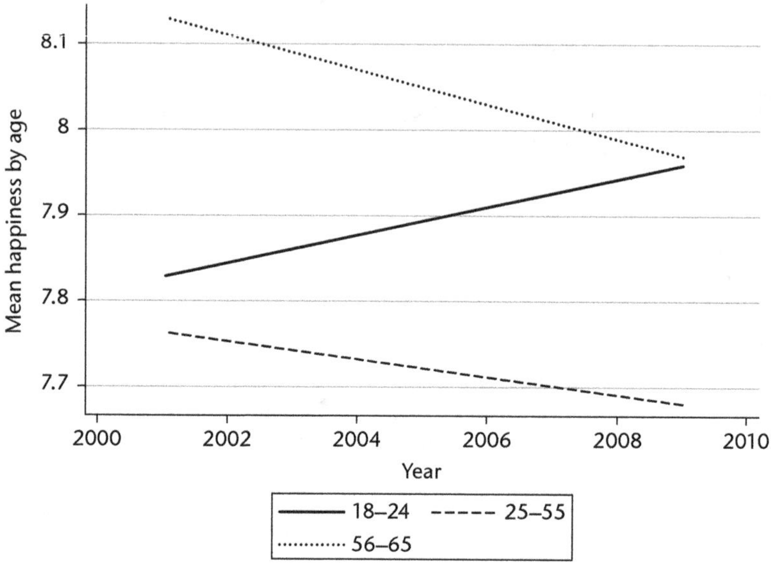

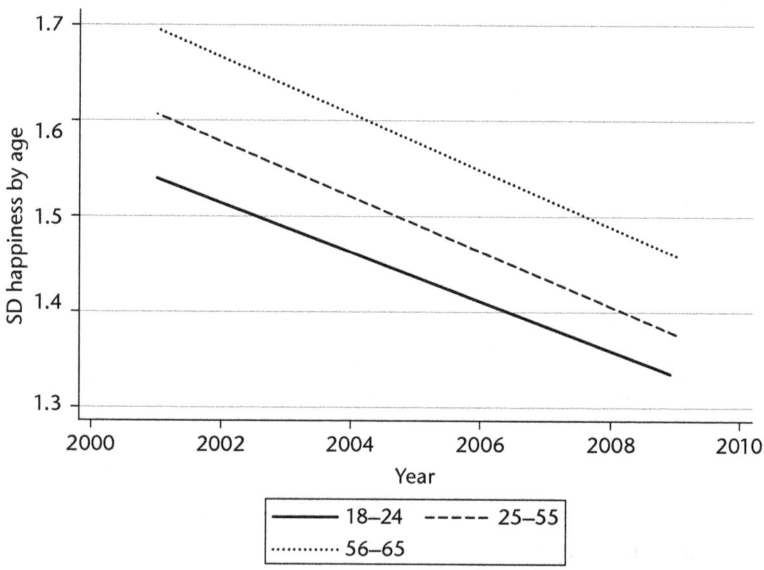

Figure 2.A7. (*Continued*)

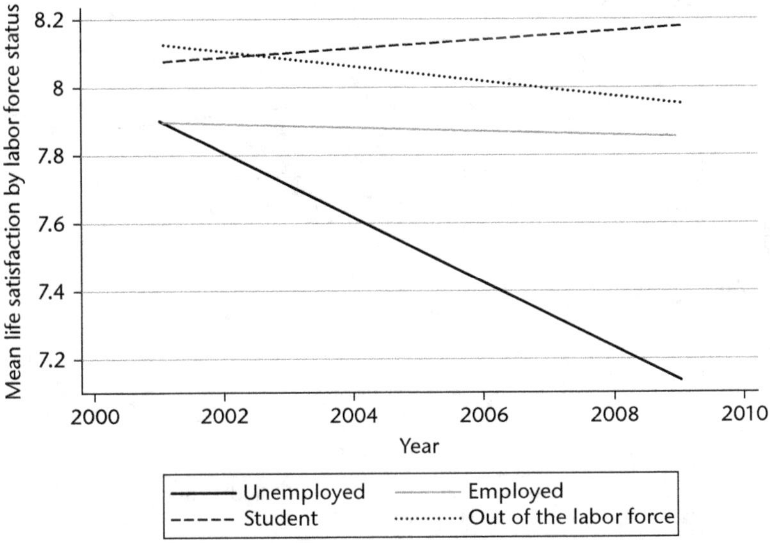

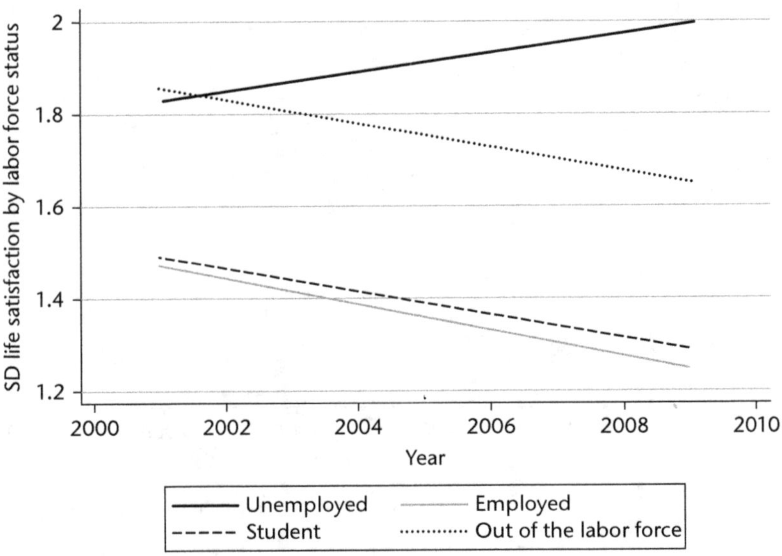

Figure 2.A7. *(Continued)*

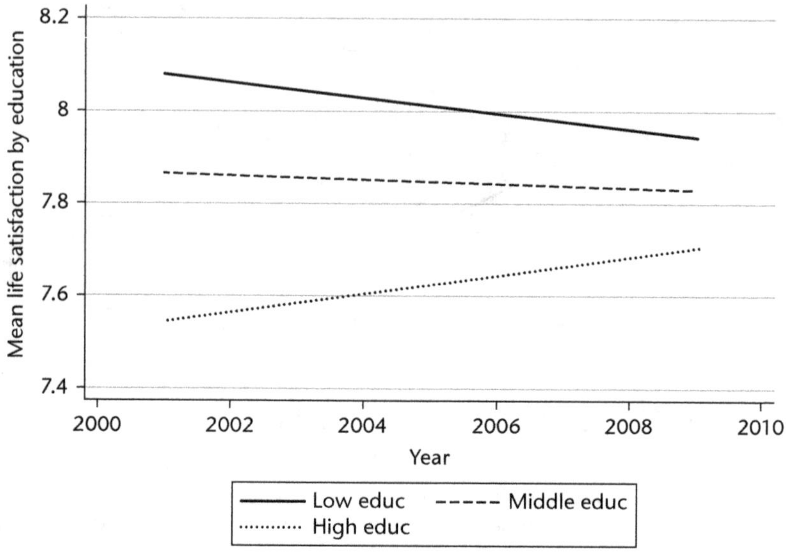

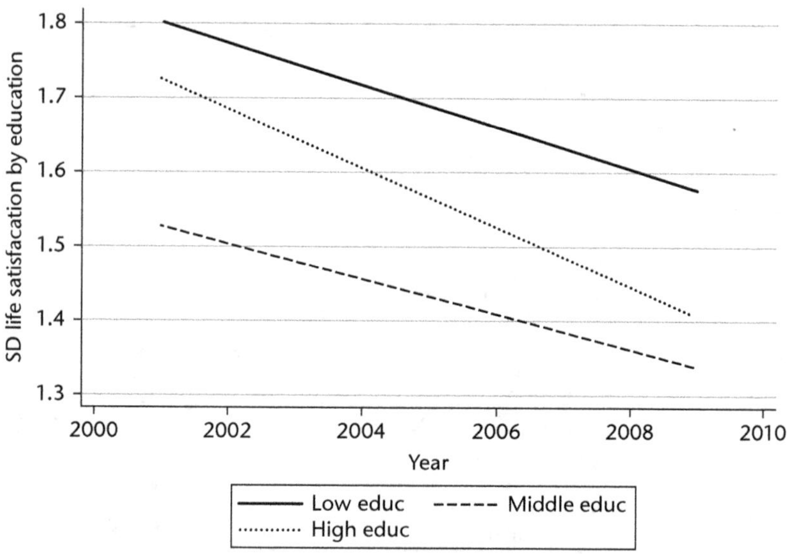

Figure 2.A7. (*Continued*)

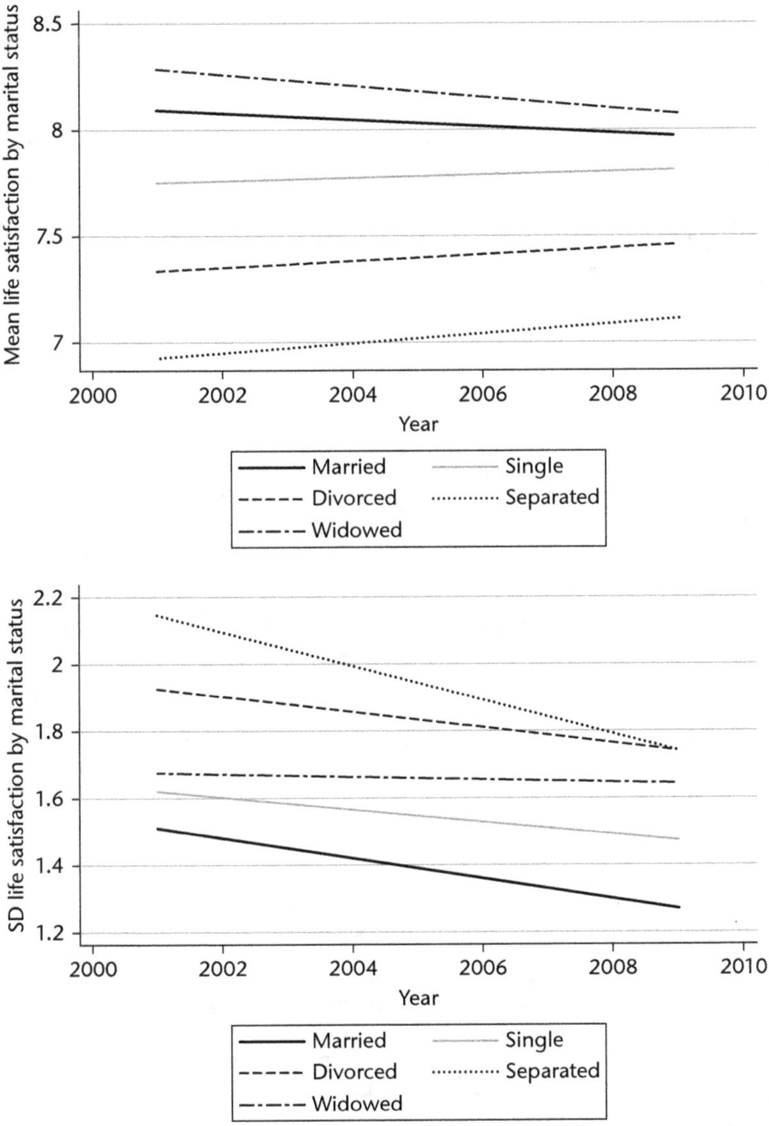

Figure 2.A7. Variance decomposition by demographic groups: HILDA

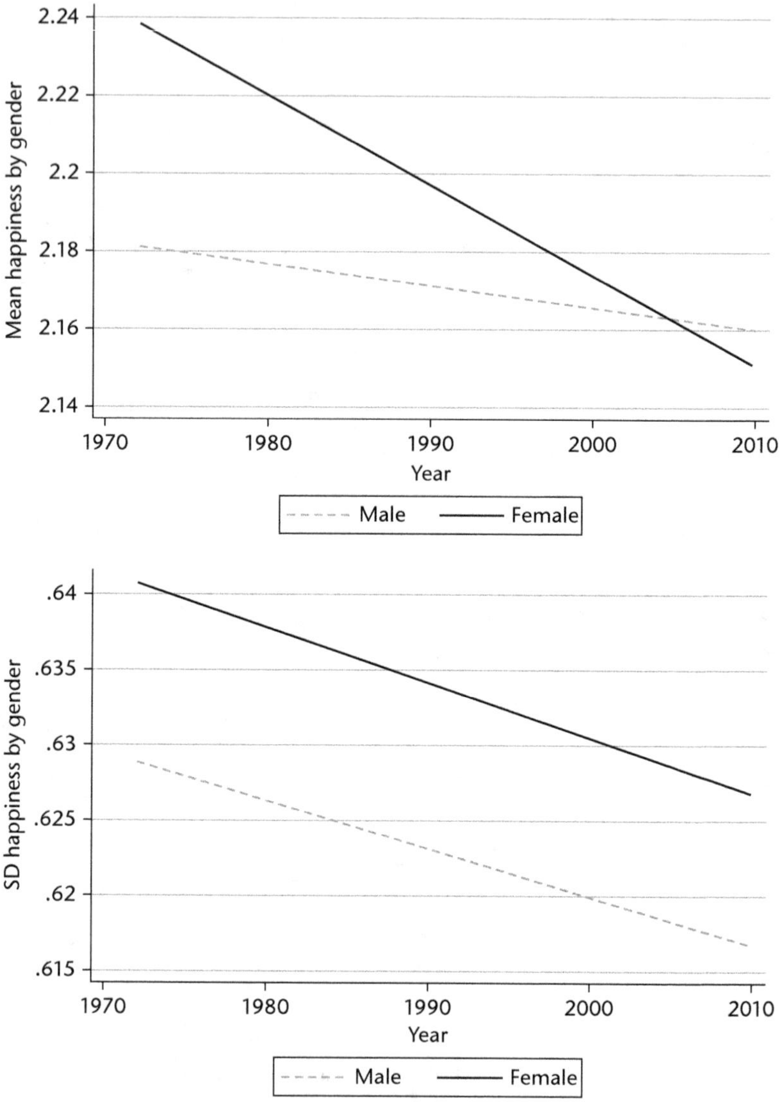

Figure 2.A8. (*Continued*)

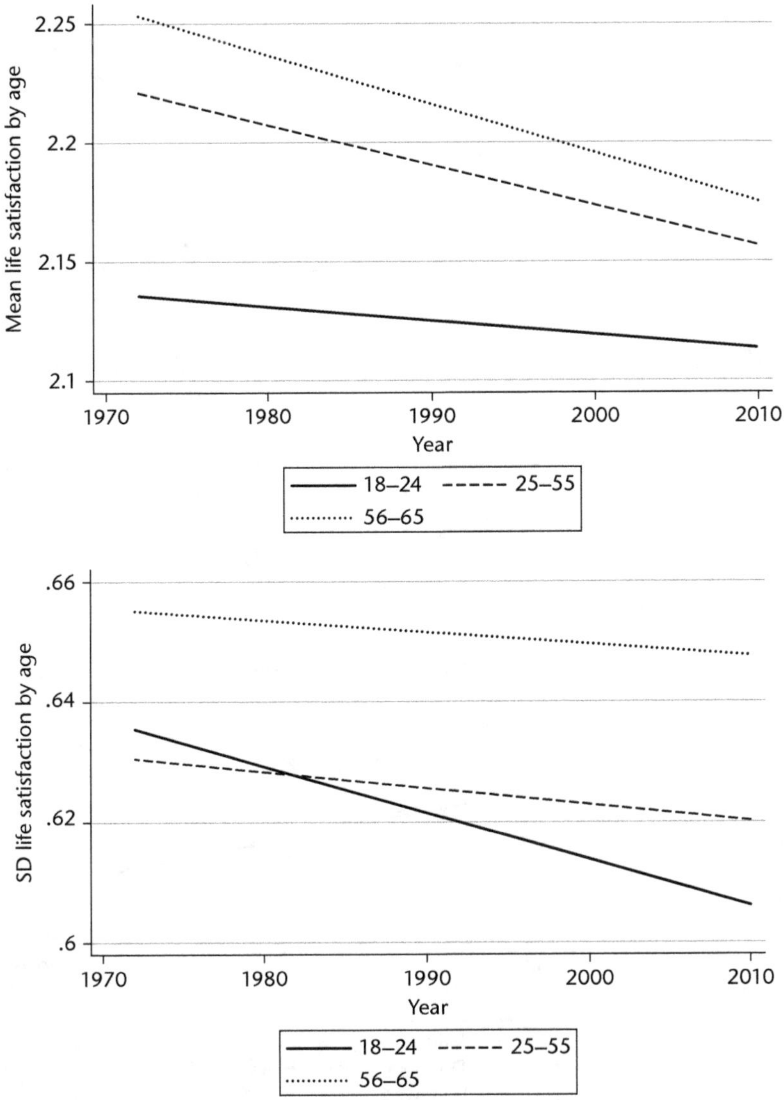

Figure 2.A8. (*Continued*)

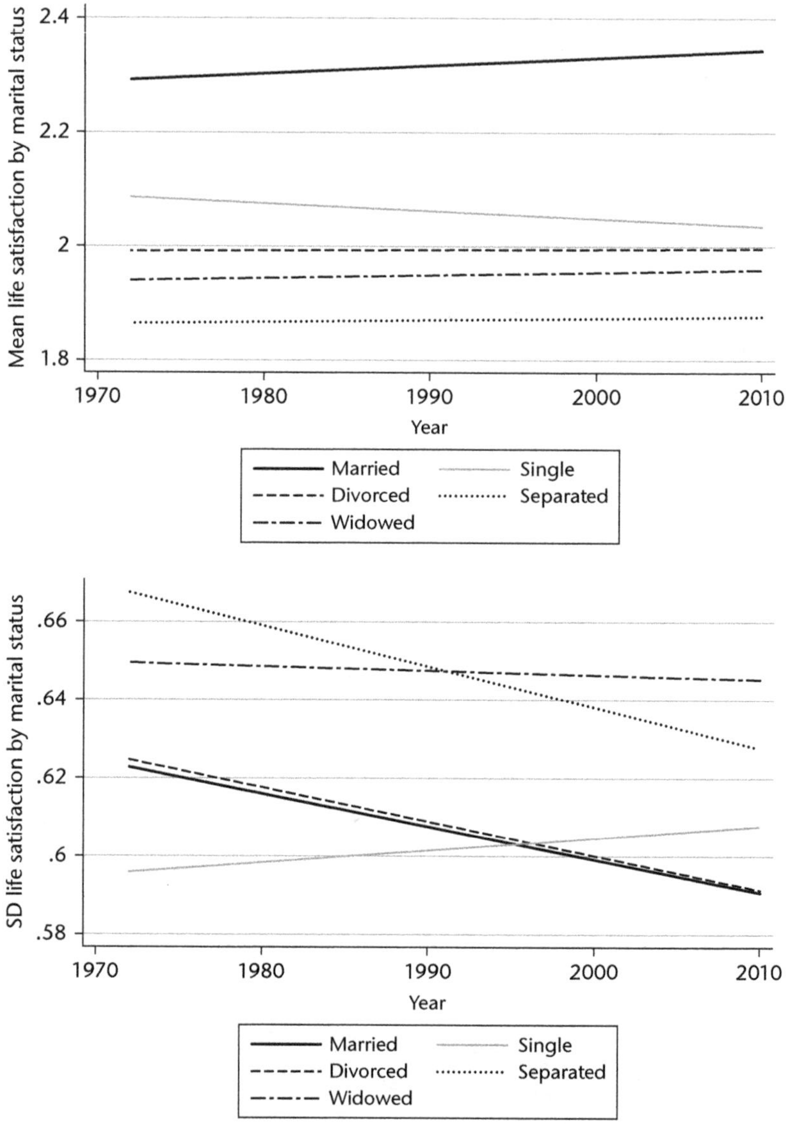

Figure 2.A8. (*Continued*)

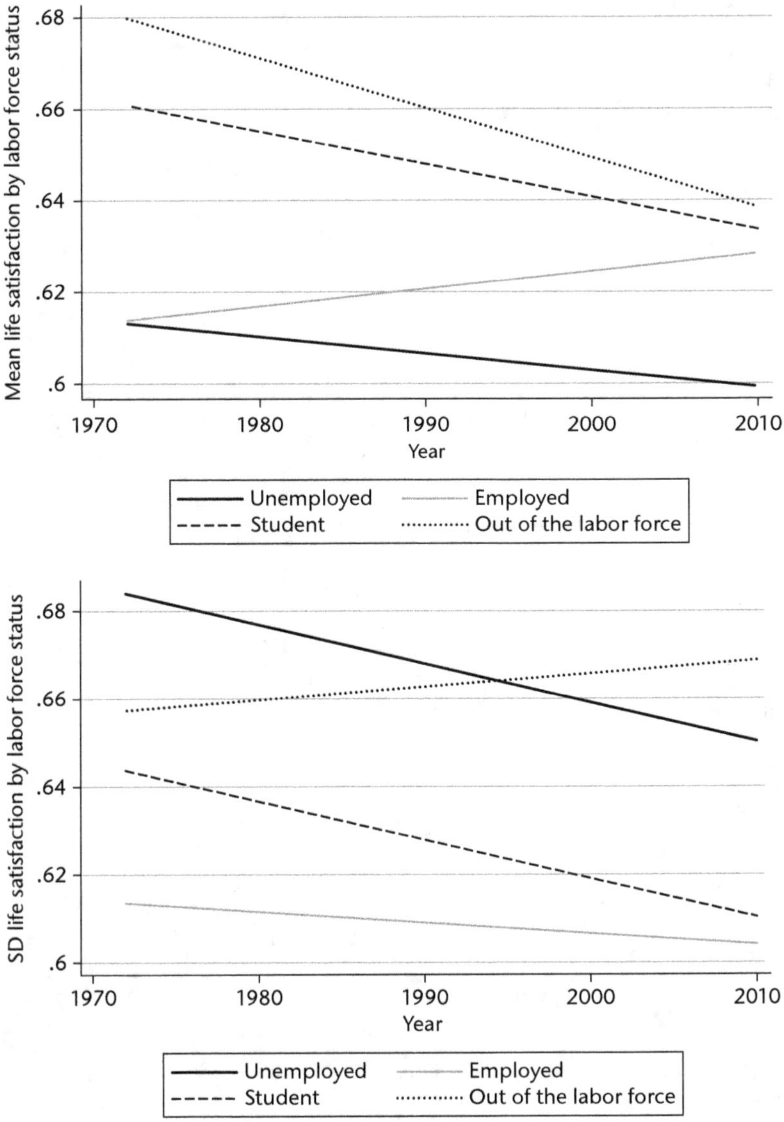

Figure 2.A8. (*Continued*)

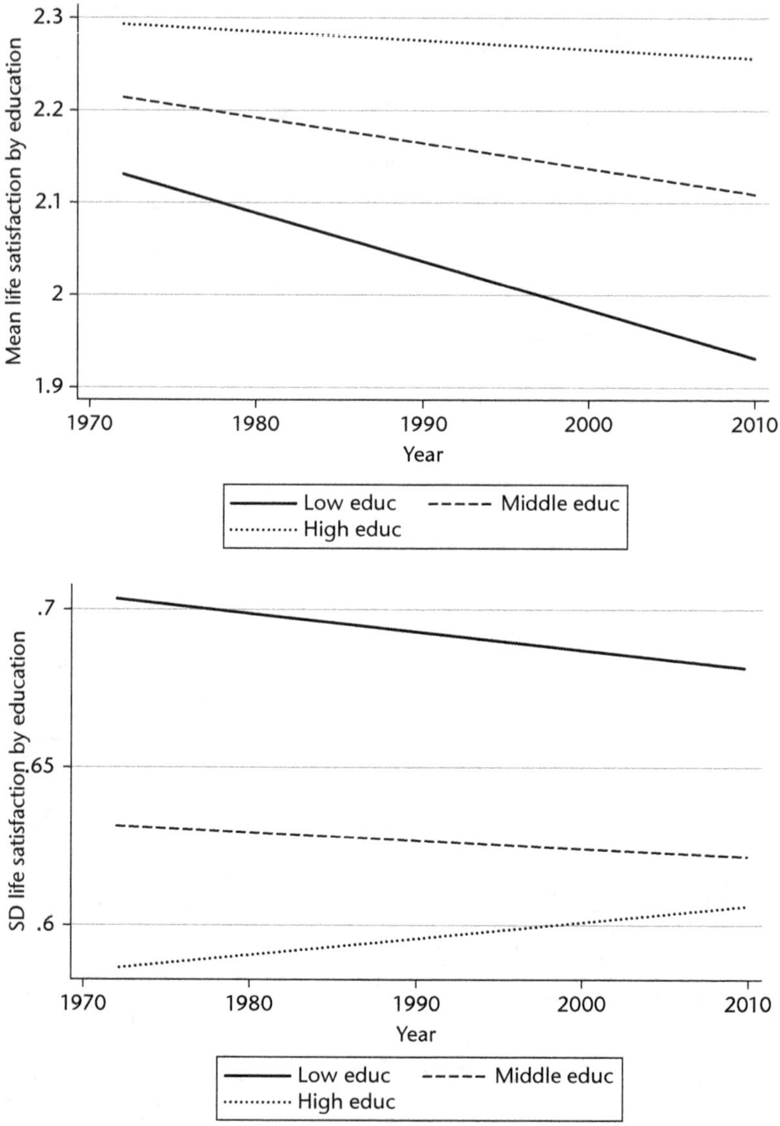

Figure 2.A8. Variance decomposition by demographic groups: GSS

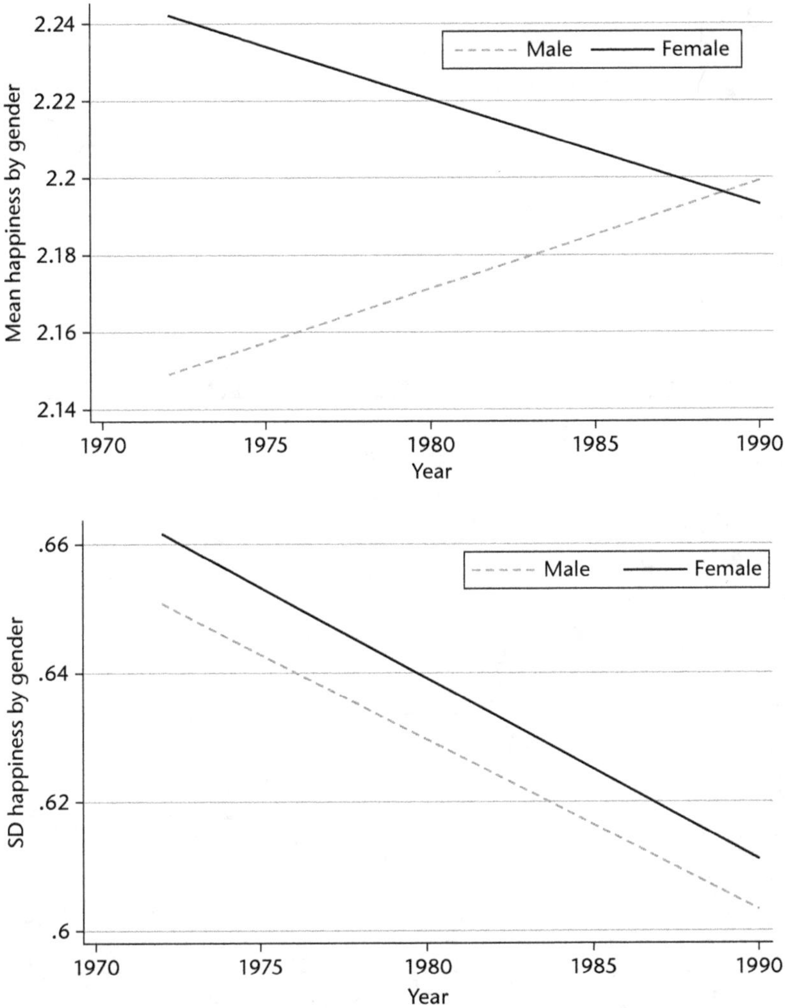

Figure 2.A9. (*Continued*)

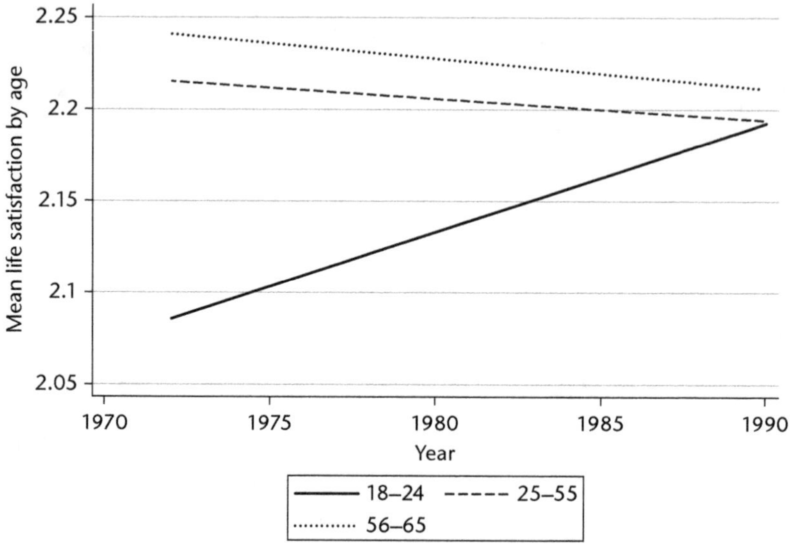

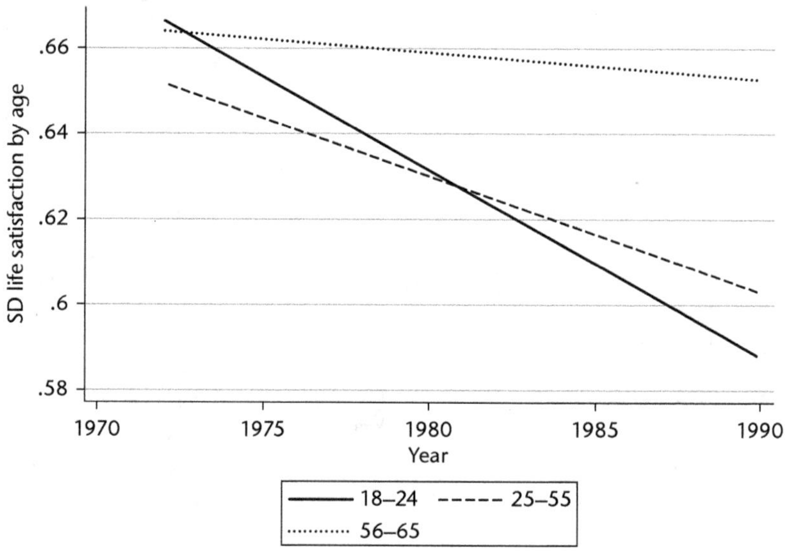

Figure 2.A9. (*Continued*)

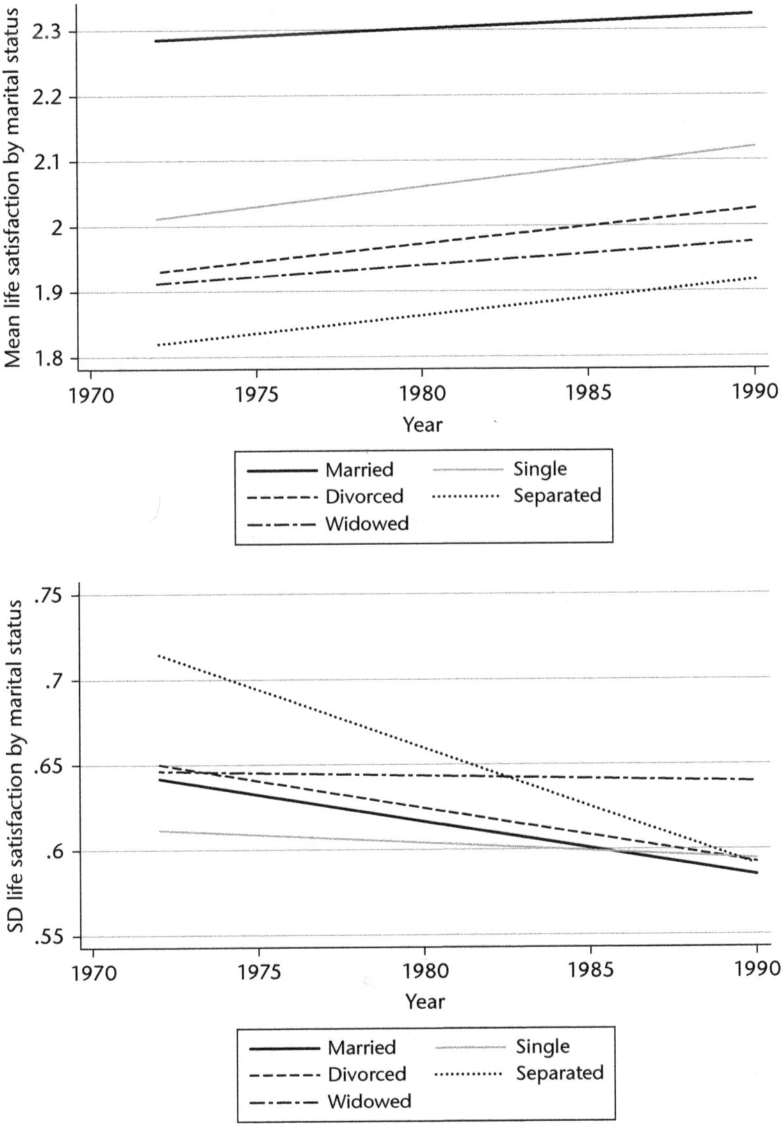

Figure 2.A9. *(Continued)*

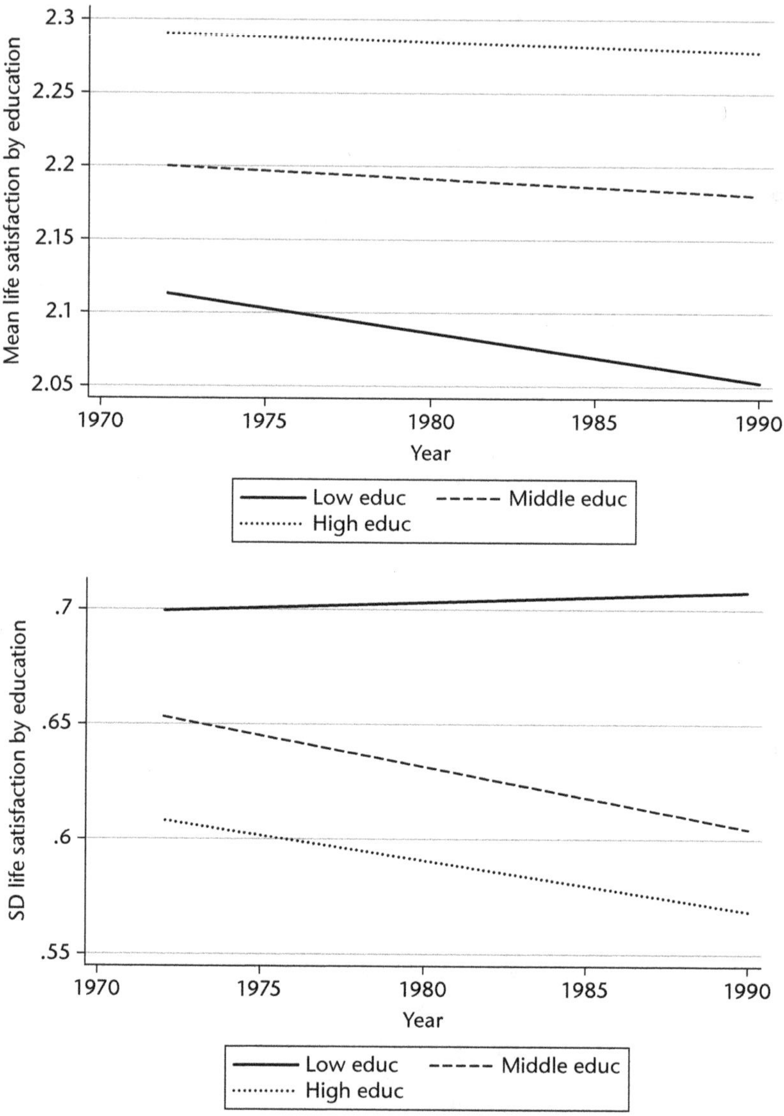

Figure 2.A9. (*Continued*)

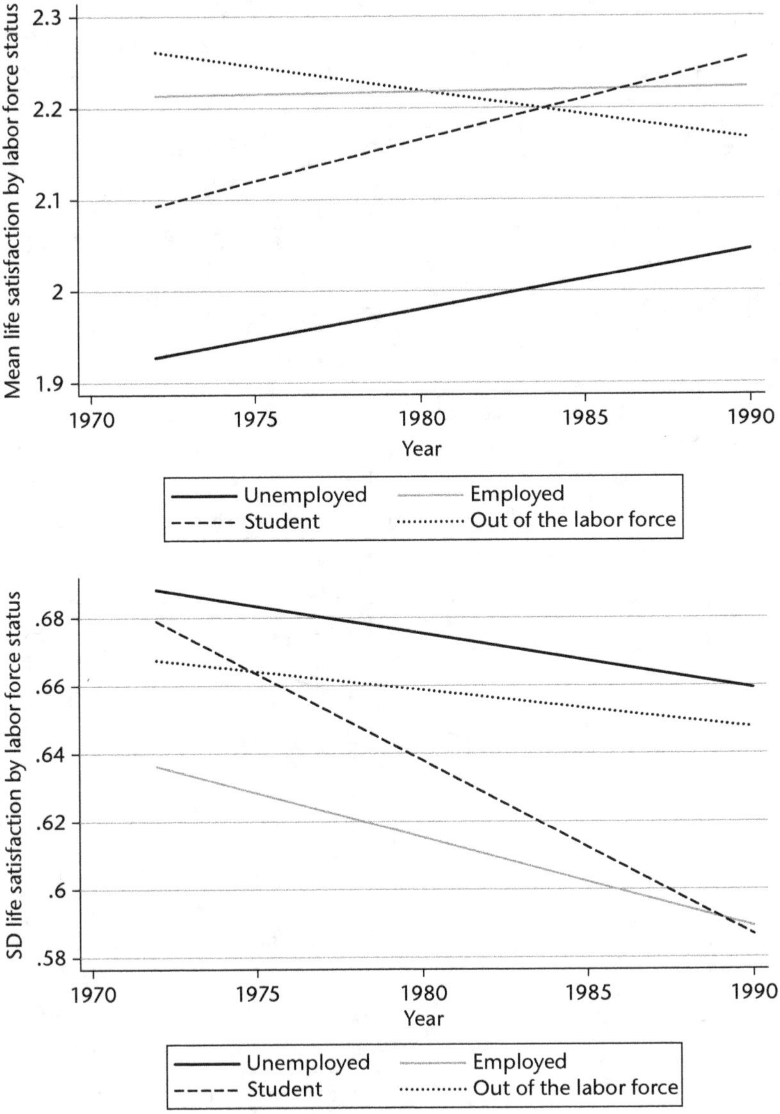

Figure 2.A9. Variance decomposition by demographic groups: GSS (1970–90)

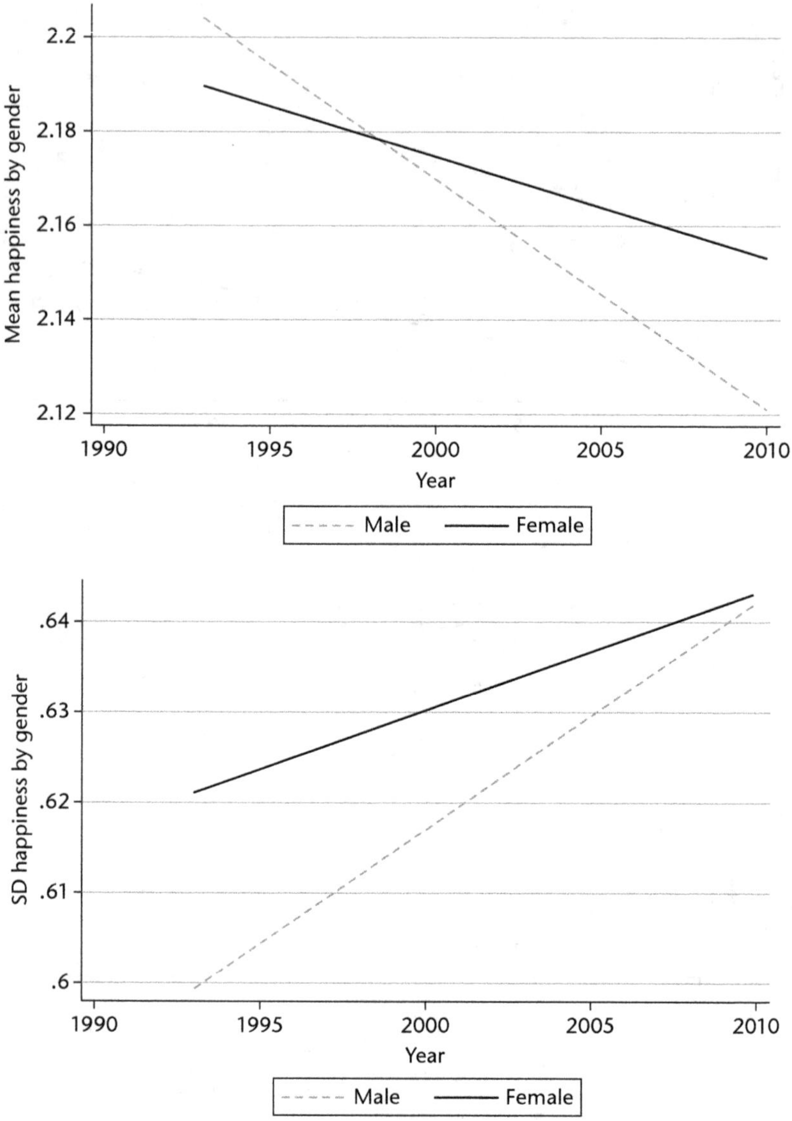

Figure 2.A10. (*Continued*)

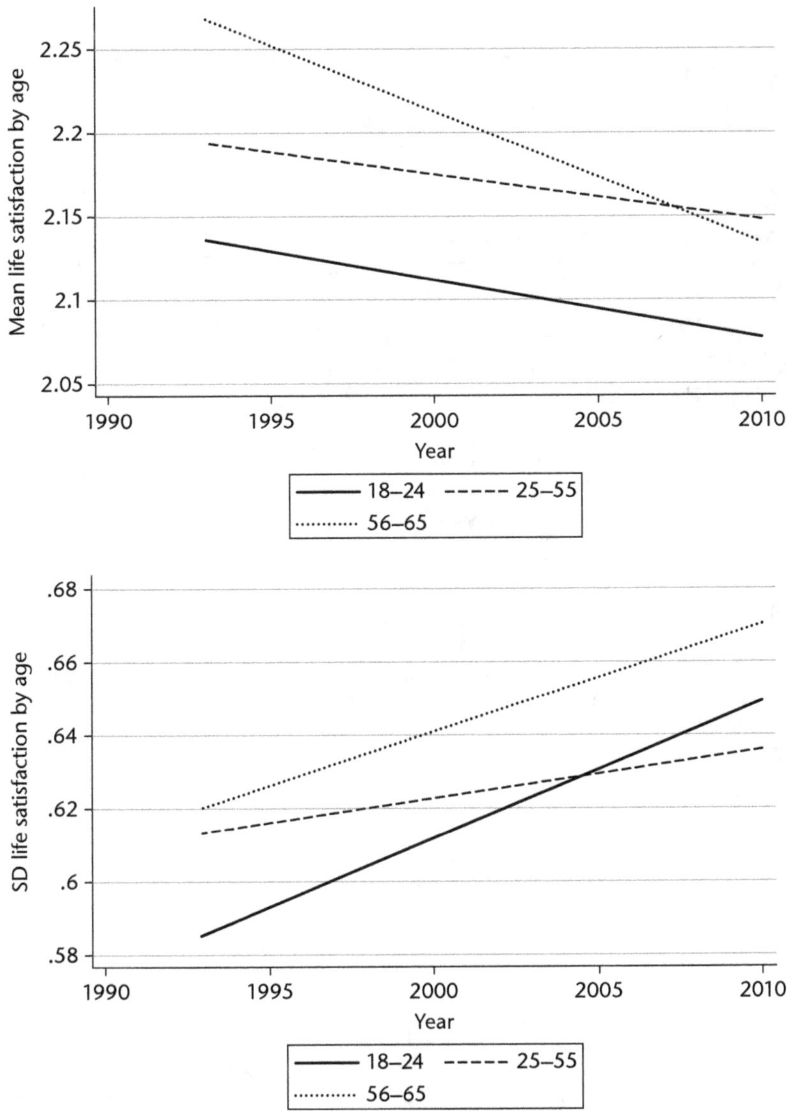

Figure 2.A10. (*Continued*)

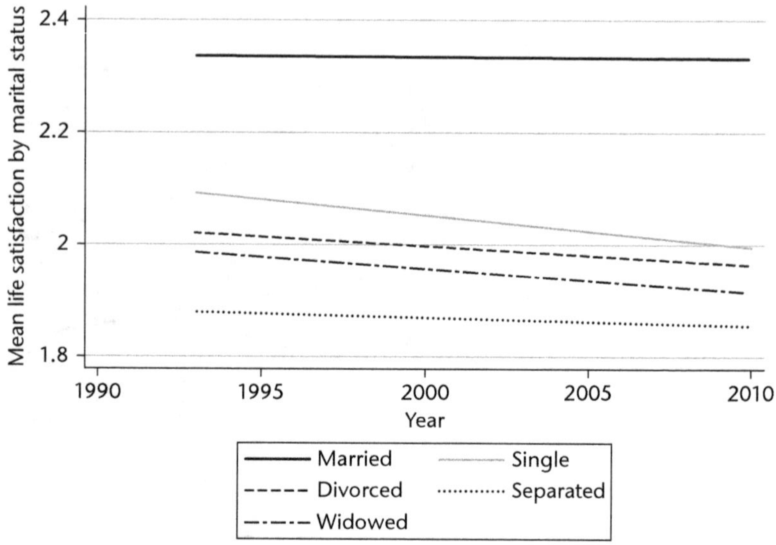

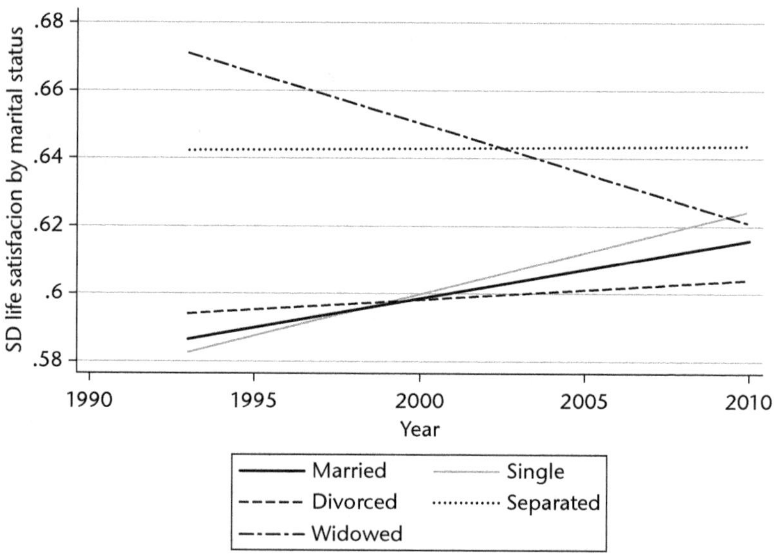

Figure 2.A10. *(Continued)*

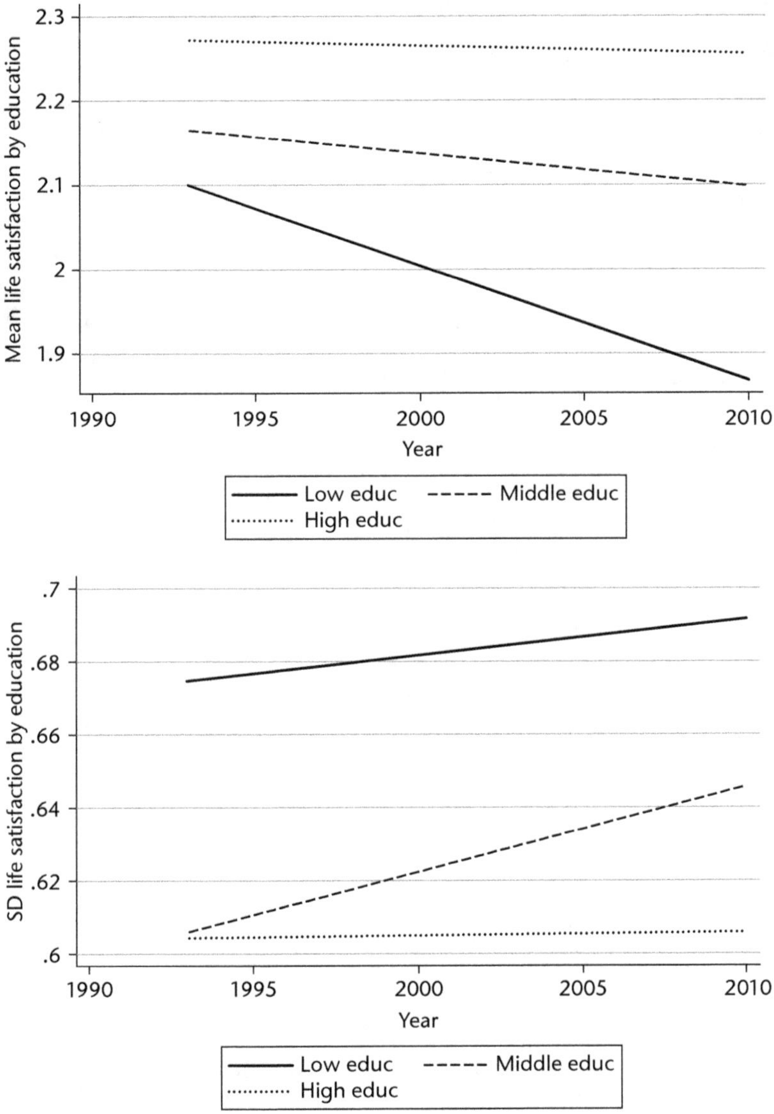

Figure 2.A10. *(Continued)*

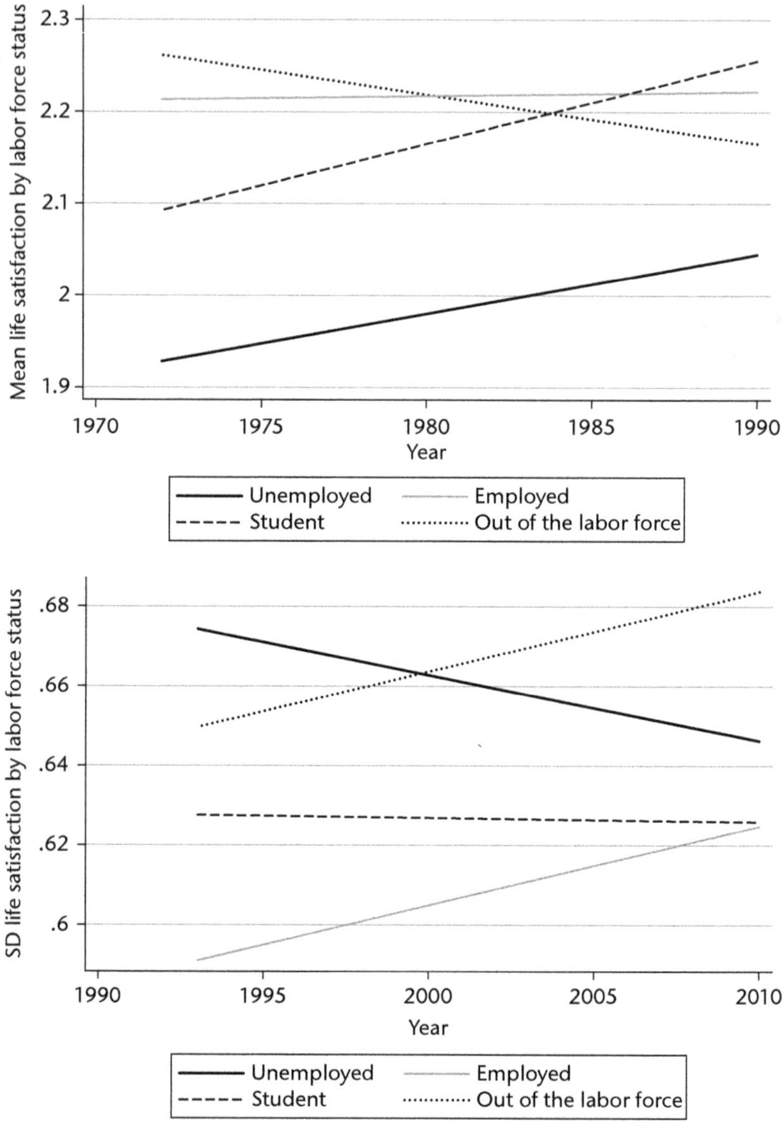

Figure 2.A10. Variance decomposition by demographic groups: GSS (1991–2010)

Table 2.A1. Descriptive statistics: World Values Survey

Variable	Obs.	Mean	Std. Dev.	Min	Max
	(1)	(2)	(3)	(4)	(5)
Life satisfaction	200887	6.53	2.47	1	10
SD life satisfaction	203071	2.21	0.35	1.41	3.35
Ln income	182735	1.35	0.63	0	2.3
Women	204914	0.52	0.50	0	1
Age 18–24	204993	0.19	0.39	0	1
Age 25–55	204993	0.70	0.46	0	1
Age 56–65	204993	0.11	0.31	0	1
Married	201619	0.65	0.48	0	1
Divorced	201619	0.03	0.17	0	1
Separated	201619	0.02	0.13	0	1
Single	201619	0.26	0.44	0	1
Widowed	201619	0.03	0.18	0	1
Out of labor force	197205	0.21	0.41	0	1
Student	197205	0.08	0.27	0	1
Unemployed	197205	0.10	0.30	0	1
Employed	197205	0.47	0.50	0	1
Low educ	189005	0.34	0.47	0	1
Middle educ	189005	0.44	0.50	0	1
High educ	189005	0.22	0.41	0	1
GDP per capita	202528	8843.9	13121.8	233.8	93367
Mean log deviation	200475	0.15	0.05	0.04	0.32
Rule of law	126376	0.06	1.01	−1.86	1.98
Control of corruption	126376	0.12	1.09	−1.56	2.44
Voice and accountability	126376	0.10	0.92	−1.7	1.7
Year	212402			1981	2008

Table 2.A2. Descriptive statistics: BHPS (1996–2008)

Variable	Obs	Mean	Std. Dev	Min	Max
	(1)	(2)	(3)	(4)	(5)
Life satisfaction	119234	5.15	1.26	1	7
SD life satisfaction	119234	1.26	0.03	1.20	1.31
SD life satisfaction/ mean	119234	0.25	0.01	0.23	0.26
GDP per capita	133736	35535	2791	30110	39462
SD income	133736	22968	3234	16642	28259
Women	133736	0.54	0.50	0	1
Age 18–24	133736	0.12	0.33	0	1
Age 25–55	133736	0.69	0.46	0	1
Age 56–65	133736	0.17	0.38	0	1
Low educ	133736	0.21	0.15	0	1
Middle educ	133736	0.60	0.17	0	1
High educ	133736	0.19	0.14	0	1
Out of labor force	133736	0.21	0.41	0	1
Student	133736	0.04	0.19	0	1
Unemployed	133736	0.04	0.20	0	1
Employed	133736	0.62	0.49	0	1
One child	133736	0.18	0.39	0	1
Two children	133736	0.14	0.34	0	1
Three children	133736	0.06	0.23	0	1
Married	133736	0.69	0.46	0	1
Single	133736	0.21	0.41	0	1
Divorced	133736	0.06	0.24	0	1
Separated	133736	0.02	0.14	0	1
Widowed	133736	0.02	0.14	0	1

Table 2.A3. Descriptive statistics: GSOEP (1984–2009)

Variable	Obs	Mean	Std. Dev.	Min	Max
	(1)	(2)	(3)	(4)	(5)
Life satisfaction	275207	7.15	1.78	0	10
SD life satisfaction	315609	1.77	0.11	1.67	2.11
SD life satifaction/mean	315609	0.25	0.01	0.23	0.28
GDP per head	315609	25075	7080	12872	37060
SD income	315609	31433	23473	11221	87639
Women	315609	0.50	0.49	0	1
Age 18–24	315609	0.10	0.31	0	1
Age 25–55	315609	0.73	0.44	0	1
Age 56–65	315609	0.15	0.35	0	1
Low education	265939	0.28	0.45	0	1
Middle education	265939	0.30	0.46	0	1
High education	265939	0.32	0.47	0	1
Out of labor force	287219	0.20	0.12	0	1
Student	287219	0.02	0.04	0	1
Unemployed	287219	0.02	0.15	0	1
Employed	287219	0.70	0.45	0	1
One child	315609	0.20	0.40	0	1
Two children	315609	0.14	0.35	0	1
Three children	315609	0.14	0.35	0	1
Married	274947	0.64	0.47	0	1
Single	274947	0.25	0.38	0	1
Divorced	274947	0.06	0.29	0	1
Separated	274947	0.03	0.17	0	1
Widowed	274947	0.02	0.12	0	1

Table 2.A4. Descriptive statistics: GSS (1972–2010)

Variable	Obs	Mean	Std. Dev	Min	Max
	(1)	(2)	(3)	(4)	(5)
Happy	41383	2.18	0.63	1	3
SD happiness	45316	0.63	0.02	0.60	0.67
SD happiness/mean	45316	0.29	0.01	0.27	0.31
GDP per capita	45316	32732	7103	21912	43131
SD income	12653	31628	12600	7936	46689
Women	45316	1.55	0.50	1	2
Age 18–24	45316	0.12	0.33	0	1
Age 25–55	45316	0.73	0.44	0	1
Age 56–65	45316	0.14	0.35	0	1
Low education	45316	0.09	0.29	0	1
Middle education	45316	0.62	0.48	0	1
High education	45316	0.28	0.45	0	1
Out of labor force	45316	0.18	0.39	0	1
Student	45316	0.04	0.19	0	1
Unemployed	45316	0.06	0.24	0	1
Employed	45316	0.70	0.46	0	1
One child	45316	0.17	0.37	0	1
Two children	45316	0.25	0.43	0	1
Three children	45316	0.29	0.45	0	1
Married	45316	0.56	0.50	0	1
Single	45316	0.23	0.42	0	1
Divorced	45316	0.13	0.34	0	1
Separated	45316	0.04	0.19	0	1
Widowed	45316	0.03	0.18	0	1

Table 2.A5. Descriptive statistics: HILDA (2001–2009)

Variable	Obs	Mean	Std. Dev	Min	Max
	(1)	(2)	(3)	(4)	(5)
Life satisfaction	93275	7.80	1.51	0	10
SD life satisfaction	93327	1.50	0.08	1.41	1.67
SD life satisfaction/ mean	93327	0.19	0.01	0.18	0.21
GDP per capita	93327	34833	1441	32350	36482
SD income	93327	36064	4493	30446	42993
Women	93327	1.52	0.50	1	2
Age 18–24	93327	0.15	0.36	0	1
Age 25–55	93327	0.69	0.46	0	1
Age 56–65	93327	0.16	0.36	0	1
Low educ	93327	0.23	0.42	0	1
Middle educ	93327	0.73	0.44	0	1
High educ	93327	0.03	0.17	0	1
Out of labor force	93327	0.16	0.37	0	1
Student	93327	0.02	0.15	0	1
Unemployed	93327	0.06	0.24	0	1
Employed	93327	0.75	0.43	0	1
One child	93327	0.12	0.33	0	1
Two children	93327	0.27	0.44	0	1
Three children	93327	0.26	0.44	0	1
Married	93327	0.66	0.47	0	1
Single	93327	0.23	0.42	0	1
Divorced	93327	0.06	0.24	0	1
Separated	93327	0.03	0.18	0	1
Widowed	93327	0.01	0.12	0	1

Table 2.A6. World Values Survey: RIF estimates of the variance of life satisfaction across countries

	(1)	(2)	(3)	(4)	(5)	(6)
Ln GDP per capita	−0.528*** (0.0159)	−0.552*** (0.0162)	−0.687*** (0.0214)	−0.199*** (0.0290)	−0.0222 (0.0300)	−0.267*** (0.0243)
Mean Ln deviation		7.739*** (0.491)	5.260*** (0.552)	6.530*** (0.486)	8.928*** (0.490)	9.360*** (0.493)
Social expenditure			0.00876** (0.00357)			
Rule of law				−0.929*** (0.0386)		
Control of corruption					−1.114*** (0.0371)	
Voice and accountability						−1.104*** (0.0383)
Observations	126035	122681	86534	106628	106628	106628
R-squared	0.041	0.043	0.048	0.054	0.057	0.056

Other controls: Year fixed effects, age categories, gender, number of children, education, employment status, marital status. Standard errors are clustered at the country level. Weighted estimates.

Table 2.A7. World Values Survey: RIF estimates of variance of life satisfaction over time

	(1)	(2)	(3)
Ln GDP per capita	−0.849***	−0.892***	−0.892***
	(0.0756)	(0.0766)	(0.111)
Mean Ln Deviation		4.265***	2.685**
		(0.924)	(1.165)
Social expenditures			−0.0658***
			(0.0160)
Female	−0.0758*	−0.0828*	−0.0843*
	(0.0431)	(0.0438)	(0.0506)
Age 25–55	0.265***	0.244***	0.269***
	(0.0660)	(0.0670)	(0.0776)
Age 56–65	0.595***	0.584***	0.528***
	(0.0926)	(0.0941)	(0.108)
One child	−0.139*	−0.154*	−0.0398
	(0.0808)	(0.0819)	(0.0888)
Two children	−0.0825	−0.0991	−0.129
	(0.0785)	(0.0796)	(0.0871)
Three children	−0.118	−0.140*	0.0736
	(0.0799)	(0.0810)	(0.0900)
Married	0.0322	0.0818	0.0576
	(0.0776)	(0.0787)	(0.0850)
Divorced	0.787***	0.823***	0.815***
	(0.131)	(0.133)	(0.149)
Separated	1.016***	1.058***	1.300***
	(0.163)	(0.166)	(0.181)
Widowed	1.089***	1.157***	0.959***
	(0.135)	(0.137)	(0.157)
Not in labor force	0.223***	0.220***	0.293***
	(0.0587)	(0.0597)	(0.0687)
Student	0.0301	0.0508	0.344***
	(0.0877)	(0.0889)	(0.0990)
Unemployed	1.516***	1.520***	1.555***
	(0.0718)	(0.0732)	(0.0814)
Medium education	−0.757***	−0.771***	−0.974***
	(0.0496)	(0.0505)	(0.0576)
High education	−1.124***	−1.126***	−1.465***
	(0.0597)	(0.0607)	(0.0702)
Observations	126035	122681	86534
R-squared	0.073	0.073	0.064

Note: the regression includes country fixed effects. Standard errors are clustered at the country level. Weighted estimates.

3

Poor, or Just Feeling Poor? On Using Subjective Data in Measuring Poverty

*Martin Ravallion**

3.1 Introduction

Development monitoring and policy evaluation efforts have traditionally put a high weight on progress against poverty, defined in terms of household consumption or income as measured in surveys.[1] It is well recognized that household consumption or income aggregates need to be normalized for cost-of-living differences, including differences in household size, although there are differing views on how the normalization should be done. It has also come to be recognized that neither income nor consumption (even with seemingly appropriate normalizations) can be considered a sufficient statistic for welfare. Standard survey methods allow a fairly complete accounting of the market goods consumed (including own-farm products). However, there are important non-market goods that are typically excluded, such as access to public services for health care or schooling. And household aggregate income or consumption reveals nothing directly about distribution within the household.

There have been attempts to define development indices that allow for these "non-income" factors. An early example was Morris's (1979)

* For comments on the chapter the author is grateful to Kathleen Beegle, Nobuo Yoshida, Ekaterina Zhuravskaya, and seminar/conference participants at the Paris School of Economics and the World Bank.

[1] For example, since the mid-1990s the World Bank—the largest international development agency—has deemed poverty reduction to be its "overarching goal." The first of the United Nation's Millennium Development Goals is to halve the 1990s' income or consumption poverty rate for the developing world by 2015.

"Physical Quality of Life Index," which is an average of literacy, infant mortality, and life expectancy. A now famous example is the "Human Development Index" (HDI), which aggregates life expectancy and education, along with income.[2] A recent example is the "Multidimensional Poverty Index" (MPI) of Alkire and Santos (2010). This combines ten components: two for health (malnutrition and child mortality); two for education (years of schooling and school enrollment); and six for "living standards" (including both access to services and proxies for household wealth).[3]

All such composite indices confront the problem of setting the trade-offs (relative weights) across their dimensions. This is essentially ad hoc in all these measures.[4] And there are objections that can be raised. For example, Ravallion (2012a) points out that the HDI puts a remarkably low monetary value on an extra year of life in very poor countries, and a very high value in rich ones.[5] The HDI's weight on schooling in poor countries is also far higher than its weight on longevity, for no obvious reason. Recognizing that welfare is "multidimensional," and that income is an incomplete metric, does not mean we can credibly collapse the multiple dimensions into a single, unidimensional space. The essential problem is that we do not know the prices for valuation. (Indeed, if we knew them we would presumably have already formed a measure of full income.) Prevailing practice is essentially to make ad hoc assumptions about the welfare function (and hence the weights).

The main aim of this chapter is to review the issues raised by using subjective assessments of welfare (or "well-being"—I use the terms interchangeably) in both deciding who is "poor" and calibrating multidimensional welfare measures. This is not a survey of the literature. Rather, the aim is to assess the case for and against the use of subjective data for this purpose and to identify key knowledge gaps.

Scientific research on subjective well-being emerged in the 1960s in psychology (where the emphasis was on measuring and explaining

[2] The index has been published since 1990 in the UNDP's *Human Development Reports*; see, for example, UNDP (2010).

[3] For further discussion of the various approaches to measuring multidimensional poverty see Tsui (2002), Bourguignon and Chakravarty (2003), Alkire and Foster (2007), Wagle (2008), and Ravallion (2011).

[4] Furthermore, the weights are rarely explicit in the space of the postulated core dimensions of welfare. Instead, the weights are only made explicit in a derived space of pre-defined functions of those dimensions. Thus indices such as the HDI and MPI lack transparency about their assumed trade-offs. For further discussion of this point see Ravallion (2011).

[5] The implicit value of an extra year of life in the new HDI introduced by UNDP (2010) varies from 0.50 per person year in the poorest country to about $9,000 per person year in the richest (Ravallion, 2012a).

"happiness" as a state of mind) and economics (where the emphasis was on calibrating welfare functions, including setting equivalence scales).[6] The core data have long been respondents' self-assessments in sample surveys. Each respondent is asked to rate her "economic welfare," or a broader concept such as "satisfaction with life" or "happiness," on an ordinal scale (sometimes called a "Cantril ladder," after Cantril, 1965). Or the respondent provides money metrics of points on qualitative welfare scales, such as the minimum income needed to "make ends meet" (Hagenaars and Van Praag, 1985; Kapteyn et al., 1988) or for multiple points on a ladder (Van Praag, 1968).

However, it would be fair to say that the use of such data in poverty and welfare measurement has stayed at the fringes of practice. In the eyes of some observers, such as Bertrand and Mullainathan (2001), the long-standing scepticism among economists about subjective questions is well founded, notably when these data are used as dependent variables. And poverty measurement is a field in which they are dependent variables.

This chapter offers a more positive, but still qualified, view on the scope for using subjective data in calibrating poverty measures. There are trade-offs. Subjective data come with problems, and the chapter tries to identify the main concerns. But it should be acknowledged that these data can provide welfare-relevant information that is simply not available in standard objective data—information that addresses some classic problems of applied welfare economics. After reviewing the economic foundations of the objective approach to poverty measurement in the next section, the bulk of the chapter examines the subjective approach. Section 3.3 sets out some basic theory and compares the two approaches, while Section 3.4 provides examples. Section 3.5 discusses the problems faced in implementing the subjective approach and some potential fixes.

3.2 Poverty Measurement and Non-income Dimensions of Welfare

There are various "objective" approaches to measuring poverty, including setting poverty lines (Ravallion, 2012b). The approach with firmest roots in economics allows in principle for multiple "non-income" dimensions of welfare, although these enter in a specific way, namely

[6] An early contribution to the quantification of "happiness" in surveys was Cantril's (1965) idea of the "ladder of life." Early applications of subjective welfare concepts in economics included Van Praag (1968), Kapteyn and Van Praag (1976), and Easterlin (1974).

as shifters of the "basic needs" demand vector needed to attain the poverty level of welfare. This section reviews this approach, as a prelude to discussing the potential role of subjective data.

The core idea is a utility function for individual i of the form $u(q_i, x_i)$, where q_i is a vector of the quantities of commodities consumed and x_i is a vector of welfare-relevant "non-income" characteristics, including demographic characteristics of the household. The utility maximizing consumption vector is denoted $q(p_i, y_i, x_i)$ at price vector p_i and total expenditure on consumption y_i. The implied indirect utility function is $v(p_i, y_i, x_i)$, giving the maximum attainable welfare at prevailing prices and characteristics. On inverting we obtain the expenditure function $e(p_i, x_i, u)$ giving the minimum cost of utility u for person i when facing prices p_i.

In applying this standard model to poverty measurement, poverty is thought of as being absolute in the space of welfare. The minimum utility that is deemed necessary to escape poverty is denoted u_z. The *welfare-consistent poverty lines* are then given by:

$$z_i^u = e(p_i, x_i, u_z)(i = 1,..., N) \tag{1}$$

On exploiting the standard properties of the expenditure function, this can be re-written as:

$$z_i^u = p_i q^c(p_i, x_i, u_z) \tag{2}$$

where $q^c(p_i, x_i, u_z)$ is the vector of utility-compensated demands. Thus we see that the welfare-consistent poverty line is the cost of a bundle of "basic consumption needs," given by the vector of utility-compensated demands at the reference level of utility defining who is poor in the welfare space. The measure of aggregate poverty can then be defined on the vector of welfare ratios, $\{y_i / z_i^u, i = 1,...,N\}$.[7] The "poverty rate" or "headcount index of poverty" is the proportion of the population with $y_i / z_i^u \leq 1$.[8]

Three remarks are in order. First, notice that, even though individuals are ranked by their consumption expenditure, y_i, the implied poverty rate is consistent with the multidimensional welfare function, $u(q_i, x_i)$. This comes from the fact that a person is "welfare poor,"

[7] The term "welfare ratios" is due to Blackorby and Donaldson (1987) who discuss the advantages of this welfare metric over money-metric utility or "equivalent income functions."

[8] A well-known problem with this measure is that it ignores distribution below the line; for example, if the poorest person becomes worse off or an inequality-increasing

meaning that $u_i \leq u_z$, if and only if she is consumption poor, defined as $y_i \leq z_i^u$. (This follows immediately from the fact that the expenditure function is the inverse of the indirect utility function.) The fact that one uses an income poverty measure does not mean one thinks of welfare as only depending on income. However, for income-based poverty measurement to be welfare-consistent it is imperative that the poverty lines are adjusted for all relevant non-income dimensions of welfare. Adjustment for prices is common, but the only other adjustments typically done are for (almost invariably) household size and (sometimes) demographic composition. It is in the practice of this approach that concerns about omitted "non-income" dimensions of welfare become salient.

Second, note that this framework allows for a measure of relative income poverty. One can readily allow for a relative poverty line by supposing that the vector x includes mean income of some reference group. If people derive utility from relative position then an absolute poverty line in the space of welfare will translate into a relative line in the space of commodities (Ravallion, 1998, 2008b).

Third, the basic model above can be extended to encompass Sen's (1985) argument that welfare should be thought of in terms of a person's capabilities—the functionings ("beings and doings") that a person is able to achieve. By this view, poverty means not having an income sufficient to support specific normative functionings.[9] A more general definition of the poverty line is proposed in Ravallion (1998, 2012b) whereby a person's functionings are determined by the goods she consumes and her characteristics. (Functionings may also vary with the mean consumption of an appropriate reference group.) One can further postulate that utility is derived directly from functionings and interpret $u(q_i, x_i)$ as a derived utility function, after solving out the functionings. Again, individual choices of q_i maximize utility. Thus one can also postulate solutions for functionings, showing how they depend on income, prices, and characteristics. "Functioning consistency" for a set of poverty lines requires that certain normative functionings are reached at the poverty line.[10]

transfer is made among the poor then the headcount index is unchanged. There is a large literature on alternative measures; for a survey see Zheng (1997).

[9] For example, following Atkinson and Bourguignon (2001), one can think of the normative functionings as comprising "survival needs" and minimum "social inclusion costs" for participating in social and economic activity.

[10] A more complete discussion can be found in Ravallion (2012b).

The real challenges are in putting these ideas into practice. This requires that we address two classic problems in applied welfare economics. The first can be called the *referencing problem*: what is the reference level of utility (or other functionings) that anchors the poverty line? (This is an instance of a general problem of reference-dependence, including in welfare measurement.) It is tempting to say this choice is arbitrary, and to hope that it is innocuous. But the choice of the reference in poverty measurement is far from arbitrary, since (in general) it affects the resulting poverty measure. This speaks to the importance of testing the sensitivity of poverty comparisons to the choice of reference, as it determines the level of the poverty line.[11]

The second problem is the *identification problem*. Even if we agree on the poverty line in the welfare space, we also need to know the expenditure function in (1). Standard practice is to calibrate its parameters from data on consumer demands. The problem is that individuals vary in characteristics, such as their household size and demographic composition, which can influence welfare in ways that may not be evident in consumer demand behavior. More precisely, if demands $q(p_i, y_i, x_i)$ can be integrated back to a utility function $u(q_i, x_i)$ then the same demands also maximize the broader welfare function $w[u(q_i, x_i), x_i]$. Thus there is no unique utility function that can be inferred from market demands alone.[12] We need stronger identifying assumptions, or more data. The rest of this chapter will consider the scope for using data on self-assessed welfare for addressing these problems.

3.3 Anchoring Poverty Measures to Subjective Welfare

There are essentially two approaches to collecting subjective data on welfare. The first uses qualitative categories in the welfare space. An example is the "economic ladder question" (ELQ): "Imagine six steps, where on the bottom, the first step, stand the poorest people, and on the highest step, the sixth, stand the rich (show a picture of the steps). On which step are you today?" A popular indicator of overall welfare has been the "satisfaction with life" (SWL) question: "Overall, how satisfied (content, happy) are you with your life? Are you (1) very

[11] This idea is made explicit and formalized in the use of stochastic dominance criteria for ordinal poverty comparisons (Atkinson, 1987; Foster and Shorrocks, 1988).

[12] This point has long been recognized; see Pollak and Wales (1979), Pollak (1991), and Browning (1992).

unsatisfied; (2) unsatisfied; (3) neither unsatisfied nor satisfied; (4) satisfied; (5) very satisfied?" The ELQ is arguably better suited to poverty measurement as it is tied to a concept of economic welfare, while ideas such as SWL or "happiness" are broader and more nebulous in scope.

The second approach asks for a money metric of subjective welfare. An example is the "minimum income question" (MIQ): "What income level do you personally consider to be absolutely minimal? That is to say that with less you could not make ends meet." This can be thought of as a special case of Van Praag's (1968) "income evaluation question," which asks what income is considered "very bad," "bad," "not good," "not bad," "good," "very good."

There are three main ways in which such data have been used to inform poverty measurement. The first is as a means of testing objective poverty lines, by regressing self-rated welfare on income normalized by the poverty line *plus* the variables that went into the construction of the poverty line, which should be jointly insignificant if those lines accord with subjective welfare.[13] The second is to calibrate a composite welfare index using the subjective welfare regression coefficients as the weights.[14] The third way is to derive a poverty line in the income space, defined as the income level at which some critical level of subjective welfare is reached in expectation. Notice that, as long as higher income is valued positively in subjective welfare, the latter two methods are equivalent in terms of their implied poverty rate (proportion of the population living in poverty) for any given poverty line in the space of subjective welfare. As noted in the previous section, the fact that one uses income as the ranking variable does not mean that one is ignoring non-income dimensions of welfare, given that these are allowed to alter the poverty line consistently with their welfare weight.[15]

It is well recognized that there are differences in self-assessments that do not pertain to economic welfare. One might define as poor all those who put themselves below some fixed rung of the ELQ or all those with income less than their answer to the MIQ. However, one must allow for heterogeneity, such that people at the same standard

[13] This approach is outlined in Ravallion and Lokshin (2002) and illustrated using Russia's poverty lines.

[14] Examples are found in Ferrer-i-Carbonell and Van Praag (2001) and Kingdon and Knight (2006).

[15] This point is a common source of confusion in the more applied literature and policy-related discussions on multidimensional poverty measurement where "income poverty" is often counterpointed to "multidimensional poverty." Plainly the two approaches are equivalent when calibrated to the same welfare function.

of living can give different answers on subjective welfare. These variations could stem from idiosyncratic "mood" effects, personality traits, or simply errors.

So it is not one's stated perception of own welfare in an interview that should be taken to be the relevant metric, as this is bound to contain many factors that one would not deem relevant. Rather, the subjective questions are used to calibrate an interpersonally comparable welfare function based on observed covariates deemed to be relevant on a priori grounds. It is the role of these data sources in *calibration* that is the focus of this chapter.

Let us take a closer look at one approach. This recognizes that any definition of poverty must be broadly accepted in the specific context it is being used. It makes little sense to use a poor country's poverty line in a rich country; indeed, it is unlikely that anyone in the US or Western Europe lives below the poverty lines found in the poorest countries, at around \$1 a day. And if one used the US poverty line in India (say) one would find that all but 5 percent of the population is poor (Ravallion, 2010); it is extremely unlikely that most Indians would agree, and nor does a poverty rate of 95 percent help much in thinking about how best to fight poverty in India. The idea of a "social subjective poverty line" (SSPL) is a natural way of defining poverty in a specific context. The SSPL can be defined as the income below which people tend to think they are poor in the specific setting and above which they tend to think they are not poor.

The standard representation of this approach in the literature is essentially a statistical model of the following form. Let $y_i^{\min}$ denote the answer given by person i to the MIQ and write:

$$y_i^{\min} = E(y_i^{\min} | p_i, y_i, x_i) + \varepsilon_i \quad (3)$$

where $E(y_i^{\min} | p_i, y_i, x_i)$ is the conditional mean—the regression function—given actual income y, which lies in the interval $[y_0, y_1]$, prices and other relevant characteristics, and ε_i is a zero-mean error term. It is assumed that $E(y_i^{\min} | p_i, y_i, x_i)$ is strictly increasing in y. It is reasonable to assume that the y_0 is insufficient $(E(y^{\min} | p_i, y_0, x_i) > y_0)$ while, at the other extreme, y_1 is more than adequate $(E(y^{\min} | p_i, y_1, x_i) < y_1)$. Then it is plain that there exists a unique fixed point:

$$E[y_i^{\min} | p_i, z(p_i, x_i), x_i] = z(p_i, x_i) \quad (4)$$

The SSPL is the (unique) solution of (4) for $z(p_i, x_i)$. If higher p or x is associated with higher $y^{\min}$ then a higher SSPL will be required.

The conceptual links between the objective utility-based approach (Section 3.2) and these two approaches to subjective welfare—the direct approach of asking the respondent's position on a welfare ladder and the approach of asking for a monetary valuation—have never been clear in the literature, and the three approaches have largely existed independently. It is of interest to ask under what conditions they will be consistent in terms of whom they identify as "poor." Clearly this requires that all three are anchored to the same continuous welfare function. It is evident that the direct approach will be consistent with the objective utility-based approach as long as the ordinal qualitative questions asked of respondents stem from the same welfare index. This is a judgment call, and some observers may not accept that (say) SWL is driven by "utility."

Establishing consistency for the SSPL approach requires that we introduce some economic structure into the statistical model of the SSPL. We can assume that the MIQ attempts to find $y_i^{\min}$ such that:

$$v(p_i, y_i^{\min}, x_i) = u_i^r \tag{5}$$

where u_i^r is the level of utility that person i thinks is implied by "making ends meet." This is assumed in turn to be a strictly increasing function of actual utility:

$$u_i^r = \phi[v(p_i, y_i, x_i)] \tag{6}$$

Equation 3 can now be interpreted as the solution of (5) and (6) for $y_i^{\min}$. The SSPL in the income space is then found as the solution to:

$$v(p_i, z_i, x_i) = \phi[v(p_i, z_i, x_i)] \tag{7}$$

But now we see that there is also a SSPL in welfare space, u_z, at which point:

$$u_z = \phi(u_z) \tag{8}$$

(The solution is unique if $\phi(u_0) > u_0$ and $\phi(u_1) < u_1$, where utility is bounded below by u_0 and above by u_1 Comparing (7) and (8) we see that $u_z = v(p_i, z_i, x_i)$. The SSPL—the point at which $y_i^{\min} = y_i$—also identifies those who just reach the implicit welfare poverty line u_z and the set of people who are welfare poor ($u_i < u_z$) is the same as the set of income poor ($y_i < z_i$). Thus, under these conditions, the SSPL approach can be said to be consistent with the other two approaches, in that they identify the same people as poor and deliver the same poverty rate.

3.4 Methods and Examples

The most common method of empirical investigation in this literature has been a regression of the survey responses on subjective welfare on individual and household characteristics, including age, gender, income, education, employment status, and household demographics.[16] Typically the researcher has data on subjective welfare (*SW*) across *N* survey respondents and a set of covariates (*X*, including some suitable non-linear function of income) and postulates a regression model of the form:

$$SW_i = \alpha + \beta X_i + \varepsilon_i (i = 1, \dots, N) \quad (9)$$

where the error term, ε, is uncorrelated with *X*. If using ordinal data from a ladder question then an ordered response estimator is typically used, such as the ordered probit, in which case (9) is the underlying continuous variable generating the ordinal responses relative to thresholds that are taken to be fixed. If instead one is using the MIQ, then $y_i^{\min}$ is the dependent variable.

This section provides an overview of some of the lessons to date in estimating such a model. The next section will discuss a number of issues in estimating such a regression.

Recall that one of the conditions for existence of a SSPL is that subjective welfare is an increasing function of income. This is invariably indicated in cross-sectional studies; indeed, I have not seen an exception in the literature, though some studies find stronger income effects than others.[17] Stevenson and Wolfers (2008) argue that the income effect on subjective well-being is robust across countries, within countries, and over time.

There have been some estimates of SSPLs.[18] Interestingly, the estimates to date suggest that the overall poverty rate based on the SSPL

[16] Examples include van Praag (1968), van de Stadt et al. (1985), Clark and Oswald (1994, 1996), Kapteyn et al. (1998), Easterlin (1995), Oswald (1997), Winkelmann and Winkelmann (1998), Pradhan and Ravallion (2000), McBride (2001), Ravallion and Lokshin (2001, 2002, 2010), Graham and Pettinato (2002), Senik (2004), Luttmer (2005), Ferrer-i-Carbonell (2005), Herrera et al. (2006), Bishop and Luo (2006), Kingdon and Knight (2006, 2007), Fafchamps and Shilpi (2009), Knight and Gunatilaka (2010), and Castilla (2010).

[17] Clark et al. (2008) review the literature on the income effect on subjective welfare.

[18] I focus on application to developing countries. The applications to date include Pradhan and Ravallion (2000) using data for Jamaica and Nepal, Ferrer-i-Carbonell and Van Praag (2001) for Russia, Taddesse and Shimeles (2005) for Ethiopia, Gustafsson (2004) for urban China, Lokshin et al. (2006) for Madagascar, Bishop and Luo (2006) for urban China, and Carletto and Zezza (2006) for Albania.

is roughly similar to that implied by objective poverty lines.[19] It may well be that the choice of parameters in the "objective" absolute lines already approximated the expected SSPL in the specific context.

However, the *structure* of the poverty profile has turned out to be different in some respects. While objective poverty lines for developing countries often imply that larger households are poorer, this is not typically the case in cross-sectional studies using the subjective approach, which tends to suggest greater economies of scale in consumption than normally assumed. For example, in using the ELQ to test the welfare consistency of prevailing objective poverty lines for Russia, Ravallion and Lokshin (2002) find some striking differences in the properties of the equivalence scale. The objective poverty lines had an elasticity of 0.8 to household size, while the subjective indicator called instead for an elasticity half this size.[20]

Subjective data have thrown new light on the long-standing debate on whether poverty is "absolute" or "relative." The position one takes on this issue is crucial to whether one believes that economic growth reduces poverty. If the poverty line has an elasticity of zero to the poverty line then growth tends to reduce poverty, but this ceases to be true at an elasticity of one (Ravallion, 2003). However, one finds little support for the idea of a relative poverty line set at a constant proportion of the current mean income. Poverty lines calibrated to subjective welfare tend to rise with mean income but with an elasticity less than unity, suggesting that they are more like the "weakly relative poverty lines" defined by Ravallion and Chen (2011). Hagenaars and Van Praag (1985) estimated an elasticity of 0.51 for eight European countries. For the US, Kilpatrick (1973) estimated an elasticity of about 0.6 for subjective poverty lines and De Vos and Garner (1991) found an own-income elasticity of the US subjective poverty line of 0.43.

A number of papers have reported evidence of effects on subjective welfare that can be interpreted as indicative of "relative deprivation," meaning that self-assessed well-being tends to fall as social

[19] An exception to this finding is reported for the U.S. by de Vos and Garner (1991), where the SSPL is well above the prevailing (absolute) line, though the U.S. line has not been updated in real terms since the 1960s; a more current absolute line for the U.S. would probably be closer to the SSPL.

[20] Similarly, see Pradhan and Ravallion (2000), using data for Jamaica and Nepal, Bishop and Luo (2006), using data for urban China, and Rojas (2007), using data for Mexico. For a more general discussion of economies of scale in consumption in developing countries see Lanjouw and Ravallion (1995).

comparators become better off, at given "own income."[21] Luttmer (2005) reports regressions for subjective welfare in the US that imply a particularly strong relativism, whereby own income does not matter to subjective well-being independently of income relative to the mean in the area of residence. (The next section points to some reasons to question this finding.) The bulk of the evidence has been for relatively rich countries. The work that has been done for developing countries has been less supportive. Senik (2004), Kingdon and Knight (2007), and Ravallion and Lokshin (2010) tested for relative deprivation effects in self-reported happiness in Russia, South Africa, and Malawi respectively and found rather little support for the idea and even evidence of *positive* external effects of higher "neighbors' income," rather than the negative effect predicted by the theory of relative deprivation.

Using survey data for one of the world's poorest countries, Malawi, Ravallion and Lokshin (2010) studied the relationship between responses to the "SWL" question and household consumption per person and how that relationship varied with the respondents' assessments of the economic welfare of their friends and neighbors. Ravallion and Lokshin found that SWL increases with consumption, as expected. However, higher economic welfare of friends or neighbors tended to come with higher SWL at given own consumption. So this does not support the theory of relative deprivation (as this would imply lower welfare with richer friends or neighbors, at given own consumption). However, the parametric models with controls presented in Ravallion and Lokshin (2010) revealed that concerns about relative deprivation emerged among the richer Malawians, who tended to be concentrated in urban areas.

These findings are echoed in the responses to survey questions on whether poverty is perceived as absolute or relative reported by Corazzini et al. (2011), which suggest that respondents coming from richer backgrounds see poverty as more relative, though not to the point that absolute poverty is seen as unimportant.

Some of the literature has also thrown light on the role played by expectations. Ravallion and Lokshin (2002) find strong lagged income effects on subjective welfare in Russia, consistent with the view that that those on a positive (negative) income trajectory are likely to rate

[21] See Oswald (1997), Frank (1997), Frey and Stutzer (2002), Clark, Frijters, and Shields (2008), and Clark and Senik (2010). Reviewing the evidence, Frey and Stutzer assert that "There is little doubt that people compare themselves to other people and do not use absolute judgments" (p. 412). This would seem to be overstated.

their welfare higher (lower) than others at given current income (and other covariates).[22]

Knight and Gunatilaka (2012) argue that "aspirations" for higher income also matter negatively to subjective welfare, and that this mitigates appreciably the direct income effect. Using data for rural China they proxy "aspiration income" by answers to a version of the MIQ and find that the latter has a significant negative coefficient in predicting SWL and "satisfaction with income." Aspiration income is in turn found to be an increasing function of own income (consistent with past research on the SSPL). They interpret their results as evidence of an "hedonic treadmill" whereby higher actual income need not raise happiness given offsetting effects on aspirations.[23] However, once one allows for latent heterogeneity in subjective welfare there are other interpretations of the Knight–Gunatilaka finding, as discussed in the next section.

A number of papers have found evidence that unemployment lowers subjective welfare at given income.[24] This is not what the standard economic model of work-leisure choice would suggest, since unemployment at given income implies greater leisure, which is assumed to yield utility. (The welfare cost of unemployment is seen to be through the lost income.) There may well be an independent disutility of unemployment that is missing from the standard model, possibly associated with the quantity constraints on choice that involuntary unemployment entails or possibly stemming from social status roles played by employment. However, the welfare effect attributed to unemployment may also stem from latent heterogeneity in personality traits, which is one of the issues to which the next section turns.

3.5 Problems in Using Subjective Data in Measuring Poverty

Subjective data can offer a direct lens on welfare that is not available in standard objective data. But are subjective questions reliable, in the sense that one gets similar answers under similar circumstances?

[22] Ravallion and Lokshin (2000) also find that Russians on a positive (negative) income trajectory are also less (more) likely to support redistribution from the rich to the poor.

[23] The authors note the endogeneity concern and provide instrumental variables (IV) estimates although it is not obvious that there is any theoretically valid IV for this problem.

[24] Examples include Clark and Oswald (1994), Theodossiou (1998), Winkelmann and Winkelmann (1998), and Ravallion and Lokshin (2001).

Studies of SWL or "happiness" have found a worryingly high degree of variability. For example, Kristensen and Westergaard-Nielsen (2007) found that 20 percent of survey respondents in Europe gave a different answer on job satisfaction when asked twice within the same interview. Krueger and Schkade (2008) studied reported SWL for the same people interviewed two weeks apart and found the correlation coefficient was only 0.6.

In the present context, it is not the reliability of the subjective welfare scores themselves that is of greatest concern, but the reliability of the regressions for subjective welfare, as used in calibrating SSPLs, or measuring welfare more generally. If the likely errors in subjective welfare data are white noise—classical measurement errors—we would not be concerned; the R^2 will be lower but the regression coefficients will still be unbiased under standard assumptions. However, there are good reasons to expect the errors in subjective data to be correlated with other explanatory variables of interest, as argued by Bertrand and Mullainathan (2001) and Ravallion and Lokshin (2001). That does not mean the regressions are useless. Biases can almost never be ruled out. The real issue is how large the biases are in practice, and whether they can overturn key conclusions, such as whether larger households are poorer or whether economic growth reduces poverty.

This section tries to assess what appear to be the main concerns about the specification and interpretation of regressions for subjective welfare.

3.5.1 *Welfare-irrelevant Covariates and Missing Data on Welfare-relevant Covariates*

To assert that subjective welfare regressions should override prior normative judgments puts a lot of weight on those regressions. There are concerns about both the variables included and the variables left out.

Not everything that helps predict self-assessed welfare will be considered relevant to measuring poverty (or assessing welfare more broadly). In principle one can partition the X vector in equation (9) into two types of variables: those that are deemed (on a priori grounds) to be relevant to assessing welfare and those that are controls for other factors, with the latter fixed at reference values (common to all individuals) when measuring welfare or poverty.[25] Thus the welfare metric becomes a predicted value *as if* the individual had the reference characteristics.

[25] This is proposed by Ravallion (1990) in the context of measuring undernutrition, though the analytics are formally identical.

Personality traits are a case in point. These clearly influence self-assessed well-being. While these differences are not often data, this is starting to change. Suppose that we control for personality in a regression for (say) SWL. The idea of a poverty line that is set at a higher level for people with certain personalities, at given levels of other relevant factors, is probably not going to gain much acceptance. Personality is unlikely to be given independent weight.

And some more readily observed covariates may well be acting as proxies for personality. For example, a common finding in the literature is that unemployment reduces subjective welfare at a given level of income. If one included unemployment in defining the poverty line then one would conclude that the unemployed should have a higher poverty line than the employed, *ceteris paribus*. Yet other "objective" approaches to setting a poverty line would not suggest that the unemployed need more income to attain the same level of welfare. And that may be the right call if the trade-off between income and unemployment implied by a subjective welfare regression is being distorted by latent personality traits.

Nor are the available data for X ever likely to embrace all that matters to welfare. This approach is unlikely to provide a sufficient statistic for multidimensional poverty comparisons. (And it is unlikely that any approach would.) To estimate the regression function we ideally have the X's from the same individuals as the indicator of subjective welfare. There is bound to be some relevant dimension of welfare left out, but hopefully available in some separate survey. In practice, multidimensional poverty measurement is invariably going to be a matter of devising a defensible set of multiple indices rather than one single composite index (Ravallion, 2011).

3.5.2 *Survey Design and Measurement Errors*

Measurement errors are present in all areas of applied research. Naturally there are errors in survey responses on subjective welfare or its determinants. Three examples follow of why such errors matter to the conclusions drawn about the determinants of subjective welfare.

(i) Incomes or consumptions are measured with error. Sometimes the income measure was built up from a detailed questionnaire, which is likely to be more reliable than other measures found in the literature based on very few questions—or even just one, "what is your income?" The scope for attenuation bias in estimating the income gradient in subjective welfare is plain.

(ii) An attenuation bias in estimates of the income (or other) gradient in subjective welfare can also arise from psychological adaptation to adverse circumstances. Poor people may try to cope with deprivation in ways that attenuate the true income gradient in subjective assessments of their well-being. For example, Lokshin and Ravallion (2008) found that the income gradient in the self-assessed health status of Russians was greatly attenuated relative to that in their objective health status. This is consistent with adaptation.

(iii) Recall that a common method of testing for welfare costs of relative deprivation is by regressing self-assessed welfare on both own income and the mean income of "neighbors"—typically the mean income of survey respondents in a geographic area that includes the respondent. However, the latter could just be picking up a spatial autocorrelation in income measurement errors, giving spurious social effects.

The measurement of comparison-group welfare also poses a problem. In the near-universal approach in the literature, the researcher must make an a priori judgment about the relevant comparison group. Yet this can vary greatly from person to person. It has been argued that "comparisons are most salient if individuals perceive the reference person or group as in some way similar to themselves" (Kahneman and Varey, 1991, p. 140). But that is based on the individual's own judgment, given idiosyncratic informational and social factors that a researcher would have a very hard time observing in any systematic way. Neither psychological nor economic theories of relative deprivation offer much insight into what constitutes the relevant comparison group. The researcher must make some potentially strong identifying assumptions.

There are also concerns about survey design and implementation effects, including sensitivity to how questions are asked and the context. It is known that precisely how, and in what circumstances, one asks subjective questions matters to the results. In survey data for Britain, Taylor (2006) finds that those interviewed on a Friday report significantly greater job satisfaction and less mental stress than those interviewed midweek, controlling for other observed factors. Also for Britain, Conti and Pudney (2011) find that seemingly small changes in how questions on satisfaction with work were asked led to large changes in the answers obtained, particularly for women. Moreover, they find that the measurement errors are not ignorable, in that the distortions influence findings on the determinants of job satisfaction. They also find evidence of a "put on a good show for the visitor effect" (Conti and Pudney, 2011, p. 1093)—whereby there is an upward bias in reported welfare in open oral interviews relative to when the questionnaire is completed in private—and a "not in front of the children effect" (p. 1093), whereby there was another upward bias when children were present at the interview. These biases were found to be larger for women. Bertrand and Mullainathan (2001) give other examples of how the ordering and wording of subjective questions can alter responses.

Such problems are not confined to subjective questions. Seemingly objective questions can entail similar biases. My favorite (undocumented) example is from a colleague who was doing field work piloting a questionnaire and found a markedly higher literacy rate for a given population and date when asking "are you literate?" than when using a direct test by showing one sentence on a card and asking what it said. (In this case the bias was greater for men.) While we do not normally think of literacy or schooling as subjective, such variables are not immune to the same biases.

Some of the long-standing questions on subjective welfare in the literature seem problematic when one considers the scope for measurement error. While the MIQ offers an elegant solution to the problem of determining the SSPL, it comes with a problem, and it is a problem that is likely to be especially serious in developing-country settings. The problem is that the income concept respondents to the MIQ have in mind need not correspond to that used by the analyst in estimating the SSPL. This will bias the SSPL (Kapteyn et al., 1988; Tummers, 1994). In applying the MIQ in many developing countries, one will also find that "income" is not a well-defined concept, particularly (but not only) in rural areas. It is not at all clear whether one could get sensible answers to the MIQ.

To address this concern, Pradhan and Ravallion (2000) propose a method for estimating the SSPL based on qualitative data on consumption adequacy. Instead of asking respondents the precise minimum consumption that they need, Pradhan and Ravallion simply asked whether their current consumptions are adequate. For example, their adequacy question for food takes the form:

> Concerning your family's food consumption over the past one month, which of the following is true?
>
> | | |
> |---|---|
> | Less than adequate | 1 |
> | Just adequate | 2 |
> | More than adequate | 3 |
>
> "Adequate" means no more nor less than what you consider to be the minimum consumption needs of your family.

The question is then repeated for other components of consumption (for both market and non-market goods and services).

This provides a multidimensional alternative to the one-dimensional and difficult MIQ. The method exploits the structure of consumption—essentially providing a subjective welfare function for each component of basic needs. The SSPL can be defined as the level of total spending above which respondents say (on average) that their expenditures are adequate for all their needs or some sub-set. Under certain technical conditions, a unique solution for the SSPL can then be obtained from the estimated parameters of a set of regressions for consumption adequacy: Pradhan and Ravallion (2000) provide a detailed exposition.

3.5.3 *Non-ignorable Latent Heterogeneity*

By "latent heterogeneity" I mean that observationally similar people give different responses about their welfare. Such heterogeneity is plausible. Different people are likely to have different ideas about what it means to be "rich" or "poor," or "satisfied" with one's life or not, leading them to interpret survey questions on subjective welfare differently.[26] For example, the Young Lives Project (2009) reports the comment of a six-year-old in rural Vietnam, named Duy, as saying that "We are nearly rich as we have a new cupboard, but we haven't got a washing machine." Duy clearly has a different idea of what it means to be "rich" than those in Vietnam more familiar with the living conditions of the truly rich. Survey respondents can be expected to interpret subjective questions relative to their personal frame of reference, which will depend on latent aspects of their own knowledge and experience. It is unlikely that all such sources of heterogeneity could be captured in the typically observed covariates in surveys.

Such heterogeneity will clearly make it hard to credibly use subjective data in making interpersonal comparisons of welfare. But does it matter to inferences drawn from regressions, as might be used to set weights on the observables? In the standard ordered probit estimator one assumes that the ordinal responses to ladder-type

[26] While this chapter focuses on heterogeneity in scales, there are other concerns with survey design. For example, Conti and Pudney (2011) find that minor re-designs in questions on satisfaction of life/work led to large changes in answers, particularly for women, finding that distortions in responses influence findings with respect to correlates of women's job satisfaction. For an overview of the concerns about inferring welfare effects from subjective data see Ravallion (2012).

questions on subjective welfare are generated by a latent continuous variable and that the thresholds—the values of the underlying welfare metric at which ordinal responses on the stipulated scales change—are constant parameters, the same for all respondents. If that does not hold, and the scales vary systematically with the postulated covariates of welfare, then we will lose our ability to draw valid inferences from the regression about the appropriate weights on those covariates. The heterogeneity can then said to be "non-ignorable" statistically.

There are a number of reasons to be concerned about such non-ignorable heterogeneity. It has been argued by psychologists and economists that relatively stable (though not necessarily fixed) personality traits influence behavior in a wide range of domains, including behaviors relevant to realized economic welfare.[27] It appears likely that latent personality traits would be correlated with the observed socioeconomic characteristics that are often postulated as relevant to a multidimensional welfare index, as argued by Ravallion and Lokshin (2001). People with a latent tendency for depression may well be less likely to take care of their physical health. Unemployment may also be more likely for people with certain personality traits, such as one's "work ethic." These differences can be thought of as either differences in the meaning attached to the scales used in subjective welfare questions or a difference in the latent subjective welfare itself.

To give a sharp example, suppose subjective welfare depends on income and personality, and we are interested in identifying the income poverty line corresponding to some fixed level of subjective welfare. Personality is unobserved (and so relegated to the regression error term), but is known to also affect earnings and (hence) income.[28] It is readily verified that if the combined effect of the latent personality traits that raise subjective welfare is to increase (decrease) labor market earnings then we will underestimate (overestimate) the SSPL.

We may want to control for personality in measuring poverty, but we can't if it is not data. For example, we can agree that people with fewer opportunities for schooling are poorer at given current income. In data we see that schooling is associated with higher subjective

[27] See, for example, Goldberg (1993) and Heckman (2011). These traits can change over a life time, but can be treated as roughly constant over periods of a few years or more.

[28] Evidence on this can be found in Mueller and Plug (2006). Also see the discussion in Heckman (2011).

welfare at given current income (possibly reflecting higher expected future income for those with more schooling). Thus, welfare consistency appears to demand that we use a higher income poverty line for people with less schooling. However, schooling attainments depend on individual personality as well as opportunities. For example, there is evidence that more conscientious people acquire more schooling.[29] At the same time, it can be assumed that more conscientious people tend to delay gratification in other aspects of their life, which may well mean that they report lower current subjective welfare at given current income than do others. Then a regression for subjective welfare ignoring the personality differences will tend to lead one to underestimate the required gradient in poverty lines needed to compensate for differences in schooling opportunities.

Even with similar personalities (or statistically ignorable differences) different people may apply different criteria for scaling their welfare. They have different ideas about what it means to be "rich" or "poor," or what it means to be "satisfied" or not with one's life. Again, latent heterogeneity in factors that are essentially irrelevant to welfare but influence responses to subjective welfare questions can cast doubt on the implied interpersonal comparisons of welfare from subjective data. If such heterogeneity were purely random then it would not invalidate inferences from such regressions (at least for linear models). Thus it has been argued in the literature that, while interpersonal welfare comparisons are invalidated by heterogeneous scales, the regressions are likely to be robust to such heterogeneity.[30]

However, that claim is of doubtful veracity. As already noted, it is a well-established idea that people assess their welfare relative to some "comparison group" such as neighbors or co-workers. This argument has emphasized relativist welfare comparisons. It has also been argued that reference groups play an important role in expectations formation.[31] It is a small step from these ideas to the proposition that survey respondents answer questions with reference to their immediate experiences and that this may well be highly localized in some relevant social or geographic dimensions. People will answer subjective questions relative to their personal frame of reference, which depends on the respondent's own knowledge and experience and therefore is

[29] Reported in Heckman (2011), using data for Germany.

[30] For example, Frey and Stutzer (2002) note the possibility of heterogeneity in the scales used in self-reported welfare questions but claim that this does not invalidate regression models for such data.

[31] For more recent discussions and evidence see Ravallion and Lokshin (2000) and Senik (2004).

likely to vary systematically with the characteristics of that person, including objective measures of economic welfare.

For example, it can be conjectured that people living in poor areas of a developing country tend to have a more limited knowledge of the full range of levels of living found in the society as a whole. Someone living in a poor, remote village who has only infrequently left the village and gone no further than the district town is likely to rate her welfare higher than someone with the same real income who lives in a city and sees far greater affluence around her. Similarly, it can be conjectured that well-off people are often unaware of how poor some people are, and may thus rate their own welfare lower on the scale.

This can be called a frame-of-reference bias (FORB) (Ravallion, 2008b). The potential for FORB raises concerns about the (enumerable) regression models found in past literature. Consider, for example, the many papers that have used subjective welfare regressions to test for reference-group effects, such as whether higher neighbors' income makes one feel worse off through perceptions of relative deprivation. It seems likely that the same reference group also influences the respondents' interpretation of scales used in subjective questions. The reference group acts as both the comparator in assessing relative position and a key element of the information set used by respondents when interpreting the scales.

So a cloud of doubt hangs over subjective welfare regressions, arising from concerns about likely heterogeneity in the interpretation of the scales used to measure subjective welfare. This heterogeneity undoubtedly reduces the power of standard covariates in explaining perceived welfare. More worrying, however, is the possibility that the heterogeneity in scales is leading to biased inferences from studies of subjective welfare, including biases in identifying its income gradient, as well as the effects of other variables such as education, employment status, and relative economic position. Bias arises if these variables are correlated with the latent heterogeneity in scales. It can be conjectured that poorer people tend to have more limited horizons in life, due to more limited experiences with the extent of the disparities in levels of living in society as a whole; a poor person's idea of what it means to be "rich" may then be very different to that of a middle- or upper-income person with a very different frame of reference. This may be correlated with certain attributes of the household.

Recognizing the existence of latent heterogeneity in subjective welfare can also alter the interpretation of some of the regressions found in the literature. Consider, for example, the interesting argument by Knight and Gunatilaka (2012) about the existence of an "hedonic treadmill" in China. Recall that this was based on a regression of SWL against both answers to the MIQ (taken to proxy "aspiration income") and actual income (with controls for some other observed covariates, which can be ignored for expository purposes). However, the answers to the MIQ may simply be picking up latent heterogeneity in subjective welfare. Indeed, it can be readily shown that the economic model of the SSPL outlined in Section 3.3 implies that any latent individual characteristic that increases welfare will reduce y_i^{min} at given own income.[32] The MIQ variable may not be measuring aspirations at all, but simply acting as a (negative) control for omitted effects on subjective welfare. This will increase precision and (probably) reduce bias in estimating the income effect, which is strong in the Knight and Gunatilaka regressions. But this is clearly a very different interpretation to the idea of an hedonic treadmill.

We have seen how much latent heterogeneity can confound the interpretation of subjective welfare regressions. What can be done about the problem? One possible solution is to control for these differences directly. Psychologists have developed various tests that can be implemented in surveys.[33] However, it is not as yet common to have such data collected in the surveys needed to study the determinants of subjective welfare. The next subsection considers an econometric method of neutralizing latent heterogeneity.

3.5.4 *Addressing Latent Heterogeneity Using Panel Data*

Panel data on subjective welfare and covariates have been proposed as one solution to the problem of latent heterogeneity. If we have longitudinal data on self-assessed welfare (*SW*) and covariates (*X*) we can postulate a model of the form:

$$SW_{it} = \alpha + \beta X_{it} + \eta_i + \varepsilon_{it} \; (i = 1,...,N; t = 1,...,T) \qquad (10)$$

where the error term has two components: a time-invariant effect, η_i, capturing (say) personality traits, for which $Cov(\eta_i, X_{it}) \neq 0$, and an innovation error term, ε_{it} with $Cov(\varepsilon_{it}, X_{it}) = 0$. Thus the non-ignorable heterogeneity is assumed to be entirely captured by η_i. One can question

[32] To see this, consider the simplified version of equations (5) and (6) where utility depends on own-income but there is a latent heterogeneity term, so utility is $v(y_i) + \eta_i$. The MIQ solves: $v(y_i^{min}) + \eta_i = \phi[v(y_i) + \eta_i]$. Differentiating w.r.t. η_i holding own-income constant we find that: $\partial y_i^{min} / \partial \eta_i = [\phi'(\cdot) - 1] / v'(y_i^{min})$. The conditions for existence of a unique SSPL in utility space imply that $\phi'(\cdot) < 1$ at least locally. Then $\partial y_i^{min} / \partial \eta_i < 0$.

[33] The Pearlin scale is an example (Pearlin and Schooler, 1978).

whether this econometric specification adequately captures the way heterogeneity impacts on subjective welfare; I will return to this point after considering some examples.

In what appears to have been the first panel data study of subjective welfare, van de Stadt et al. (1985) modeled a money metric of subjective welfare in the Netherlands. They did not allow for latent individual effects correlated with the covariates, but they did allow for dynamics by including the lagged subjective welfare measure as a regressor, which picks up at least some of the heterogeneity. More recently, the papers by Winkelmann and Winkelmann (1998), Ravallion and Lokshin (2001), and Senik (2004) allowed for a time-invariant latent individual effect when modeling subjective welfare data. I will discuss the example of the Ravallion and Lokshin paper in more detail as this provides insights into the implications of allowing for latent heterogeneity for standard regression results on the determinants of subjective welfare.

Using panel data for Russia on responses to the ELQ, Ravallion and Lokshin confirmed some of the results of past studies using single cross-sections, but not others. Household income was found to be a highly significant predictor of self-rated economic welfare. Controlling for household income, individual income was a far weaker predictor, suggesting that there is some degree of income pooling. Health shocks lowered subjective economic welfare at given values of other variables in their model, including incomes.

However, the demographic effects found in cross-sectional studies (notably of household size, at given income per capita) were not found to be robust. The extent of the scale economy of household size in individual subjective welfare suggested by a number of papers in the literature may well reflect latent personality effects on the demographic characteristics of the respondent's household.

In keeping with past work, Ravallion and Lokshin found evidence of an income-compensated welfare cost of unemployment. They argue that the most plausible interpretation is that the current welfare loss arises from some combination of lower expected future incomes and more uncertain incomes, the latter arising from greater exposure to uninsured risk outside the formal employment sector. They found that it would take a large gain in current income to compensate for becoming unemployed.

However, their results also point to a number of qualifications on past findings about the welfare effects of unemployment. While becoming unemployed entails a large welfare loss, that loss is not fully restored when an unemployed person gets a job, except via the income gain.

This implies a long-term welfare loss from even transient unemployment at given income. It also suggests that high unemployment benefits do not attract people out of work, but they may well discourage a return to work. However, the unemployment effect was not found to be robust to restricting the sample to those for whom incomes were almost certainly better measured. This suggests that there could well be a bias in past estimates of the (income-compensated) welfare effect of unemployment, arising from the structure of income measurement errors.

These panel data models impose considerable structure on the way in which latent heterogeneity is deemed to matter to subjective welfare, namely that it takes the form of a individual specific time-invariant and additive component of the error term. I turn next to another source of data that offers a more flexible and robust way of addressing concerns about latent heterogeneity in scales.

3.5.5 *Using Vignettes to Address Heterogeneity in Scales*

The essential idea of vignettes in this context is to include in the survey (or a sub-sample) reasonably detailed descriptions of the lives of certain stylized individuals and ask the respondent the same subjective question about those vignettes that was posed about the respondent herself.

Vignettes have been used in a number of recent studies of subjective data on (inter alia) health status, political efficacy, and job satisfaction. King et al. (2004) and King and Wand (2007) designed vignettes to establish common points on the heterogeneous reference scales regarding political efficacy in China and Mexico. Kristensen and Johansson (2008) used vignettes in anchoring subjective scales for job satisfaction. Bago d'Uva et al. (2008) used them for correcting self-assessed health data for reporting bias. Vignettes have also been used in testing the competence of doctors (Das et al., 2008). Kapteyn et al. (2008) used vignettes to compare life satisfaction between respondents in the United States and the Netherlands.

Beegle, Himelein, and Ravallion (BHR) (2012) used vignettes to provide various tests for bias due to latent heterogeneity in individual scales of subjective welfare.[34] Their tests entailed adding vignettes to a national household survey for Tajikistan in 2007. Respondents

[34] This can be thought of as a contribution to ongoing efforts to employ qualitative data to help validate standard "objective" metrics of welfare and poverty. For an overview of various approaches see Shaffer (2013).

placed these vignettes on the same six-step ladder used to report their own subjective economic welfare. BHR performed three sets of tests for bias. In their first test, they found some significant covariates for vignette responses among the regressors commonly used to explain subjective welfare. However, the effects were neither very strong nor consistent across different vignettes.

In their second and third tests, BHR explored the extent of bias due to the aforementioned frame-of-reference effect by embedding vignette rankings by households in standard regressions for subjective welfare. BHR did this in two ways: they included vignettes among the covariates and, to address endogeneity concerns with this approach, also recalibrated the self-assessments of welfare to accord with the heterogeneity in scales revealed by the vignette responses. The striking finding of these tests is that the bias is negligible with respect to the "income effect" on subjective welfare as well as other covariates. Based on this study, concerns that past uses of subjective economic welfare data are compromised by systematic differences in the meaning given to the scales used appear to be unwarranted.

A third test by BHR involved estimating an explicit model of the heterogeneity in scales, whereby the thresholds are modeled as functions of covariates, assuming that the structure of this heterogeneity is common between "own welfare" and the vignettes.[35] As usual, there is assumed to be a continuous latent variable for the respondents' self-rated welfare, but now the thresholds are explicit functions of a vector of explanatory variables. The extra information on the vignette responses provides the basis for identification, under the assumption that the thresholds for self-assessed welfare are determined identically as for these thresholds in the vignette responses. This is a natural assumption to make. Without the vignettes, identification would only be possible under questionable assumptions about the nonlinearity of the functional forms involved. Thus BHR were able to model determinants of the thresholds separately to those of the latent continuous variable for subjective welfare.

[35] Here BHR followed an approach developed by King et al. (2004), who proposed an econometric method ("CHOPIT") for modeling the same type of data use by BHR in which there is an equation for both the latent response of interest and one for the vignettes, with the two equations estimated jointly.

This approach revealed similar results on the factors influencing subjective welfare, but also threw new light on the heterogeneity in scales. In particular, BHR found that poorer households tend to have a narrower range in the thresholds used in identifying where they lie and where the vignettes lie on the subjective welfare ladder.

A frame-of-reference effect on subjective welfare is evident in BHR's findings; people with different socioeconomic backgrounds use systematically different scales in responding to questions on their welfare. However, BHR's results do not suggest that this is an important source of bias in past efforts to model the objective determinants of subjective welfare, and for retrieving SSPLs.

Ravallion, Himelein, and Beegle (RHB) (2013) assess the robustness of BHR's findings using similar data for selected areas in two quite different developing countries, Guatemala and Tanzania. As in the Tajikistan survey, respondents were asked to score stylized vignettes, as well as their own household. Similarly to BHR, they find only small biases are induced in the coefficients on widely used regressors for subjective poverty and welfare.

However, the RHB paper goes further into assessing the robustness of interpersonal comparisons of welfare (including subjective poverty measures) based on self-assessments of economic welfare. Measures of "subjective poverty" are becoming common.[36] These measures tell us what proportion of survey respondents place themselves on the bottom rung (or possibly second-lowest rung) of a welfare ladder from "poor" to "rich." But if the rungs of the welfare ladder are not understood the same way by different respondents, it is unclear what meaning can be attached to such measures. To help address this concern, RHB propose a new approach to measuring subjective poverty. Instead of asking what proportion of respondents say they are on the lowest rung of the welfare ladder, RHB ask what proportion report that their own welfare is no greater than the poorest vignette. RHB found that subjective poverty measures increase, given the presence of scale heterogeneity. In two of the three countries (Tajikistan and Tanzania) the increase is large. There is considerable scale heterogeneity among the poor. While the overall poverty ranking of the three countries is unaffected, the large change in levels resulting from addressing scale heterogeneity raises concerns over using a simple subjective welfare measure to assess and compare poverty.

[36] Examples include Mangahas (1995), Ravallion and Lokshin (2002), Carletto and Zezza (2006), and Posel and Rogan (2013).

More work of this sort is needed. But from the two studies so far we can conclude that diverse scales are in evidence, casting doubt on the meaning of widely used summary measures such as subjective poverty rates. Nonetheless, only small biases are induced in the coefficients on widely used regressors for subjective poverty and welfare.

3.5.6 *Latent Heterogeneity in Weights*

So far the discussion has focused on the problem of heterogeneity in self-assessed welfare, interpreted as either an additive effect on the underlying continuous welfare level or in the ordinal scales used in the survey. However, there is another concern that has received little or no attention in this context.

Recall that one objective of the exercise is to use subjective welfare data to help determine the weights on various non-income dimensions of welfare—to inform choices in constructing a multidimensional index of poverty. It appears very likely that different people have different weights given that non-market goods are included, and so there is no market mechanism to bring marginal rates of substitution into parity across people.

What then does the standard subjective welfare regression give us? It appears to be widely thought that the regression coefficients can be interpreted as the average weights for the population.[37] However, that interpretation requires some rather strong behavioral assumptions. To see why, note first that the differences in weights across the sample will end up in the error term of the regression model. Then a key issue is whether the heterogeneity in the weighted idiosyncratic welfare determinants is correlated with the dimensions of welfare in which one is interested. If it is, then we have an example of what (in the context of impact evaluations) Heckman et al. (2006) term "essential heterogeneity." In the present context, let us continue to suppose that subjective welfare is a linear function of X_i, as in equation (9) with $Cov(X_i, \varepsilon_i) = 0$, but now allow the weights to vary across people, so that $\beta_i = \bar{\beta} + \gamma_i$ is the weight for person i and $\bar{\beta}$ is the population mean weight. Then equation (9) becomes:

$$SW_i = \alpha + \beta_i X_i + \varepsilon_i = \alpha + \bar{\beta} X_i + (\varepsilon_i + \gamma_i X_i) \tag{11}$$

[37] See, for example, the discussion in Kingdon and Knight (2006).

The composite error term in parentheses contains the heterogeneity in weights. Now it is far from clear what standard subjective welfare regressions are telling us. Even if $Cov(X_i, \varepsilon_i) = 0$, a linear regression model for subjective welfare will not in general deliver the mean weights in the population in large samples. That requires that the interaction effects between the latent differences in weights and the values taken by the covariates are orthogonal to those covariates, i.e. that $Cov(X_i, \gamma_i X_i) = 0$. However, we can easily imagine that people with high weights on some welfare dimension tend to be better endowed with that dimension $Cov(X_i, \gamma_i X_i) > 0$; this may reflect parental decisions on schooling, say. Then (ignoring all other problems) the regression coefficient will tend to overestimate the mean weight. Alternatively, suppose that people with low innate attributes (such as health) tend to put a higher value on those attributes; then one could find that $Cov(X_i, \gamma_i X_i) < 0$. We will underestimate the mean weight.

Thus the likely heterogeneity in the weights attached to non-market goods clouds inferences from subjective welfare regressions. Indeed, while one would presumably like to find weights appropriate to the trade-offs of poor people, it is far from clear that the weights implied by standard regressions are appropriate. One could try to model the heterogeneity in weights by adding interaction effects. This will presumably help, although latent heterogeneity in weights can never be ruled out.

A possible direction for research is to use surveys to try to focus directly on the subjective trade-offs adopted by respondents. This would require more complicated and difficult survey questions, but a not dissimilar approach has been used with some success for inferring attributes of preferences, such as risk aversion or valuations of environmental factors.

3.6 Conclusions

Subjective data offer to expand the information set traditionally used for assessing welfare and measuring poverty. Self-assessed welfare is not equated with welfare. Rather, the promise of subjective data is to help identify the weights on the dimensions of welfare for which prices are missing (or unreliable) and in determining the SSPL—below which people tend to think they are poor, but above which they do not.

Some variables with explanatory power for subjective welfare may not be relevant for measuring poverty. Personality traits, for example, are expected to influence self-assessed welfare but are unlikely to carry much weight in deciding if one person is poorer than another. And even when personality traits are not data, they are likely to influence the observed covariates of self-assessed welfare. In the end, one cannot escape the need for normative judgments about what should be included in a measure of poverty.

The existence of confounding "non-welfare" factors in survey-based measures of subjective welfare is a continuing concern. Practitioners should not presume that these variables are statistically harmless for the purpose at hand. There are a number of reasons for expecting biases in the subjective welfare regressions found in the literature, especially those using cross-sectional data. However, some encouragement can also be found in the recent literature. For example, while there are frame-of-reference effects—whereby the scales in subjective questions are interpreted differently depending on the respondent's knowledge and experience—the biases turned out to be quite small in the one study to date using vignettes to eliminate the heterogeneity in subjective scales for a developing country.

A potentially important problem that has received no attention (to my knowledge) is latent heterogeneity across individuals in their welfare weights—as must be expected for non-market goods. Those weights may well reflect endowments of the welfare covariates, or the covariates may come to reflect the differing weights. Then we do not know whose trade-offs the subjective welfare regression is giving us; we would like to use weights favored by poor people, but that cannot be assured. Further research might usefully explore the possibilities of deriving a locally valid estimator using innovative survey or experimental methods to identify personal trade-offs.

References

Alkire, Sabina and James Foster, 2007, "Counting and Multidimensional Poverty Measurement," Oxford Poverty and Human Development Initiative, Working Paper 7, University of Oxford.

Alkire, Sabina and Maria Emma Santos, 2010, "Acute Multidimensional Poverty: A New Index for Developing Countries," Oxford Poverty and Human Development Initiative, Working Paper 38, University of Oxford.

Atkinson, Anthony B., 1987, "On the Measurement of Poverty," *Econometrica* 55: 749–64.

Atkinson, Anthony B. and Francois Bourguignon, 2001, "Poverty and Inclusion from a World Perspective." In Joseph Stiglitz and Pierre-Alain Muet (Eds.) *Governance, Equity, and Global Markets*. Oxford: Oxford University Press.

Bago d'Uva, T., E. Van Doorslaer, M. Lindeboom, and O. O'Donnell, 2008, "Does Reporting Heterogeneity Bias the Measurement of Health Disparities?" *Health Economics* 17(3): 351–75.

Beegle, Kathleen, Kristen Himelein, and Martin Ravallion, 2012, "Frame-of-Reference Bias in Subjective Welfare Regressions," *Journal of Economic Behavior and Organization* 81: 556–70.

Bertrand, Marianne and Sendhil Mullainathan, 2001, "Do People Mean What They Say? Implications for Subjective Survey Data," *American Economic Review, Papers and Proceedings* 91(2): 67–72.

Bishop, John A. and Feijun Luo, 2006, "Economic Transition and Subjective Poverty in Urban China," *Review of Income and Wealth* 52(4): 625–41.

Blackorby, Charles and David Donaldson, 1987, "Welfare Ratios and Distributionally Sensitive Cost–Benefit Analysis," *Journal of Public Economics* 34: 265–90.

Bourguignon, Francois and Satya Chakravarty, 2003, "The Measurement of Multidimensional Poverty," *Journal of Economic Inequality* 1: 25–49.

Browning, Martin, 1992, "Children and Household Economic Behavior," *Journal of Economic Literature* 30(3): 1434–75.

Cantril, Hadley, 1965, *The Pattern of Human Concerns*, New Brunswick: Rutgers University Press.

Carletto, Gero and Alberto Zezza, 2006, "Being Poor, Feeling Poor: Combining Objective and Subjective Measures of Welfare in Albania," *Journal of Development Studies* 42(5): 739–60.

Castilla, Carolina, 2010, "Subjective Poverty and Reference-Dependence Income over Time, Aspirations and Reference Groups," UNU-WIDER Working Paper 2010/76.

Clark, Andrew E., Paul Frijters, and Michael A. Shields, 2008, "Relative Income, Happiness and Utility: An Explanation for the Easterlin Paradox and Other Puzzles," *Journal of Economic Literature* 46(1): 95–144.

Clark, Andrew E., and Andrew J. Oswald, 1994, "Unhappiness and Unemployment," *Economic Journal* 104: 648–59.

Clark, Andrew E., and Andrew J. Oswald, 1996, "Satisfaction and Comparison Income", *Journal of Public Economics* 61: 359–81.

Clark, Andrew E., and Claudia Senik, 2010, "Who Compares to Whom? The Anatomy of Income Comparisons in Europe," *Economic Journal* 120: 573–94.

Conti, Gabriella and Stephen Pudney, 2011, "Survey Design and the Analysis of Satisfaction," *Review of Economics and Statistics* 93(3): 1087–93.

Corazzini, Luca, Lucio Esposito, and Francesca Majorano, 2011, "Exploring the Absolutist vs. Relativist Perception of Poverty using Cross-Country Questionnaire Survey," *Journal of Economic Psychology* 32(2): 273–83.

Das, Jishnu, Jeff Hammer, and Ken Leonard, 2008, "The Quality of Medical Advice in Low-income Countries," *Journal of Economic Perspectives* 22(2): 93–114.

De Vos, Klaas and Thesia Garner, 1991, "An Evaluation of Subjective Poverty Definitions: Comparing Results from the U.S. and the Netherlands," *Review of Income and Wealth* 37(3): 267–85.

Easterlin, Richard A., 1974, "Does Economic Growth Improve the Human Lot? Some Empirical Evidence," in P.A. David and W.R. Melvin (Eds.) *Nations and Households in Economic Growth*, Palo Alto: Stanford University Press, pp. 89–125.

Fafchamps, M., and F. Shipli, 2009, "Isolation and Subjective Welfare: Evidence from South Asia," *Economic Development and Cultural Change*, 57(4), 641–83.

Ferrer-i-Carbonell, Ada, 2005, "Income and Well-being: An Empirical Analysis of the Comparison Income Effect," *Journal of Public Economics*, 89, 997–1019.

Ferrer-i-Carbonell, Ada and Bernard Van Praag, 2001, "Poverty in Russia," *Journal of Happiness Studies* 2: 147–72.

Foster, James, and A.F. Shorrocks, 1988, "Poverty Orderings," *Econometrica* 56: 173–7.

Frank, Robert H., 1997, "The Frame of Reference as a Public Good," *Economic Journal*, 107, 1832–47.

Frey, B., and A. Stutzer, 2002, "What Can Economists Learn from Happiness Research?" *Journal of Economic Literature*, XL, 402–35.

Goldberg, L.R., 1993, "The Structure of Phenotypic Personality Traits," *American Psychologist* 48(1): 26–34.

Graham, Carol, and Stefano Pettinato, 2002, "Frustrated Achievers: Winners, Losers, and Subjective Well-being in New Market Economies," *Journal of Development Studies* 38(4): 100–40.

Groedhart, T., V. Halberstadt, A. Kapteyn, and B. Van Praag, 1977, "The Poverty Line: Concept and Measurement," *Journal of Human Resources* 12: 503–20.

Gustafsson Bjo, Li Shi, and Hiroshi Sato, 2004, "Can a Subjective Poverty Line be Applied to China? Assessing Poverty among Urban Residents in 1999," *Journal of International Development* 16: 1089–107.

Hagenaars, Aldi, and Bernard van Praag, 1985, "A Synthesis of Poverty Line Definitions," *Review of Income and Wealth* 31(2): 139–54.

Heckman, James, 2011, "Integrating Personality Psychology into Economics," NBER Working Paper 17378.

Heckman, James, Serio Urzua, and Edward Vytlacil, 2006, "Understanding Instrumental Variables in Models with Essential Heterogeneity," *Review of Economics and Statistics* 88(3): 389–432.

Herrera, Javier, Mireille Razafindrakoto, and François Roubaud, 2006, "The Determinants of Subjective Poverty: A Comparative Analysis Between Madagascar and Peru," Paris: DIAL Working Paper DT/2006–01.

Kahneman, D., and C. Varey, 1991, "Notes on the Psychology of Utility," in J. Elster and J. Roemer (Eds.) *Interpersonal Comparisons of Well-being*. Cambridge: Cambridge University Press.

Kapteyn, Arie, 1994, "The Measurement of Household Cost Functions: Revealed Preference versus Subjective Measures," *Journal of Population Economics* 7: 333–50.

Kapteyn, Arie, P. Kooreman, and R. Willemse, 1988, "Some Methodological Issues in the Implementation of Subjective Poverty Definitions," *Journal of Human Resources* 23: 222–42.

Kapteyn, Arie, J. Smith, and A. Van Soest, 2008, "Comparing Life Satisfaction," Working Paper WR-623, Rand Cooperation.

Kapteyn, Arie and Bernard Van Praag, 1976, "A New Approach to the Construction of Family Equivalence Scales," *European Economic Review* 7: 313–35.

Kilpatrick, Robert, 1973, "The Income Elasticity of the Poverty Line," *Review of Economics and Statistics* 55(3): 327–32.

King, G., C. Murray, J. Salomon, and A. Tandon, 2004, "Enhancing the Validity and Cross-Cultural Comparability of Measurement in Survey Research," *American Political Science Review* 98(1): 191–207.

King, G., and J. Wand, 2007, "Comparing Incomparable Survey Responses: Evaluating and Selecting Anchoring Vignettes," *Political Analysis* 15(1): 46–66.

Kingdon, Geeta, and John Knight, 2006, "Subjective Well-being Poverty vs. Income Poverty and Capabilities Poverty?" *Journal of Development Studies* 42(7): 1199–224.

Kingdon, Geeta, and John Knight, 2007, "Community, Comparisons and Subjective Well-being in a Divided Society," *Journal of Economic Behavior and Organization* 64(1): 69–90.

Knight, John, and Ramani Gunatilaka, 2010, "The Rural-Urban Divide in China: Income but not Happiness?" *Journal of Development Studies* 46(3): 506–34.

Knight, John, and Ramani Gunatilaka, 2012, "Income, Aspirations and the Hedonic Treadmill in a Poor Society," *Journal of Economic Behavior and Organization*, 82(1): 67–81.

Kristensen, Nicolai, and E. Johansson, 2008, "New Evidence on Cross-Country Differences in Job Satisfaction Using Vignettes," *Labor Economics* 15(1): 96–117.

Kristensen, Nicolai, and Niels Westergaard-Nielsen, 2007, "Reliability of Job Satisfaction Measures," *Journal of Happiness Studies* 8: 273–92.

Krueger, Alan B., and David Schkade, 2008, "The Reliability of Subjective Well-being Measures," *Journal of Public Economics* 92(8–9): 1833–45.

Lanjouw, Peter, and Martin Ravallion, 1995, "Poverty and Household Size," *Economic Journal* 105: 1415–35.

Lokshin, Michael, and Martin Ravallion, 2008, "Testing for an Economic Gradient in Health Status Using Subjective Data," *Health Economics* 17: 1237–59.

Lokshin, Michael, Nithin Umapathi, and Stefano Paternostro, 2006, "Robustness of Subjective Welfare Analysis in a Poor Developing Country: Madagascar 2001," *Journal of Development Studies* 42(4): 559–91.

Luttmer, Erzo F.P., 2005, "Neighbors as Negatives: Relative Earnings and Well-being," *Quarterly Journal of Economics* 120(3): 963–1002.

Mangahas, M., 1995, "Self-rated Poverty in the Philippines," *International Journal of Public Opinion Research* 7(1), 40–55.

Morris, M.D., 1979, *Measuring the Condition of the World's Poor: The Physical Quality of Life Index,* Washington, DC: Overseas Development Council.

Mueller, Gerrit, and Erik Plug, 2006, "Estimating the Effect of Personality on Male and Female Earnings," *Industrial and Labor Relations Review* 60(1): 3–22.

Oswald, Andrew, 1997, "Happiness and Economic Performance," *Economic Journal* 107: 1815–31.

Pearlin, Leonard, and Carmi Schooler, 1978, "The Structure of Coping," *Journal of Health and Social Behaviour* 19: 2–21.

Pollak, Robert, 1991, "Welfare Comparisons and Situation Comparisons," *Journal of Econometrics* 50: 31–48.

Pollak, Robert, and Terence Wales, 1979, "Welfare Comparison and Equivalence Scale," *American Economic Review* 69: 216–21.

Posel, D., and M. Rogan, 2013, "Measured as Poor *versus* Feeling Poor: Comparing Objective and Subjective Poverty Rates in South Africa," Paper prepared for the UNU-WIDER Conference, Helsinki, Finland.

Pradhan, Menno, and Martin Ravallion, 2000, "Measuring Poverty Using Qualitative Perceptions of Consumption Adequacy," *Review of Economics and Statistics* 82: 462–71.

Ravallion, Martin, 1990, "Income Effects on Undernutrition," *Economic Development and Cultural Change,* 38: 489–516.

Ravallion, Martin, 1994, *Poverty Comparisons.* Switzerland: Harwood Academic Press.

Ravallion, Martin, 1998, *Poverty Lines in Theory and Practice.* Living Standards Measurement Study Paper 133. Washington DC: World Bank.

Ravallion, Martin, 2003, "The Debate on Globalization, Poverty and Inequality: Why Measurement Matters," *International Affairs,* 79(4): 739–54.

Ravallion, Martin, 2008a, "Poverty Lines," in Larry Blume and Steven Durlauf (Eds.) *The New Palgrave Dictionary of Economics,* 2nd edition. London: Palgrave Macmillan.

Ravallion, Martin, 2008b, "On the Welfarist Rationale for Relative Poverty Lines," in Kaushik Basu and Ravi Kanbur (Eds.) *Social Welfare, Moral Philosophy, and Development: Essays in Honour of Amartya Sen's Seventy-fifth Birthday,* Oxford: Oxford University Press.

Ravallion, Martin, 2010, "The Developing World's Bulging (but Vulnerable) Middle Class," *World Development* 38(4): 445–54.

Ravallion, Martin, 2011, "On Multidimensional Indices of Poverty," *Journal of Economic Inequality,* 9(2): 235–48.

Ravallion, Martin, 2012a, "Troubling Tradeoffs in the Human Development Index," *Journal of Development Economics,* 99: 201–9.

Ravallion, Martin, 2012b, "Poverty Lines Across the World," in Philip N. Jefferson (Ed.) *Oxford Handbook of the Economics of Poverty.* Oxford: Oxford University Press.

Ravallion, Martin, and Shaohua Chen, 2011, "Weakly Relative Poverty," *Review of Economics and Statistics* 93(4): 1251–61.

Ravallion, Martin, Kristen Himelein, and Kathleen Beegle, 2013, "Can Subjective Questions on Economic Welfare Be Trusted? Evidence for Three Developing Countries," Policy Research Working Paper, World Bank, Washington DC.

Ravallion, Martin, and Michael Lokshin, 2000, "Who Wants to Redistribute? The Tunnel Effect in 1990s Russia," *Journal of Public Economics* 76(1): 87–104.

Ravallion, Martin, and Michael Lokshin, 2001, "Identifying Welfare Effects from Subjective Questions," *Economica*, 68: 335–57.

Ravallion, Martin, and Michael Lokshin, 2002, "Self-assessed Economic Welfare in Russia." *European Economic Review* 46: 1453–73.

Ravallion, Martin, and Michael Lokshin, 2006, "Testing Poverty Lines", *Review of Income and Wealth* 52(3): 399–421.

Ravallion, Martin and Michael Lokshin, 2010, "Who Cares about Relative Deprivation?" *Journal of Economic Behavior and Organization*, 73(2): 171–85.

Rojas, Mariano, 2007, "A Subjective Well-being Equivalence Scale for Mexico: Estimation and Poverty and Income-distribution Implications," *Oxford Development Studies* 35(3): 273–93.

Scitovsky, Tibor, 1978, *The Joyless Economy*. Oxford: Oxford University Press.

Sen, Amartya, 1983, "Poor, Relatively Speaking," *Oxford Economic Papers* 35(2): 153–69.

Sen, Amartya, 1985, *Commodities and Capabilities*. Amsterdam: North-Holland.

Sen, Amartya, 1992, *Inequality Reexamined*. Oxford: Oxford University Press.

Senik, Claudia, 2004, "When Information Dominates Comparison: Learning from Russian Subjective Panel Data," *Journal of Public Economics* 88, 2099–123.

Shaffer, Paul, 2013, "Ten Years of 'Q-Squared': Implications for Understanding and Explaining Poverty," *World Development* 45: 269–85.

Slesnick, Daniel T., 1993, "Gaining Ground: Poverty in the Postwar United States," *Journal of Political Economy* 101(1): 1–38.

Solnick, Sara, and David Hemenway, 1998, "Is More Always Better? A Survey on Positional Concerns," *Journal of Economic Behavior and Organization* 37: 373–83.

Stevenson, Betsey, and Justin Wolfers, 2008, "Economic Growth and Subjective Well-being: Reassessing the Easterlin Paradox," NBER Working Paper 14282, National Bureau of Economic Research, Cambridge, Massachusetts.

Taddesse, Mekonnen, and Abebe Shimeles, 2005, "Perceptions of Welfare and Poverty: Analysis of the Qualitative Responses of Urban Households," in Arne Bigsten, Abebe Shimeles and Bereket Kebede (Eds.), *Poverty, Income Distribution and Labour Markets in Ethiopia*. Uppsala, Sweden: Nordic Africa Institute.

Taylor, Mark P., 2006, "Tell Me Why I Don't Like Mondays: Investigating Day-of-the-Week Effects on Job Satisfaction and Psychological Well-being," *Journal of the Royal Statistical Society: Series A (Statistics in Society)* 169(1): 127–42.

Theodossiou, I., 1998, "The Effects of Low-Pay and Unemployment on Psychological Well-being: A Logistic Regression Approach," *Journal of Health Economics* 17: 85–104.

Townsend, Peter, 1979, *Poverty in the United Kingdom*. Harmondsworth, Middlesex: Penguin Books.

Tsui, Kai-Yuen, 2002, "Multidimensional Poverty Indices," *Social Choice and Welfare* 19: 69–93.

Tummers, Martijn, 1994, "The Effect of Systematic Misperception of Income on the Subjective Poverty Line," in Richard Blundell, Ian Preston, and Ian Walker (Eds.) *The Measurement of Household Welfare*. Cambridge: Cambridge University Press.

United Nations Development Program (UNDP), 2010, *Human Development Report*. New York: UNDP.

Van Praag, Bernard, 1968, *Individual Welfare Functions and Consumer Behavior*. Amsterdam: North-Holland.

Van Praag, Bernard, 1994, "Ordinal and Cardinal Utility: An Integration of the Two Dimensions of the Welfare Concept," in Richard Blundell, Ian Preston, and Ian Walker (Eds.) *The Measurement of Household Welfare*. Cambridge: Cambridge University Press.

van de Stadt, Huib, Arie Kapteyn, and Sara van de Geer, 1985, "The Relativity of Utility: Evidence from Panel Data," *Review of Economics and Statistics* 67: 179–87.

Wagle, Udaya, 2008, *Multidimensional Poverty Measurement: Concepts and Applications*. New York: Springer.

Winkelmann, Liliana and Rainer Winkelmann, 1998, "Why Are the Unemployed So Unhappy? Evidence from Panel Data," *Economica* 65: 1–15.

Young Lives Project, 2009, "Duy's Story: A Profile from Young Lives in Vietnam," Young Lives Project, Department of International Development, University of Oxford.

Zheng, Buhong, 1997, "Aggregate Poverty Measures," *Journal of Economic Surveys* 11(2): 123–40.

Discussion: Ekaterina Zhuravskaya

It is an honor to be here. Thank you very much for the opportunity to listen to these very insightful talks. I enjoyed reading Martin's chapter and found it very interesting.

The main motivating question of the analysis in this chapter is that despite the fact that development economics is not a new field, the question "how many people are poor in a society" does not have a straight answer even now. This is an unsatisfactory state of the profession and Martin tells us that there are many reasons why this is the case. The main reason is that income is only one out of many objective dimensions of economic well-being, and there are others such as education, health, engagement in society, freedom, inequality, etc. The problem is how to create a composite index of all of these and how to generate weights. So far the practice is that the weights applied are ad hoc. This practice has so far been determined by politicians, motivated by political objectives, although usually referring to "scientific" methods. This is the first problem.

The second is that whatever the objective dimensions of economic well-being are, the subjective dimensions seem to be different. This is what we learned from the contributions presented in this conference. With the same objective indicators, some individuals in a society feel poorer than others, i.e. less well-off. This variation certainly has long-term development implications. Think for instance about what is happening in Hungary. It has been shown that Hungary is one standard deviation lower in happiness compared to what objective indicators would have predicted. This has long-term political implications and, through policy choices, long-term economic implications also.

Martin asks whether one can define a poverty line using subjective well-being measures. Here the answer seems to be moderately positive. Martin considers, step by step, various problems, which actually exist in this literature. I am not going to repeat them, but the important thing is that some of them have not been considered before—in particular the hypothesis that at each level of well-being, the weights attached to any single dimension may be different.

How does Martin answer this? He says that, first, we should be concerned with whether we can actually solve these intellectual problems and define a poverty line using subjective well-being measures. Here his answer seems to be moderately optimistic given that the subjective well-being literature can inform us about the relevant debate, but what he then does is to consider, step by step, the various problems which the subjective well-being literature faces. I am not going to repeat these here, as they are well described in Martin's work. It is important to note that some of the issues that Martin raises here have not been considered before, and are of great importance. In particular, Martin points out that at each level of well-being, the weights attached to any single dimension may be different.

My first concern is that we need to think more about the purpose of the exercise: Why do we want to measure poverty or why do we need a poverty line? There are two possibilities. The first is for positive analysis: as researchers, we want to understand the determinants of poverty. The second is normative: as practitioners, we apply poverty lines in order to be able to bring as many people as possible out of poverty. It seems to me that the actual discussion depends on which stand we take and on our underlying motivation. As researchers, it is not clear that we need to draw a poverty line in order to study the determinants of subjective well-being. If we think as practitioners, the situation is different: the question about the poverty line becomes meaningful and important. Yet this is where the use of subjective indicators starts being problematic. In most societies, there is an understanding about who is poor, and if you ask people in developing countries, in all villages, "Who is poor in your village?" then people, most of the time, will have no problem in saying who that is. However, the real problem is to use these answers for direct policy interventions. If we do so, people will immediately start giving strategic answers, and the picture will be severely distorted. The question I am raising here is yet another challenge to add to the list of challenges that Martin has talked about. How can we measure poverty from the point of view of subjective well-being? In particular, to the extent that subjective indicators cannot be checked via objective measures, we cannot use them directly for policy, as people will learn how to distort their answers knowing that policy will depend on them. We need incentive-compatible measures, but as the determinants of subjective indicators vary across individuals and societies, incentive-compatible measures may not be feasible.

In principle, however important subjective well-being is, there is large scope for policy action without needing to think about subjective indicators at all. The World Bank has been working on a number of indicators—hunger, malnutrition, children of primary school age out of school—that are very strongly correlated with subjective well-being. These indicators are objective and one does not need to answer methodological questions about identification in order to act on them. Generally, all of the main concerns about subjective well-being are products of the rich world. The Easterlin paradox would be a good example of that. This is not to say that there are no poor in rich societies, but who is considered to be poor and where is the poverty line is de facto a political question. I can give you several examples. For instance, how is the poverty line adjusted for inflation? In many countries, this adjustment is completely ad hoc. But using subjective indicators for this would certainly make this problem even more political.

An additional challenge is that the very definition of poverty may affect subjective feelings of being poor. When politicians fix the poverty line at whatever level, people who learn about it and find themselves below the line may suddenly feel sorry for themselves and their subjective well-being may fall. Maybe this is one of the reasons why the SSPL poverty lines are in fact very close to the objective ones.

My final point is that if we think about which policies are most effective in improving subjective well-being in poor countries among the poor (conditional on objective observables), the answer might be indoctrination. For example, the vast majority of lower-class individuals in the Soviet Union were sure that they were fortunate to be born there, because everywhere else, they believed, life was much worse. This type of policy is widely used by autocrats across the globe. In order to improve subjective well-being, a politician just needs to convince people that the situation everywhere else is even worse.

General Discussion

Claudia Senik underlined that the problem of unobserved individual heterogeneity is not particular to subjective variables. As soon as one estimates a relationship between two variables, no matter whether they are objective or subjective, one has to deal with this problem. What is particular to subjective variables is the potential heterogeneity in the way in which people translate their experienced well-being into declared well-being. This scaling problem is the only specific problem here. But Martin's chapter suggests that this "scaling" heterogeneity is actually not a real problem. Another point is that the discrepancy between subjective and objective measures of poverty should not be seen as a weakness of the data. On the contrary, this is a useful source of information and brings up research questions: a number of behavioral analyses have been motivated by this discrepancy. Richard Easterlin noted that, as suggested by the psychology literature, the problem is that there are so many sources of bias that it is hard to be sure about the right measure. However, the issue is whether the problems are such that they dramatically change the outcomes. What we really want to know is if societies are making progress on well-being or not. He recalled that the Bureau of Labor Statistics in the United States identified fifteen different measures of poverty, and the level of poverty varied according to these measures, from 10 percent to 30 percent. But they generated these measures over 15–20 years and the impressive thing was that, year by year, the measures all changed in the same direction and almost by the same magnitude. So what matters is not which one was the right measure, but if people became worse or better off. It seems to him that the issue is not so much how to measure poverty or subjective well-being, but to take a measure or some group of measures, and look at them over time. Are they showing the same thing basically or are they making progress? Martin Ravallion insisted that we should be worried about the heterogeneity in scales, but he remained careful about the results from the vignette studies. His overall take is that subjective well-being regressions are reasonably robust. Regarding the question of looking over time, one should keep in mind that we are talking about developing countries. This is a big issue, when we are looking at the effects of substantial economic growth, and the scales could well change, notably with the changes in reference groups. It seems quite likely that scales will change as developing countries go through structural change. Then it is not clear what can be inferred from long-term comparisons of average self-assessed welfare.

4

Subjective Well-being and Social Evaluation: A Case Study of China*

John Knight and Ramani Gunatilaka

4.1 Introduction

China's remarkable rate of economic growth since the start of economic reform is generally assumed to have raised the economic welfare of the Chinese people dramatically. This is regarded as self-evident from the facts that, in less than three decades, average real income per capita rose by more than six times and that more than 300 million people were lifted out of "dollar a day" poverty (Ravallion and Chen, 2007). Moreover, within a quarter of a century China's "human development index" rose from 0.37 to 0.68 (UNDP, 2010: Table 2). For us to question whether economic growth has raised happiness in China appears either absurd or disingenuous.

Nevertheless, starting with the pioneering work of Easterlin (1974), economists have increasingly asked this question of advanced economies. It has been shown that in several economies—including the United States, Japan, the United Kingdom, France, Germany, Italy, and the Netherlands—income per capita rose consistently over one or more decades, and yet the mean subjective well-being score remained roughly constant (for instance, Blanchflower and Oswald, 2004; Easterlin, 2009). By contrast, Stevenson and Wolfers (2009) report a cross-country equation indicating that, within countries over

* Chapter initially prepared for the CEPREMAP Workshop on Well-being and Development held in the Paris School of Economics, March 9, 2012. We are grateful to Xiaobo Zhang (our discussant), Dick Easterlin, and Martin Ravallion for helpful comments.

time but given a common slope, happiness increases with income. However, a re-specification allowing country slopes to differ produces an average value of the country coefficients that is negative, albeit not significantly so (Krueger, 2009: 99). There is indeed something odd to be explained.

Very few such studies have apparently been made for developing countries, probably owing to a lack of relevant time series data on subjective well-being. However, one would expect that the happiness of people in poor countries is determined in a different way. For instance, it is arguable that the greatest concern of poor people is to meet their basic physical needs for food, shelter, and clothing, whereas non-poor people are more concerned with their position and achievement in relation to society. Thus, absolute income might be important to happiness at low levels of income, but relative income might be more important at higher levels.[1]

The chapter is divided into two main parts. In the first part we ask: are the findings for the advanced economies true also for China? We present time-series evidence to suggest that this is indeed the case. Although the lack of appropriate time-series data prevents us from directly analyzing the reasons why happiness has not risen in China, we consider the reasons indirectly on the basis of four papers reporting research on subjective well-being in China by means of a cross-section national household survey (Knight et al., 2009; Knight and Gunatilaka, 2010a, 2010b, 2012). This part follows the argument of our summary paper (Knight and Gunatilaka, 2011), but without explaining the methodology or providing the detailed empirical estimates.

In the second main part of the chapter we ask: can our measures of and explanations for subjective well-being be used for purposes of social evaluation? Ultimately a value judgment is required. We examine other potential criteria for social progress, and contrast them with the subjective well-being criterion. This leads to a discussion of the case for and against viewing subjective well-being in normative as well as positive terms. A subjective well-being function is estimated that is intended to encompass the other indicators by including them as explanatory variables.

[1] As Kingdon and Knight (2007) found for South Africa, a country with high income inequality. Whereas the effect of absolute income on subjective well-being was significantly positive for both groups, the effect of relative income on subjective well-being was insignificant for the poor but important for the non-poor.

4.2. Can Subjective Well-being Be Explained?

4.2.1 *Background*

This section provides some background evidence on subjective well-being (we use the terms subjective well-being, happiness, and satisfaction with life interchangeably). Kahneman and Krueger (2006) present a graph obtained from the Gallup Organization, which had conducted surveys of respondents in China in four years ranging from 1994 to 2005. The percentage of respondents who were somewhat satisfied or very satisfied with life fell monotonically by 15 percent over that period, and the proportion of respondents who were somewhat dissatisfied or very dissatisfied thus rose monotonically. Yet over that period household real income per capita rose annually on average by 3.7 percent in rural China and by 5.4 percent in urban China. Easterlin and Sawangfa (2010) provide evidence of the trend in reported life satisfaction or happiness in China from three sources: the Gallup survey, the Asiabarometer survey, and the World Values Survey. The results are shown in Table 4.1. In each case the average life satisfaction score fell: from 2.82 in 1997 to 2.67 in 2004; from 3.73 in 2003 to 3.68 in 2007; and from 6.83 in 1995 to 6.76 in 2007, respectively (each survey used different units). The happiness score in the World Values Survey also fell, from 3.05 in 1995 to 2.94 in 2007. Unfortunately, these time

Table 4.1. Mean life satisfaction or happiness in China over time

	About 1995	About 2000	About 2005
Life satisfaction score			
Gallup survey (1–4 scale)	2.82	2.78	2.67
Year:	1997	1999	2004
Asiabarometer survey (1–5 scale)		3.73	3.68
Year:		2003	2006
World Values Survey (1–10 scale)	6.83	6.53	6.76
Year:	1995	2001	2007
Happiness score			
World Values Survey (1–5 scale)	3.05	2.87	2.94
Year:	1995	2001	2007

Sources: Easterlin and Sawangfa (2010); World Values Survey, data for China.

Notes: An earlier World Values Survey is excluded because it was confined to the urban population. The 1995 World Values Survey covered central China (two-thirds of the national population) and the 2001 and 2007 surveys were intended to be nationally representative. The 1994 Gallup survey is excluded because it had five rather than four response categories.

series data sets are not rich enough to permit direct analysis of the reasons for their trends.

The question being posed therefore cannot be dismissed out of hand. It is worth exploring further. To do so, it is necessary to review the reasons that have been put forward for the "Easterlin paradox" (Easterlin, 1974, 1995). Easterlin's own explanation, both in his original paper and subsequently, is that subjective well-being is a positive function of income but a negative function of aspirations, and that aspirations rise along with income, so cancelling out the positive effect of income. Moreover, the reason why aspirations tend to rise with absolute income is that they are influenced by relative income.

Any explanation would have to deal with the obvious fact that nearly everyone, in rich as well as poor countries, if asked, would say they wanted more income, other things being equal; and, if offered more income, would reveal their preference for it. Easterlin's explanation provides an answer: people want more income because they wish to raise their relative income, or they recognize that the incomes of their comparator groups will rise, or they fail to recognize that their aspirations will rise as well as their income. Thus, people run on a "hedonic treadmill."

A potential criticism of the Easterlin paradox is that people redefine their happiness scores over time. For instance, if people adjust their aspirations to the utility they normally experience, an improvement in their normal utility would lead them to report no higher happiness than previously, even if they were experiencing higher utility than previously. People are thus on an "aspirations treadmill" and not a "hedonic treadmill." A test of this argument requires separate measures of "experienced utility" ("net affect," or feelings) and of subjective well-being (life satisfaction). Kahneman and Krueger (2006) present evidence suggesting that measures of net affect show as much adaptation as do measures of life satisfaction, and accordingly reject this criticism. In any case, there is no consensus that there is such a thing as utility independent of aspirations—that is, that the utility which a person experiences can be separated from their perception of happiness, however formed.

On the other hand, there is now a considerable literature providing evidence—largely for advanced economies—that happiness is sensitive to relative income (for instance, Frank, 1997; Clark and Oswald, 1998; Frey and Stutzer, 2002; Luttmer, 2004; Di Tella et al., 2006; Graham and Felton, 2006; Clark et al., 2008). The effect of reference-group income is normally negative but a couple of studies have shown it to be positive (Senik, 2004; Kingdon and Knight,

2007). There is also evidence-based research showing that aspirations are important to subjective well-being (Stutzer, 2003; di Tella et al., 2003; di Tella et al., 2007; Easterlin, 2004). The research provides the justification for examining the effect of economic growth on happiness within the framework of Easterlin's explanation for his paradox.

4.2.2 *Survey, Data, and Method*

The data used in this chapter come from the national household survey, relating to 2002, of the China Household Income Project (CHIP). This is the third CHIP cross-section national household survey, containing rich socioeconomic information. This and the previous two surveys (1988 and 1995) were designed by the research team, with hypotheses in mind, but only the 2002 survey contained questions on subjective well-being.

There were just a couple of subjective well-being questions in the questionnaires for the sub-samples of (registered) urban resident households and rural–urban migrant households, but the questionnaire for rural households contained a specially designed module on subjective well-being. The analysis has to be based on a snapshot picture with no panel element. The chapter pioneers the analysis of the question being posed but it can only be a suggestive beginning.

The subjective well-being question that is available for all three sub-samples can be translated as "how happy are you nowadays?" Five answers were offered: very happy, happy, so-so, unhappy, and not at all happy. This forms the dependent variable in much of the analysis. It was treated either as an ordinal or as a cardinal measure, involving either ordered probit or OLS estimation. In line with the methodological study by Ferrer-i-Carbonnel and Frijters (2004), we found no substantive differences between the results using the two measures, and accordingly we report only the cardinal results, since they are easier to interpret. The household head, or its main member present, was asked the question; the respondent is identified.

The explanatory variables in the happiness equations are a set of individual, household, and community socioeconomic characteristics. We distinguish what we term basic variables, conventional economic variables, comparison variables, insecurity variables, and attitudinal variables. We retain the specifications taken from the four papers but, to simplify, we do not present the tables (available in the summary paper Knight and Gunatilaka, 2011) and generally discuss only those variables of most relevance to our theme.

The coefficients in the happiness functions represent associations and not necessarily the hypothesized causal relationships. They might instead reflect the influence of unobserved variables on both the dependent and the independent variable, or reverse causation. In some cases we shall suggest reasons why the independent variable might have a causal effect on happiness but without establishing causation, either because the variable is not germane to the main argument or because a valid instrument is not available. If the interpretation is important to our story—as in the case of income—we try to isolate the effect of exogenous variation in the independent variable by means of instrumenting.

4.2.3 *Rural Happiness*

We begin with rural happiness, drawing on Knight et al. (2009) which analyzes its determinants or correlates. Despite the fact that rural dwellers have relatively low incomes and have been left behind in China's economic development, it appears that rural China is not a hotbed of dissatisfaction with life. No less than 62 percent of the sample reported being happy or very happy, and only 9 percent were not happy or not at all happy. With very happy having a score of 4, happy 3, so-so 2, unhappy 1, and not at all happy 0, the mean score was 2.67. Nevertheless, there is much variation in happiness scores, and this variation can be well explained by the variables in the survey.

Many of the coefficients in the rural happiness equations are statistically significant, have predictable signs, and display the regularities that are common to many happiness studies around the world. For instance, the age–happiness profile has a U-shaped pattern, and being female, being married, and being in good health all raise happiness. The conventional economic variables affect happiness, in line with basic economic theory, but the contributions of ln income and net wealth (positive), as well as of working hours (negative), are weak. We instrumented the income variable in case it was endogenous. The effect was to raise the coefficient on ln income. We had expected unobserved characteristics, such as a happy disposition, to raise both income and happiness, so producing upward bias in the OLS equation. The downward bias suggested either that aspirations raise income but lower happiness, or that there is attenuation bias resulting from measurement error. Even then, the effect of a doubling of income was to raise the happiness score by less than 0.4 points.

Despite the apparent unimportance of income for happiness, 64 percent of the unhappy gave lack of income as the reason for their unhappiness. A possible explanation for these discrepant results is that happiness is not only a positive function of income but also a negative function of aspirations, and that the latter can be governed by the income of the reference group. The reference group is likely to be determined by information sets and by social interactions. Most rural people report confining their reference groups to the village: 68 percent make comparisons with their neighbors or fellow villagers.

Happiness is sensitive to respondents' perceptions of their household's position in the village income distribution (since only ten households were sampled in each village, it is not possible to use actual instead of perceived position). Five categories are distinguished: income perceived to be much above, above, at, below, and much below the village average, with the middle category being the omitted variable in the dummy variable analysis. The coefficients are large: that of the highest income category is greater than that of the lowest by 1.05 (column 2). The notion of relative deprivation, as developed by sociologists such as Runciman (1966), appears to be relevant. Thus, a rise or fall in income tends to be offset if there is a simultaneous rise or fall in village income. Aspirations appear to adjust to the income of the community, so producing a hedonic treadmill.

By contrast, income inequality in the county (as measured by the Gini coefficient of income per capita of the sampled households) is found to raise happiness. Hirschman's (1973) "tunnel effect"—the analogy of two lines of cars jammed in a tunnel—might provide the explanation: initially at least, the movement of one line raises expectations that the other will also move. Thus, county income inequality might serve as a "demonstration effect" of possible progress in the future.

Reference time is relevant as well as reference income: those whose current living standards are considered to be higher than five years ago are happier than those whose living standards are now lower. By comparison with static expectations, those who expect an increase in income over the next five years have a higher current happiness score while those who expect a decrease have a lower score, other things being equal. This is inconsistent with the standard assumption that current utility depends on current consumption and not on expected future consumption; it suggests that people internalize their future states into their current happiness. That being the case, it is consistent with the psychological research findings (for instance, Rabin, 1998) that people tend to base their aspirations on current incomes, and that they are better able to project their income into the future than their aspirations.

There is some more evidence that aspirations are important for happiness. We can distinguish those whose comparators are within and those whose comparators are beyond the village. Relative income within the village appears to be less important, and the coefficients showing the effect of future income on current happiness all have lower values, in the case of those with reference groups beyond the village. This suggests that the aspirations, relative to current income, of villagers with wider horizons are raised by the higher incomes of their comparators.

We introduced a set of attitudinal variables into our happiness functions, in an attempt to explore otherwise hidden influences. The significant coefficients suggest that rural people who derive their satisfaction with life more from personal relationships and less from material goods and services are happier, other things being equal, although reverse causation is also possible.

4.2.4 *Urban Happiness*

Our discussion of urban happiness draws on another paper (Knight and Gunatilaka, 2010b). Estimating urban happiness equations, we obtained the conventional results for some of the standard variables. The coefficients on the ln income variable were roughly twice the size of the coefficients in the corresponding functions for rural residents: it appears that urban people may be more materialistic, in the sense that either aspirations for or need for income are raised by urban living. When the income variable was instrumented, its coefficients lost their significance—but instrumenting appeared not to be necessary.

Our hypothesis is that urban people also experience relative deprivation. We find two indicators that relative income is important for happiness. First, households in each city were grouped into four income per capita quarters. Given the highest quarter as the reference category, the coefficients on the quarters become monotonically more and more negative, and the effect is both statistically significant and substantively important. City mean income per capita across the cities varies sufficiently for this variable not simply to reflect the variation in household incomes. Second, the log of average urban income per capita in the province of residence has a negative coefficient. In the urban case, unlike the rural case, the effect of surrounding prosperity on aspirations may arouse feelings of relative deprivation.

Those who consider income distribution, both in the nation and in the city, to be fair are happier, *ceteris paribus*, although it is unclear which way causation runs. As with rural dwellers, expected future income is important to current happiness, possibly because people internalize their future states and also assume that their aspirations in the future will be the same as their current aspirations.

There was a high rate of retrenchment from state-owned enterprises in the years prior to the survey, and retrenched workers faced great difficulties in finding re-employment. The social security system was in transition from being employer-based to insurance-based, and unemployment benefits were not reliable, so that many unemployed workers received very little. We expected the new uncertainties of urban living to depress happiness. We therefore explored the effect of insecurity on urban-dwellers' happiness.

The experience of current unemployment, and of having been laid off in the past, had a significant negative coefficient, as also did the dummy variable denoting that a worker's employing enterprise made a loss: this would increase the employee's chances of being made redundant. Emil Durkheim's (1897) notion of *anomie* might be relevant. He defined *anomie* as normlessness, when social rules break down and people do not know what to expect of each other. The remarkable economic progress, the rapid creation of markets, the withdrawal of institutional support, and the demise of ideology might have created a state of *anomie*. The survey does not possess good attitudinal questions to identify *anomie*. However, respondents were asked what they considered to be the most important social problem. Three suggestive pointers are the negative coefficients on corruption, on social polarization, and on immorality in the happiness function.

4.2.5 *A Rural–Urban Comparison*

We went on to make a comparison of rural and urban China (Knight and Gunatilaka, 2010a). China has a remarkable rural–urban divide (Knight and Song, 1999): the ratio of urban to rural household income per capita has exceeded 2.0 to 1 throughout the period of economic reform, and actually rose in recent years despite the economic reforms and marketization that partly integrated the rural and urban sectors. In 2002, the year of the survey, the ratio from the survey stood at 3.1 to 1. We would therefore expect a corresponding large divide in subjective well-being. Yet the survey also shows that, when happiness is converted into a cardinal value, the urban score is no higher than the rural score. Indeed, the reported mean urban happiness (2.5) is actually lower than the mean rural happiness (2.7). How can this result be explained?

We first calculated a standard "Oaxaca decomposition" of these mean differences in happiness using those variables in the equations that are identical in the two sub-samples. The difference in income of course simply added to the puzzle. What raised the happiness of rural people was their superior happiness generation function. Unfortunately, much of the work was being done by the difference in the intercept terms, which remained unexplained. It was necessary to produce an explanation from the separate and non-identical rural and urban happiness functions.

It is possible that in some societies there is a cultural unwillingness to report happiness, or alternatively unhappiness, and that comparisons made across culturally distinct groups might be misleading as a result. Thus a greater willingness of urban than of rural people to report being less than happy might explain our results. We cannot reject the hypothesis, but one piece of evidence points against it: rural migrant households living in the cities reported having lower average happiness than did urban households. A culture of not wishing to admit being unhappy is not observable among households that were recently part of rural society.

Our preferred explanation runs as follows. On the one hand, rural China is not a hotbed of dissatisfaction with life, despite the relative poverty and low socioeconomic status of its people in Chinese society. The basic reasons are that they have limited information sets and narrow reference groups, they expect their income to rise in the future, and they place a high value on personal and community relationships. On the other hand, the relatively low happiness of urban people despite their relatively high income and their expectations of higher income in the future has to do with the nature of the urban society that has emerged in recent years. High aspirations, governed by reference groups, appear to give rise to the relative deprivation that makes for unhappiness. In addition, the greater insecurity associated with redundancy, unemployment, and various other urban social ills also makes city-dwellers unhappy.

4.2.6 *Migrant Happiness*

Rural–urban migration in China has grown remarkably in recent years: the number of rural–urban migrants probably exceeded 130 million in 2002. Many of the migrants are temporarily in the cities but settlement is increasingly permitted. The higher income to be obtained in the city compared with the village appears to provide a strong incentive to migrate. The 2002 CHIP survey contained a unique feature—a nationally representative subsample of rural–urban migrants, that is, rural *hukou* households living in the urban areas. Their subjective well-being is analyzed in Knight and Gunatilaka (2010a). The average happiness score of these (fairly settled) migrants is lower than that of rural residents. This appears to be inconsistent with the economic theories of rural–urban migration based on utility maximization. We looked at three main possible explanations: in terms of the hardships of urban life that they experience, in terms of self-selection, and in terms of revised aspirations.

We proceeded by estimating migrant happiness functions. Again we found the usual results for several of the basic variables. The coefficient on ln income per capita is significantly positive but its values indicate that a doubling of income raises the happiness score by only 0.13 points. Although this effect is increased, to 0.35 points, the inference that income level is relatively unimportant is not altered by instrumenting the income variable. The coefficient tends to rise with length of stay, suggesting either that there is a process of self-selection or that migrants may become more materialistic as they lay down deeper urban roots. Although current income is not important to happiness, expectations of income over the next five years enter powerfully and significantly into the current happiness score. Again, this suggests that anticipated future happiness is absorbed into current happiness and that people are bad at forecasting how their aspirations will change if income changes, so that they judge their future happiness on the basis of their current aspirations. An alternative interpretation is that expected future income determines current consumption, in line with the "permanent income" theory of consumption, and that the relationship would therefore not survive if current income were replaced by current consumption in the happiness function. However, this substitution made no notable difference to the coefficients on expected income; moreover, the same result was found for the other two sub-samples.

When migrants who reported that they were unhappy or not at all happy were asked the reason for their unhappiness, over two-thirds said that their income was too low. This pointer to the possible importance of perceptions of relative deprivation is confirmed by the negative, large, and significant coefficient on per capita income of urban residents in the destination province. This effect is stronger for the migrants who had been in the city for more than the median length of time, 7.5 years. The migrants appear to compare their own situations with those of others living in their new surroundings, and increasingly to do so as they become more settled.

China's political economy accords urban *hukou* people a set of rights and privileges that are denied to rural *hukou* people residing in the cities (Knight and Song, 1999, 2005). The migrants are generally "second-class citizens." When we included various proxies for these disadvantages in the happiness function, job dissatisfaction, perceptions of discrimination against migrants, and measures of job insecurity had significant negative coefficients. The unsatisfactory conditions in which migrants live and the unpleasant and insecure nature of their employment depress happiness.

We explored the reasons why migrants were on average less happy than peasants by conducting a decomposition analysis using happiness functions with identical determinants for the migrant and rural sub-samples. The objective was to explain the migrant shortfall in mean happiness score, equal to 0.31, distinguishing between the contributions of the different mean values of the explanatory variables and those of their coefficients. The effect of characteristics was actually to increase the difference in mean happiness scores: in particular, the migrants had higher mean income. The explanation was therefore to be found in the superior happiness function of rural people. Here the expectations of future income were crucial. With static income as the reference category, the coefficients of the migrants were uniformly lower, suggesting that migrants had higher income aspirations relative to their current income. This can be expected if aspirations depend on the income of the relevant comparator group. The rural respondents are representative of rural society and so their mean income is close to the mean income of their likely comparator group. But the migrant subsample is unrepresentative of urban society: migrants tend to occupy the lower ranges of the urban income distribution. If migrants make comparisons with urban-born residents as well as with other migrants, their aspirations will be high in relation to their current income.

An equivalent exercise was conducted to decompose the difference in mean happiness between migrants and urban *hukou* residents, the migrant shortfall in happiness score being 0.11. In this case the difference in coefficients makes no net contribution to the explanation. Two differences in mean characteristics can explain all of the difference: the higher mean income of urban residents and their superior position in the urban income distribution. Position in the city income distribution has a powerful effect on happiness, and this is true for both samples. A far higher proportion of migrants than of urban residents fall into the lowest quarter of city households in terms of living standards. If the income of the relevant comparator group influences aspirations, the inferior position of migrants in the city income distribution can thus explain why they appear to have higher aspirations in relation to their current income.

There might be selection on the basis of unobserved characteristics. For instance, migrants might be inherently unhappy people who have unsuccessfully sought happiness through migration. Our test was to use the residual (actual minus predicted) happiness score as a proxy for inherent disposition and to introduce this variable into a probit equation predicting that the migrant reported urban living to yield more happiness than rural living. The coefficient was significantly positive and large, implying that the unobserved characteristic was acquired after migration. Thus, this explanation lacked empirical support.

4.2.7 *Aspiration Income and Happiness*

Our argument has centered on peoples' aspirations in relation to their income, and yet the evidence has been only indirect. We should ideally measure aspirations, or at least aspirations for income. There is a proxy for "aspiration income" in the rural data set, which is analyzed in Knight and Gunatilaka (2012).

Respondents were asked: "What is the minimum income needed to sustain the household for a year?" It was possible to justify this as a proxy for income aspirations. The strategy was first to analyze its apparent determinants and then to include income aspirations as an additional argument in the happiness functions for the rural sample that had previously been estimated.

We estimated the determinants of aspiration income, with log of household income need as the dependent variable. Among the demographic and physiological determinants of income need, good health and satisfaction with the village clinic (both reducing the need for protecting health) and size and composition of the household are important, and the age, sex, and marital status of the respondent are also relevant. The equations contain several variables that might influence aspirations for income. In particular, the coefficient on log of household income is both positive and significant. The coefficient is 0.19 (OLS) and 0.57 (IV)—that is, a doubling of actual income increases the perceived minimum income by 13 percent or 39 percent respectively. Years of education also has a significantly positive coefficient: the more education the respondent had received, the higher the income needed. With static living standard as the base category, those whose current living standard is worse than that of five years ago have a significantly higher aspiration for income. By contrast, financial assets may have a negative effect—that is, more wealth appears to provide security rather than to raise aspirations. Those whose main reference group is outside the village have higher aspiration income, as do households whose income is below their village's average household income.

At the second stage, we added the aspiration income variable to the function estimating happiness, again converted into a cardinal score. Some equations had ln per capita income need as the only aspiration variable and others had a full list of aspiration variables. When other variables that are likely to represent aspirations are introduced as well as minimum income need, they generally have significant coefficients. However, our particular interest here lies in aspiration income. As expected, the coefficient on log of household income per capita is significantly positive in the OLS specifications, with an average value of about 0.20; the coefficients are higher but not significantly positive in the (less precise) IV estimates. Log of minimum income needed has a significantly negative coefficient, averaging –0.07 in the OLS estimates; it is more negative but not significant in the IV estimates. Although the conventional statistical tests of good instruments are passed, it is not possible to find a set of instruments which reliably identify the separate effects of the two income variables. Nevertheless, this set of results provides direct, albeit only suggestive, evidence that, other things being equal, having higher aspirations for income can reduce happiness. Moreover, a comparison of the positive and negative coefficients suggests that people run on a partial "hedonic treadmill."[2]

4.3 Does Subjective Well-being Have Normative Value?

It is one thing to explain subjective well-being but another to utilize it in social evaluation. Because income can be readily quantified, most poverty research in developing countries relies on measures of household income per capita as the criterion for social progress in poverty alleviation.[3] A broader approach is to include but go beyond household income per capita in order to derive a Human Development Index or a

[2] If there are particular unobserved personal characteristics that reduce happiness, they might by way of compensation raise a person's perceived need for income. In that case the variable that we call aspiration income wholly or partly represents this compensatory effect. However, three facts taken together reduce the likelihood of this explanation being important in our case: the question about income need related to the household and not to the respondent; some other variables hypothesized to reflect aspirations for income were also found to reduce happiness; and our attempt to instrument the aspiration income variable did not persuasively eliminate its negative effect.

[3] For instance, The World Bank's Dollar-a-day Index, shown in its *World Development Report* (annual).

Human Poverty Index.[4] Sen (1983, 1984, 1990, etc.) has eschewed the metric of utility as a criterion for social evaluation, preferring instead people's "capabilities" to be or to do things of intrinsic worth. Ultimately, social evaluation requires a value judgment to be made. Accordingly, our discussion is simply about the arguments—philosophical, political, or economic—for choosing one criterion rather than another.[5]

4.3.1 *Other Indicators of Social Progress*

Different criteria can produce very different evaluations. This is illustrated by Table 4.2, which sets out a series of possible alternative measures of social welfare in China and of its changes during the period 1995–2007, each an objective rather than subjective measure. The period is chosen to correspond roughly to the period over which measures of subjective well-being, shown in Table 4.1, are available.

The results of Table 4.2 stand in sharp contrast to those of Table 4.1. Household real income per capita grew rapidly in both rural and urban China, as did real GDP per capita (by 6.3, 8.3, and 8.8 percent per annum respectively). The UNDP's Human Development Index (HDI) is a measure of achievement in three aspects of well-being: health and longevity, access to knowledge, and standard of living. China's HDI increased over the period, and it rose in international rank (the top country being 1). All three components of the HDI improved, although whereas GDP per capita was unbounded, both life expectation and the educational enrollment ratio were effectively bounded. The Human Poverty Index (HPI) measures deprivation in the same three indicators of well-being. China's HPI fell over the period, improving in all three components. The Gini coefficient of household income per capita rose rapidly in the reform years prior to 1995 but remained fairly constant in the next dozen years, at a high level (0.48 in 2007).

The World Bank publishes annual Worldwide Governance Indicators (available online). In these we see that China does well on "government

[4] For instance, the UNDP's *Human Development Report* (annual).

[5] If there are particular unobserved personal characteristics that reduce happiness, they might by way of compensation also raise a person's perceived need for income. In that case the variable that we call aspiration income wholly or partly reflects this compensatory effect. However, three facts taken together reduce the likelihood of this explanation being important in our case: the question about income need related to the household and not to the respondent; some other variables hypothesized to reflect aspirations for income were also found to reduce happiness; and our attempt to instrument the aspiration income variable did not persuasively eliminate its negative effect.

Table 4.2. Measures of socioeconomic progress in China, 1995–2007

	1995	2007	Change '95–07
Rural household real income per capita	100	208	6.3% p.a.
Urban household real income per capita	100	259	8.3% p.a.
Real GDP per capita	100	276	8.8% p.a.
Human Development Index			
Value	0.556	0.772	0.216
Rank (percentile)	61	51	–10
of which:			
Life expectancy			
Years	69.2	72.9	3.7
Index	0.74	0.80	0.06
Combined gross enrollment rate			
Percentage	64	69	5
Index	0.76	0.85	0.09
Real GDP per capita			
PPP US$ (000)	2.935	5.383	5.2% p.a.
Index	0.46	0.61	0.15
Human Poverty Index			
Value	17.1	7.7	–9.4
of which:			
Adult illiteracy rate %	18.5	6.7	–11.8
Population below real $1 a day %	29.4	15.9	–13.5
Gini coefficient of household income per capita			
Rural	0.364	0.363	–0.001
Urban	0.339	0.338	–0.001
National	0.469	0.481	0.016
Worldwide Governance Indicators			
of which:			
Government effectiveness			
Score	–0.30	+0.18	+0.48
Percentile	45	63	18
Control of corruption			
Score	–0.25	–0.59	–0.34
Percentile	43	33	–10
Voice and accountability			
Score	–0.12	–1.70	–1.58
Percentile	12	5	–7

Notes: The Worldwide Governance Indicators relate to 1996 (their first year), not 1995.

Sources: Household income per capita data: NBS (2009); human development data: UNDP (2009, 1998); Gini coefficient: Knight and Ding (2012), from the China Household Income Project (CHIP) surveys, 1995, 2007; Worldwide Governance Indicators: World Bank <info.worldbank.org/governance/wgi/index/asp>.

effectiveness," and improved over the period, but poorly on "control of corruption" and "voice and accountability," and these scores deteriorated. In 2007 China was in the seventh percentile (the bottom country being 1) on "voice and accountability," which effectively measures the ability of people to monitor and influence government conduct. With these exceptions, the various potential measures of well-being in Table 4.2 suggest that objectively measured well-being improved over the period in which measured subjective well-being remained constant.

4.3.2 *Criteria for Social Evaluation*

Should the level of happiness or satisfaction with life be the criterion for social evaluation? The criteria in terms of happiness might be modified to include not only the level but also the distribution of happiness, for instance by according a higher weight in the social welfare function to people who, according to their characteristics, are expected to be less happy. The value judgment that happiness should be used in social evaluation has been forcefully made by Layard (2005). Reasoned but cautious support for some use of happiness measures is to be found in Frey and Stutzer (2002), Kahneman and Krueger (2006), and Di Tella and MacCulloch (2006).

This approach is in accordance with traditional welfare economics, which has given utility the status of being uniquely important in assessing well-being (Sen, 2009: 272). The notion of utility—that is, units of happiness—is central to a great deal of normative as well as positive economic analysis, invariably entering the social welfare function that underlies welfare economics and thus policy prescription. Yet the profession has been loath to try to measure happiness directly. Economists normally regard reported perceptions as suspect, and they want economic agents' preferences to be revealed by their actions rather than words. They are willing to value utility at the margin, by assuming that the price of a good, or leisure, measures its marginal utility, but not to measure total utility. For this reason the quantitative economic analysis of subjective well-being is not a mainstream concern.

For the moment, let us accept that happiness is one, or even the only, relevant criterion for social evaluation. Various arguments can be put which suggest that happiness is a poor measure of well-being. At one time it was a common assumption in welfare economics that interpersonal comparisons of utility are intrinsically impossible. However, this assumption is a very restrictive basis for social evaluation. Let us assume that interpersonal comparisons are difficult but not impossible to make, and consider reasons why use of happiness scores might be unreliable.

It has been argued that utility is different from happiness, and that utility is the variable to include in the social welfare function. One version of this argument concerns the role of changing aspirations and adaptation. This raises the question: is there a distinction between reported happiness, or satisfaction with life, and "true utility"—between subjective and objective notions of utility? If people gradually adjust their aspirations to the utility that they normally experience, they might report no higher happiness from an improvement in life circumstances even if they experience higher utility. In other words, is there an "aspirations treadmill" rather than a hedonic treadmill? Di Tella and MacCulloch (2006) are skeptical on the grounds that the happiness score is correlated with other variables (such as unemployment, divorce, and brain activity) that they expect to be associated with "true utility." Kahneman and Krueger (2006), using the "day reconstruction method" of recording people's feelings during the day, create a measure of utility ("net affect," or feelings) that is separate from reported life satisfaction. They find that net affect shows no less adaptation than life satisfaction, and so reject the hypothesis.

Some empirical literature on poverty lines attempts to measure "income need" purged of the aspirational response to actual income (for instance, Van Praag and Kaptein, 1973; Goedhart et al., 1977; Colasanto et al., 1984; Pradhan and Ravallion, 2000). Minimum income functions generally show that the minimum income that a household claims to need rises with household income, *ceteris paribus*. The standard practice is to treat the level at which the minimum equals the actual income as the subjective poverty line: below that level minimum income exceeds and above it falls short of actual income. The reason for choosing the intersection rather than the average minimum income is "preference drift"—that is, people's perceived minimum income adjusts to their actual income. It is argued that the true minimum income is normally misperceived and that only at the intersection is the distortion not present. This view carries the value judgment that subjective well-being as an objective of policy against poverty should be measured after eliminating the adjustment of the minimum income that people feel they need to the income that they experience—that is, after standardizing for endogenous aspirations.[6]

[6] In fact, this measure may not fully eliminate aspirations: insofar as a rise in the income of the community over time raises aspirations generally and thus the minimum income function, the intersection income and thus the poverty line rises.

Another version of the argument is concerned with a positive issue but has normative implications. According to Becker and Raya (2008), happiness is an important determinant of utility, but not the only one. If "utility" is defined as whatever set of factors governs individual economic behavior, then happiness—as it is measured in the surveys—is one but not the only factor; Becker and Raya mention health and longevity as among the others. They regard happiness as an inadequate criterion for individual decision-making. A possible counterargument is that these other factors do affect happiness. Indeed, they might be regarded simply as instruments in the indirect or unconscious pursuit of happiness.

It might be argued that happiness scores of individuals cannot be compared because people have in mind different scales: the upper bound ("very happy") might mean one thing to A but another to B (for instance, Veenhoven, 2004). The difference in scales might arise because people have different "frames of reference"—for instance a poor person might never have experienced great happiness (Ravallion and Lokshin, 2005). The argument is less powerful if the comparisons are made within a large sample rather than between two people. In the former case, moreover, Kahneman and Krueger (2006) propose a measure (the percentage of time that the individual spends in an unpleasant state) which depends on an ordinal ranking of feelings and does not require a scaling of subjective responses, and are reassured by the fact that it bears a strong relationship to the categories of life satisfaction. Ravallion (this volume) describes an empirical test of the argument that different people use different happiness scales: by embedding "vignette" rankings in the standard happiness regression for Tajikistan, Beagle et al. (2012) found the "scale" (or frame of reference) bias in coefficients, including that on income, to be negligible. Nevertheless, there is a case for introducing vignette rankings into happiness regressions in China.

The problem of making interpersonal comparisons that might be discounted in a homogeneous sample can be more serious when comparing distinct ways of life even within a single country. Assume that person A living in a poor area, whose frame of reference is their local community, reports a higher happiness score than B, who has the same individual and household characteristics but lives in a rich area. Can it be claimed that the two individuals have the same "true utility" or "objective welfare"? If A has neither experienced great happiness nor observed it in their community, this can give rise to a scale problem. It might however mean that A, in ignorance, has lower aspirations to happiness than B, and consequently is more satisfied with life. If A's happiness is increased by community poverty and B's decreased by community wealth, the sense of relative income does indeed influence their perceived well-being. The difference in reported subjective well-being between A and B does reflect the difference in happiness that they feel. To argue instead that this difference in subjective well-being is irrelevant to social evaluation based on "objective utility" is essentially to make a value judgment.

It is possible that cultural differences are responsible for differences in reported happiness. For instance, in some cultures happiness might be overstated because happiness is positively valued, whereas in others there might be understatement because it is regarded as immodest or as tempting fate to do otherwise. Alternatively, cultural differences might indeed produce different levels of happiness that enter a social welfare function based on subjective well-being. To give examples, the unobserved presence of beneficial social networks or of high degrees of trust may be responsible for promoting happiness in some cultures. There is a problem for social evaluation if cultural differences give rise to differences in scales, but not if they simply reflect unobserved determinants of subjective well-being.

Sen (1983, 1984, 1990) went so far as to reject entirely the metric of utility for evaluative purposes. Instead, he favored the notion of capabilities and functionings—the capabilities of people to be and to do things of intrinsic worth. His criticism of the utility approach is that people adjust to their circumstances and adjust their aspirations to what is feasible.

> The more blatant forms of inequality and exploitation survive in the world by making allies of the deprived and exploited. The underdog bears the burden so well that he or she overlooks the burden itself. Discontent is replaced by acceptance... suffering and anger by cheerful endurance. (Sen, 1984: 308–9)
>
> In situations of longstanding deprivation the victims... very often make great effort to take pleasure in small mercies and cut down personal desires to modest—"realistic"—proportions. The person's deprivation, then, may not at all show up in the metrics of pleasure, desire fulfilment, etc, even though he or she might be quite unable to be adequately nourished, decently clothed, minimally educated and so on. (Sen, 1990: 45)

In other words, human beings have an elastic capacity to make the best of a bad situation, and that capacity should not enter the social welfare function. The capabilities which Sen has in mind involve both physical social functionings. Physical functionings correspond to meeting "basic needs," such as the capability to be fed, housed, and sheltered, and good health and basic education. Social functionings involve the capability to live well in society, to be accepted as a member of it, and to avoid social shame. This is likely to require that a person's income is not relatively low.

The capabilities approach is also open to criticism. It does not offer a practical criterion for evaluating the various capabilities to function, nor does it seek an aggregation of the social values of the separate capabilities. It might be argued instead that it is defensible to place value on individual freedom and thus on each individual's expressed views about their subjective well-being. Moreover, the objective of alleviating subjectively felt misery and raising people's sense of well-being is a value judgment that is widely held. The average level of subjective well-being might thus be viewed as the people's democratic expression of the society's well-being.

Sen (2009: 269–90) appeared to revise his approach to social evaluation—arguing that happiness is relevant, but not sufficient, for judging well-being. Other criteria should enter and should not be subsidiary to the happiness criterion. As in the American Declaration of Independence, people should be accorded the right, for instance, to life and liberty as well as to the pursuit of happiness. In Sen's judgment, success in the pursuit of other objectives, such as health, longevity, and knowledge, should not be judged solely by the effect that it has on happiness. For instance, the personal well-being of a Gandhi or Mandela is sacrificed for the cause of achieving political objectives. A potential counterargument is that, bearing in mind the risks involved, chosen acts of altruism are in themselves evidence that they are expected to bring happiness to the altruist, and that the alternative of failing to pursue keenly felt political objectives is expected to cause even lower happiness. Thus, people reveal their preference for greater (directly or indirectly achieved) happiness when they make choices between alternatives.

Even if this counterargument is accepted, there are reasons to treat subjective well-being on its own as an inadequate criterion for social evaluation. A good example comes directly from our results mentioned earlier. Economic policy in China is heavily biased in favor of urban people and against rural people, an outcome to be explained in terms of the underlying political economy and the greater political threat from urban people (for instance, Knight and Song, 1999). Does the higher mean happiness score of rural than of urban people mean that the current policy discrimination against them is justified?

Here the perspective in Sen (2009), that happiness is one criterion but not the only one for social evaluation, appears apposite. The policy bias which has maintained and even increased the urban/rural income ratio is inequitable. If we are willing to judge that the advancement of subjective well-being is socially valuable, it seems reasonable also to make the further value judgment that every citizen, irrespective of place of birth or residence, has a right to be treated equally in respect of such public services as education, social security, and health care. Two conclusions follow: the state's implicit social welfare function which justifies the discriminatory policies ought not to be given support by our happiness findings; and policies to raise happiness should be conditioned on fairness in the state's treatment of rural dwellers in relation to urban-dwellers.

4.3.3 *Subjective Well-being as an Encompassing Concept*

There are at least three possible concepts in relation to the objective of alleviating poverty. They can be termed "income poverty," "capabilities poverty," and, now, "subjective well-being poverty." Kingdon and Knight (2006) estimated subjective well-being functions[7] for South Africa in which the arguments were measures of income and of people's capabilities. The objective was to provide an encompassing framework within which the estimated coefficients on income and on various capabilities would yield a set of weights that were determined by the average of individual preferences.

We adopt the same approach. Tables 4.3 and 4.4 report happiness functions for both rural and urban China, in which the dependent variable is the cardinal value of the happiness score and the independent variables are, in addition to household income per capita, indicators of capabilities selected from such plausible variables as are available in the rural and urban sub-samples of the CHIP national household survey for 2002. We categorize the independent variables as economic, physical functioning, social functioning, and conditioning variables. The exercise is simply illustrative: no attempt is made to establish that the relationships are causal.

Consider the urban happiness function (Table 4.3). The economic variables (income and wealth) have positive coefficients but they are not substantial. In the full equation (column 2), for instance, a doubling of income raises the happiness score (mean value 2.51, standard deviation 0.84) by 0.10 points. For physical functionings we have proxies for health, knowledge, and shelter. Reporting good (or very good) health (as opposed to three lower categories) raises the happiness score by 0.21 in the full equation. The coefficient on years of education is negligible: any effect of education on happiness comes

[7] In fact, they estimated "ill-being" functions as their dependent variable was "subjective well-being poverty."

Table 4.3. Subjective well-being as an encompassing concept: happiness functions in urban China, 2002

	Mean or proportion	Basic model (1)	Full model (2)
Economic variables			
Log of per capita household income 2002 (Yuan)	8.85	0.2501***	0.1394***
Log of total net wealth per capita	1.68	0.1064***	0.0334
Physical functionings			
In good health	0.61	0.2670***	0.2120***
Education (years)	10.85	0.0007	−0.0026
House area per capita	18.45	0.0048***	0.0020
Social functionings			
Extent of fairness, income distribution in city	0.82		0.1818***
Living standard in second highest quarter in city	0.33		−0.1593
Living standard in third highest quarter in city	0.56		−0.4461***
Living standard in lowest quarter in city	0.10		−0.9671***
Currently laid off	0.04	−0.2613***	−0.1756**
Conditioning variables			
Male	0.45	−0.0607***	−0.0612***
Age	46.83	−0.0462***	−0.0269***
Age squared	2321.24	0.0005***	0.0003***
Married	0.94	0.1591**	0.0714
Divorced	0.01	−0.3250**	−0.3669**
Widowed	0.03	−0.0999	−0.1435
Intercept		0.7422**	1.8365***
R-squared		0.114	0.206
Number of observations		5805	5805

Notes: The dependent variable is the happiness score, with very happy = 4, happy = 3, so-so = 2, not happy = 1, and not at all happy = 0 (mean 2.51, standard deviation 0.84); ***, **, and * denote statistical significance at the 1, 5, and 10% levels respectively. Independent variables with cardinal values assigned to qualitative assessments so that greater intensity is represented by a higher value are: in good health, extent of fairness, income distribution in city. The omitted categories in the dummy variable analysis are: respondent does not have good health, is female, and is single; household's living standard is in highest quarter of city. The models have been clustered at city level for robust standard errors.

Table 4.4. Subjective well-being as an encompassing concept: happiness functions in rural China, 2002

	Mean or proportion	Basic model	Full model
		(1)	(2)
Economic variables			
Log of per capita household income 2002 (Yuan)	7.68	0.1786***	0.0866***
Log of total net wealth per capita	2.71	0.0356**	0.0369***
Physical functionings			
In good health	0.77	0.5072***	0.3989***
Education (years)	7.29	0.0056	−0.0027
House of permanent materials	0.84	0.0702	0.0271
Log of village collective expenditure per capita	8.1	0.0389***	0.0359***
Satisfied with primary school in village	2.44	0.0924***	0.0548***
Satisfied with clinic in village	2.42	0.0875***	0.0605***
Social functionings			
Household income much above village average	0.02		0.3121***
Household income above village average	0.21		0.1742***
Household income below village average	0.18		−0.3931***
Household income much below village average	0.02		−1.0417***
Phone	0.45		0.0606**
Harmony among villagers	2.87		0.1314***
Village cadre acts as spokesman	2.69		0.0611***
Conditioning variables			
Male	0.78	−0.0454	−0.0396
Age	45.24	−0.0026	−0.007
Age squared	2152.62	0.0001	0.0001
Married	0.96	−0.0642	−0.038
Divorced	0.00	−0.8202***	−0.7728***
Widowed	0.02	−0.3932**	−0.3121**
Intercept		0.0620	0.7053***
R-squared		0.167	0.263
Number of observations		5423	5423

Notes: The dependent variable is happiness score, with very happy = 4, happy = 3, so-so = 2, not happy = 1, and not at all happy = 0 (mean 2.74, standard deviation 0.85); ***, **, and * denote statistical significance at the 1, 5, and 10% levels respectively. Independent variables with cardinal values assigned to qualitative assessments so that greater intensity is represented by a higher value are: satisfied with primary school in village, satisfied with clinic in village, harmony among villagers, village cadre acts as a spokesman for the village. The omitted categories in the dummy variable analysis are: household does not have a phone, has income p.c. at village average, respondent is in good health, is male, and is single. The following variables were tried but excluded because they were not significant in either equation—physical functionings: house area p.c., household experienced a natural disaster in 2002, village has a junior middle school, has a medical insurance scheme, has an age insurance scheme; social functionings: respondent has lived out of village, number of gifts made by household, number of dinners with relatives or friends. The models have been clustered at village level for robust standard errors.

through its effect on income. House size per capita has only a very weak effect.

It is difficult to decide the best indicators of the capability to function well in a society. Adam Smith (1776: 469–71), for instance, illustrated the need to avoid shame in society through the wearing of leather shoes and linen shirts. We see the great importance of relative income: being in the bottom quarter rather than the top quarter of the city income distribution implies having a happiness score that is lower by 0.97. Being laid off also has a strong effect, even standardizing for income. The perception that the city income distribution is fair (a cardinal variable created from a Likert scale) raises happiness. Social functionings appear to be important for happiness.

Table 4.4 reports the factors associated with rural happiness. The richer rural data set yields more proxies for physical and social functionings. Income and wealth both raise happiness, but income is even less important than in urban China: a doubling of income raises happiness score (mean value 2.74, standard deviation 0.85) by 0.06 points (column 2). Among the physical functionings, good health has a powerful effect (coefficient 0.40 in the full equation), and education is again irrelevant. Our attempt to find a good proxy for the quality of shelter was not successful. For instance, having a house built of permanent materials is positive, but not significantly so. The quantity and quality of local public goods is important: village collective expenditure per capita and satisfaction with the village primary school and with the village clinic all have significantly positive effects on happiness.

Among the social functionings, relative household income per capita is again important for happiness: the difference between reporting being very much above and very much below the village average is no less than 1.35 points. Similarly, proxies for social cohesion (the degree of harmony among villagers—a cardinal value created from a Likert scale, and whether the village cadre acts as a spokesman for the villagers) raise happiness. The coefficient on possession of a phone (improving social interaction) is also significantly positive. Even in a society as poor as rural China's, the capability to function well in society appears to be important for subjective well-being.

The coefficients in these OLS equations show associations and not necessarily causal relationships. For instance, the possession of a phone might simply reflect unobserved personal characteristics which might themselves promote social functioning. Establishing causation would require a separate study. A further problem with the weights derived is that they are relevant to the sample as a whole and might therefore be inappropriate for policy against poverty. Nevertheless, this illustrative analysis is sufficient to show how the various possible criteria for social evaluation—income, physical functioning (or basic needs), and social functioning—can be encompassed by the criterion of subjective well-being. Of course, this way of incorporating the other criteria requires making the value judgment that reported average subjective well-being is sufficient for social evaluation.

4.4 Conclusion

We have addressed two main questions, one positive and the other normative. Does our analysis of subjective well-being in China explain why the national happiness score has failed to rise in recent years despite China's great economic progress? Do the measures of subjective well-being in China provide criteria for social evaluation? We are now in a position to draw conclusions.

Our main results can be summarized as follows:

1. In all three data sets—the rural, the urban, and the migrant—current income has a positive and significant effect on happiness. However, in none of these sub-samples is the coefficient on current income substantively large. Clearly, there are other, more important, determinants of individual subjective well-being.
2. This pure effect of individual income level is further weakened by the fact that economic growth will tend to raise incomes generally. Insofar as the income of the reference group rises as well as own income, the decline in relative income reduces individual happiness. As the economy grows, it is important to "keep up with the Zhous."
3. The higher the incomes to which people aspire, the lower their subjective well-being is.
4. Aspirations are influenced by people's reference groups and reference times. For rural people, the reference group is generally their fellow villagers, for urban people it is their fellow citizens within the city, and for rural–urban migrants it is also other people living in the city, urban as well as rural *hukou* holders. It is not the income of "any old Zhou" that produces feelings of relative deprivation but the income of the "Zhous you know"—those who fall into a person's reference group.

5. China's national Gini coefficient of household income per capita rose from 0.39 in 1988 to 0.47 in 2002 (Gustafsson et al., 2008, p. 19). It is likely that this rising income inequality reduced happiness, but the relationship is complicated by the importance of local reference groups and the possibility of demonstration effects as well as relative deprivation effects.
6. Aspirations for income are much influenced by reference time income, and this is governed mainly by the present. It is current income—both absolute and relative—that mainly determines aspirations for income. However, there appears also to be a "ratchet effect": previous income can also influence aspirations, so that experience of a past fall in income reduces happiness, other things being equal. In general terms, the analysis highlights the important role that aspirations play in people's perceptions of their own well-being.
7. Expectations of future income are important for current happiness. This suggests that a gloomier view of the economy's prospects could be serious for well-being, and maybe even for political stability.

Using this framework of empirical findings, we can see that the changes in the economy and in the society that stem from, or go along with, economic growth are likely to have influenced overall happiness in China. The effects of income growth itself are limited because of the resultant growth in aspirations, this being a function of both own and relative income. The importance of relative income for subjective well-being in all three sub-samples, together with rising income inequality over time, helps to explain the failure of happiness scores to rise with income levels. The new urban insecurities and uncertainties generated by economic reform and marketization have a negative impact on the subjective well-being of the growing number of urban residents. In particular, rural–urban migrants—rapidly expanding in number—suffer both from their second-class status in the cities and from the widening of their reference groups to include the more affluent urban-*hukou* population. By extending the reference groups of rural dwellers beyond the village, migration can also have the effect of reducing rural happiness. These findings help to explain why mean happiness in China appears not to have risen, and may even have fallen, in recent years.

Easterlin et al. (this volume) include two time series on mean life satisfaction in China in addition to those discussed in Table 4.1, which suggest that the mean happiness score rose somewhat after 2005 after reaching a trough in the period 2000–5.[8] Their interpretation—that unemployment began to fall and social security provision began to improve—is consistent with our explanation of some of the forces contributing to the earlier decline.

An interesting but unexamined hypothesis was raised by Xiaobo Zhang in his discussion of this chapter. It is that the rising male–female sex ratio in the young generation has increased expected and actual marriage competition for young men, and that the effect of this on household behavior and on life outcomes helps to hold down happiness. The 2002 CHIP survey provides scope for testing this hypothesis.

Qualifications are in order. We had to tackle the pervasive problem that happiness functions can generate biased coefficients on account of unobserved heterogeneity. One appropriate remedy—the use of panel data to eliminate the influence of unobserved fixed effects—was not available to us. It was therefore necessary to instrument income (and, later, aspiration income) in our cross-section analysis. However, even when the conventional statistical requirements for good instruments were met, there remained the further test of their theoretical and contextual plausibility, and this was a matter of debate and judgment.

Our analysis of the relationship between economic growth and happiness in China is only a beginning. Progress—in China as in many other countries—awaits a "second generation" of household panels which contain modules on subjective well-being designed with research questions in mind. A start could have been made in the CHIP household survey of 2007, which was the first year of an annual panel. However, their political sensitivity required that questions on happiness be excluded from the surveys of rural and of urban resident households—the implementation of which required the cooperation of the National Bureau of Statistics.

Our analysis raises, and also illuminates, some basic normative and policy issues. To what extent should subjective well-being enter into the social welfare function, and be accepted as one of the criteria for policy making? There is no right answer: ultimately, a value judgment is required. Our discussion was an attempt to set out the case for and against making this, and alternative, value judgments.

There is a case, grounded in economic theory but not incontestably so, for using subjective well-being as one of the criteria. The case has

[8] The life satisfaction score produced by Horizon Research (confined to cities) rose from 3.33 in 2002 to 3.41 in 2010, and that produced by PEW rose monotonically each year from 5.27 to 5.85 over the same period.

been criticized in several ways: that subjective well-being is misleadingly tainted by aspirations and adaptation, that happiness is not the only objective which guides people's actions, that reports of subjective well-being are unreliable because they are biased by use of different happiness scales. However, each of these arguments is in turn open to debate. Even if the case for including subjective well-being in the social welfare function is accepted, it remains possible that other criteria should be included as well.

The alternative, capabilities, approach to social evaluation discards the use of subjective well-being on account of the adaptation of the deprived to their deprivation. Instead it includes in the social welfare function the achievement of certain capabilities to function—that is, to be and to do things of intrinsic worth. However, this approach is also open to criticism, requiring as it does an externally imposed valuation of the various capabilities, not based on clear criteria for selection or aggregation.

We made an attempt to present subjective well-being as an encompassing concept by including income, physical functionings, and social functionings as inputs in the happiness equation. The estimated coefficients of the equation can be viewed as the weights that people attach to the contributions that these inputs make to their welfare, averaged over society as a whole. This approach is also open to criticism: the subjective values that people on average attach to the variables in the equation may not be an acceptable reflection of their social values, either because aspirations and adaptation are not tethered or because the social value is not well measured by the effect on happiness.

Powerful and plausible regularities were observed in the positive analysis. Thus, in making the necessary value judgment, it is difficult simply to dismiss as irrelevant people's reported perceptions of their own welfare. Our own position is that, provided it is guided by knowledge of the determinants of subjective well-being, there can be a case for including subjective well-being in the social welfare function, but also for including other criteria as well, such as concern for individual freedoms and social fairness. Subjective well-being can be appropriate not only for judging social progress but also for making policy choices.

It is government which effectively makes the value judgments about the implicit social welfare function that guides policy. There are some difficult policy trade-offs between the gains from economic growth in China and the losses from the socioeconomic changes accompanying growth, and these have not always been sufficiently recognized. For over a quarter of a century China's reformist policy makers gave the highest priority to the achievement of rapid economic growth. In the past few years, however, the balance of policy objectives has moved somewhat in the direction of creating a "Harmonious Society"—for instance, showing greater concern for reducing income inequality and for improving social security. That move can be seen as a response to the issues that underlie this chapter. Whether it is because of their threat to social stability and thus to continued Communist Party rule or for other reasons, the forces that influence subjective well-being appear to have entered the government's social welfare function.

References

Beagle, Kathleen, Kristin Himelein, and Martin Ravallion (2012). "Frame-of-reference bias in subjective welfare regressions," *Journal of Economic Behavior and Organization*, 81: 556–70.

Becker, Gary S. and Luis Raya (2008). "Comment" (on Stevenson and Wolfers), *Brookings Papers on Economic Activity*, Spring: 88–95.

Blanchflower, David and Andrew Oswald (2004). "Well-being over time in Britain and the USA," *Journal of Public Economics*, 88, 7–8: 1359–86.

Clark, Andrew and Andrew Oswald (1998). "Comparison-concave utility and following behaviour in social and economic settings," *Journal of Public Economics*, 71, 1: 133–55.

Clark, Andrew, Paul Frijters, and Michael Shields (2008). "Relative income, happiness and utility: An explanation for the Easterlin paradox and other puzzles," *Journal of Economic Literature*, 46, 1: 95–144.

Colasanto, D., A. Kaptein, and J. van der Gaag (1984). "Two subjective definitions of poverty: Results from the Wisconsin Basic Needs study," *Journal of Human Resources*, 19, 1: 127–38.

Di Tella, Rafael, John Haisken-DeNew, and Robert MacCulloch (2007). "Happiness, adaptation to income and to status in an individual panel," NBER Working Paper 13159.

Di Tella, Rafael and Robert MacCulloch (2006). "Some uses of happiness data in economics," *Journal of Economic Perspectives*, 20, 1, Winter: 25–46.

Di Tella, Rafael, Robert MacCulloch, and Andrew Oswald (2003). "The macroeconomics of happiness," *Review of Economics and Statistics*, 85, 4: 809–27.

Durkheim, Emile (1897 [1952]). *Suicide. A Study in Sociology*, translated by J.A. Spaulding and G. Simpson, London: Routledge and Kegan Paul.

Easterlin, Richard (1974). "Does economic growth improve the human lot? Some empirical evidence." In P. David and M. Reder (eds), *Nations and Households in Economic Growth: Essays in Honor of Moses Abramovitz*, New York and London: Academic Press: 98–125.

Easterlin, Richard (1995). "Will raising the incomes of all increase the happiness of all?" *Journal of Economic Behaviour and Organization*, 27, 1: 35–48.

Easterlin, Richard (2001). "Income and happiness: Towards a unified theory," *Economic Journal*, 111, 473: 465–84.

Easterlin, Richard (2008). "Lost in transition: Life satisfaction on the road to capitalism," *Journal of Economic Behavior and Organization*, 71, 2: 130–45.

Easterlin, Richard A. (2015). "Life satisfaction in the transition from socialism to capitalism: Europe and China." In Andrew E. Clark and Claudia Senik (eds), *Happiness and Economic Growth: Lessons from Developing Countries,* Oxford: Oxford University Press, 6–31.

Easterlin, Richard and Onnicha Sawangfa (2010). "Happiness and economic growth: Does the cross-section evidence predict time trends? Evidence from developing countries." In Ed Diener, Daniel Kahneman, and John Helliwell (eds), *International Differences in Well-being,* Oxford: Oxford University Press, 166–216.

Ferrer-i-Carbonnel, Ada and Paul Frijters (2004). "How important is methodology for estimates of the determinants of happiness?" *Economic Journal*, 114, 497: 640–59.

Frank, Robert (1997). "The frame of reference as a public good," *Economic Journal*, 107, November: 1832–47.

Frey, Bruno and Alois Stutzer (2002). "What can economists learn from happiness research?" *Journal of Economic Literature*, 40, 2: 402–35.

Graham, Carol and Andrew Felton (2006). "Inequality and happiness: insights from Latin America," *Journal of Economic Inequality*, 4, 1: 107–22.

Goedhart, T., V. Halberstadt, A. Kaptein, and B. Van Praag (1977). "The poverty line: concept and measurement," *Journal of Human Resources*, 12, 4: 503–22.

Gustafsson, Bjorn, Li Shi, and Terry Sicular (eds) (2008). *Inequality and Public Policy in China*, Cambridge: Cambridge University Press.

Hirschman, Albert (1973). "The changing tolerance for income inequality in the course of economic development," *Quarterly Journal of Economics*, 87, 4: 544–66.

Kahneman, Daniel and Alan Krueger (2006). "Developments in the measurement of subjective well-being," *Journal of Economic Perspectives*, 20, 1, Winter: 3–24.

Kingdon, Geeta and John Knight (2006). "Subjective well-being poverty *versus* income poverty and capabilities poverty?" *Journal of Development Studies*, 42, 7: 1199–224.

Kingdon, Geeta and John Knight (2007). "Community, comparisons and subjective well-being in a divided society," *Journal of Economic Behavior and Organization*, 64: 69–90.

Knight, John and Sai Ding (2012). *China's Remarkable Economic Growth*, Oxford: Oxford University Press.

Knight, John, Lina Song, and Ramani Gunatilaka (2009). "The determinants of subjective well-being in rural China," *China Economic Review*, 20, 4, December: 635–49.

Knight, John and Ramani Gunatilaka (2010a). "Great expectations? The subjective well-being of rural-urban migrants," *World Development*, 38, 1, January: 113–24.

Knight, John and Ramani Gunatilaka (2010b). "The rural-urban divide: Income but not happiness?," *Journal of Development Studies*, 46, 3, March: 506–34.

Knight, John and Ramani Gunatilaka (2012). "Income, aspirations and the hedonic treadmill in a poor society," *Journal of Economic Behavior and Organization*, 82: 67–81.

Knight, John and Ramani Gunatilaka (2011). "Does economic growth raise happiness in China?" *Oxford Development Studies*, 39, 1, March: 1–24.

Knight, John and Lina Song (1999). *The Rural-Urban Divide. Economic Disparities and Interactions in China*. Oxford: Oxford University Press.

Knight, John and Lina Song (2005). *Towards a Labour Market in China*, Oxford: Oxford University Press.

Luttmer, Erzo (2004). "Neighbors as negatives. Relative earnings and well-being," *Quarterly Journal of Economics*, 120, 3: 963–1002.

Pradhan, M. and M. Ravallion (2000). "Measuring poverty using qualitative perceptions of consumption adequacy," *Review of Economics and Statistics*, 82, 3: 462–71.

Rabin, Matthew (1998). "Psychology and economics," *Journal of Economic Literature*, 36, March: 11–46.

Ravallion, Martin (2015). "Poor, or just feeling poor? On using subjective data in measuring poverty." In Andrew E. Clark and Claudia Senik (eds), *Happiness and Economic Growth: Lessons from Developing Countries*, Oxford: Oxford University Press, 140–178.

Ravallion, Martin and Shaohua Chen (2007). "China's (uneven) progress against poverty," *Journal of Development Economics*, 82, 1: 1–42.

Runciman, W.G. (1966). *Relative Deprivation and Social Justice*, Berkeley: University of California Press.

Sen, Amartya (1983). "Poor, relatively speaking," *Oxford Economic Papers*, 35: 153–69.

Sen, Amartya (1984). "Rights and capabilities," in his *Resources, Values and Development*, Oxford: Basil Blackwell, 307–24.

Sen, Amartya (1990). "Development as capability expansion," in Keith Griffin and John Knight (eds), *Human Development and the International Development Strategy for the 1990s*, London: Macmillan, 41–58.

Sen, Amartya (2009). *The Idea of Justice*, London: Allen Lane.

Senik, Claudia (2004). "When information dominates comparison: Learning from Russian subjective panel data," *Journal of Public Economics*, 88: 99–123.

Smith, Adam (1776 [1976]). *An Enquiry into the Nature and Causes of the Wealth of Nations*, Oxford: Clarendon Press.

Stevenson, Betsey and Justin Wolfers (2008). "Economic growth and subjective well-being: Reassessing the Easterlin paradox," *Brookings Papers on Economic Activity*, Spring: 1–87.

Stutzer, Alois (2004). "The role of income aspirations in individual happiness," *Journal of Economic Behavior and Organization*, 54, 1: 84–109.

United Nations Development Programme (1998, 2009). *Human Development Report*, New York: UNDP.

Van Praag, Bernard and Arie Kaptein (1973). "Further evidence on the individual welfare function of income: An empirical investigation in the Netherlands," *European Economic Review*, 7: 313–35.

Discussion: Xiaobo Zhang

First of all, thanks a lot for inviting me here. I am very happy to attend this conference, to hear the giants in the field talking about their research on happiness. So if you ask me the degree of my happiness at the moment, I will give you the highest score. The problem is that in the future, my score will go down, no matter what my life circumstances.

John's chapter is a summary of a few recently published papers by John and his co-authors. I found the puzzle very interesting. Despite rapid growth in per capita income and improvement in the HDI in China, subjective well-being has barely changed, if not declined. I think it is very important to understand why. Next, John asks whether we should use subjective well-being for social evaluation.

My discussion will focus on new explanations for the paradox. Income growth itself cannot explain the decline in subjective well-being. Inequality has barely changed from 2002 to 2007, so we cannot attribute the decline in subjective well-being to rising inequality either. Also, the massive rural-to-urban migration might be a key reason: because rural people are happier than urban residents, as they move to cities, the average happiness score naturally drops. But there are still some questions: if migrants are much less happier than those staying in villages, why do they migrate to cities in the first place?

Here I want to focus on the demographic changes. China's one-child policy took place in the late 1970s. There has been one considerable consequence: a rising sex ratio imbalance (five women for every six men). Overall there are 30 million excess men on the marriage market. There have been a number of consequences for behavior: relative position really matters for marriage market outcomes and people do compare among each other. Social comparison is a very important factor to understand economic behavior. Some of my papers have looked at this. We show that parents with sons have to compete very hard to help their sons to find wives: they tend to save more (Wei and Zhang,

2011), work harder (Wei and Zhang, 2010), and build/buy bigger and more expensive houses (Wei et al., 2012).[9] They are also likely to spend more on visible goods, such as throwing extravagant banquets and extending larger gifts (Brown, Bulte, and Zhang, 2011).[10] Competition imposes a negative squeeze effect on the poor (Chen et al., 2011, and Chen and Zhang, 2012)[11] because the poor have to sacrifice their basic needs.

Let me illustrate this squeeze effect and how relative positions matter. In rural China, having one's son married is a top concern and 87 percent of marriages occur within the same county. Arranged marriages still dominate and it is important to build bigger and more expensive houses to signal the wealth of the family. In a recent paper (Wei and Zhang, 2012), we found that more than 20 percent of the rise in housing prices can be attributed to the marriage market squeeze. Also, Hopkins and Kornienko (2010)[12] argue that greater inequality of rewards hurts most people—in particular the poor—who are forced into greater effort. When traveling in rural areas, it is common to observe extravagant banquets and funerals, which to a large extent serve the purpose of social comparisons. If we do not consider status concerns, these activities do not seem like rational economic behavior. Most families keep gift books for the major social events as they need to pay back the gifts later on, mostly likely at inflated prices. To keep up with the Joneses, the poor have to carry out a larger share of social spending. This results in considerable negative consequences: children in poor families are more likely to display underweight, for example.

This mating competition can therefore offer alternative explanations for the happiness paradox in China. The marriage market squeeze can explain why rural residents still want to migrate

[9] Wei, S.-J. and X. Zhang (2010). "Sex ratios, entrepreneurship, and economic growth in the People's Republic of China." National Bureau of Economic Research (NBER) Working Paper No. 16800.

Wei, S.-J. and X. Zhang. (2011). "The competitive saving motive: evidence from rising sex ratios and savings in China." *Journal of Political Economy*, 119, 511–64.

Wei, S.-J., X. Zhang, and Y. Liu. (2012). "Status competition and housing prices." NBER Working Paper No. 18000.

[10] Brown, P., E. Bulte, and X. Zhang. (2011). "Positional spending and status seeking in rural China." *Journal of Development Economics*, 96, 139–49.

[11] Chen, X., R. Kanbur, and X. Zhang. (2011). "Peer effects, risk pooling, and status seeking. What explains gift spending escalation in rural China?" IFPRI Discussion Paper No. 01151. Chen, X., and X. Zhang. (2012). "Costly posturing: relative status, ceremonies and early child development." IFPRI Discussion Paper, No. 01206.

[12] Hopkins, E., and Kornienko, T. (2010). "Which Inequality? The Inequality of Endowments Versus the Inequality of Rewards." *American Economic Journal: Microeconomics*, 2, 106–37.

to cities despite the lower degree of happiness over there: they are forced into greater effort. Otherwise, they will have no money, no wives. This can also explain why people feel increasingly unhappy despite rising income: because they are forced to run on an increasingly fast treadmill but in the end, some people are doomed to fail. The number of unmarried men will increase as the sex ratio imbalance worsens.

There is another channel for the one-child generation. When the young were at home, they were over-protected and called "small emperors." However, after growing up, they (in particular young men) are suddenly exposed to an extremely competitive real world. The transition may undermine a person's emotions, resulting in a drop in happiness. So there are two impacts: one on the parents, and the other on the children of the one-child generation.

In the second part of his talk, John asked: "Should we care about subjective well-being?" Yes, we should care about it. In particular, if we observe a drop in happiness amid rapid economic growth, we need to figure out the underlying mechanisms. But I also agree with John that we cannot rely on subjective well-being as the social evaluation measure. If we did so, migration might be restricted by the government (but I think that this would be wrong). And also religion would be the best policy intervention.

To conclude, using a unique data set to understand the paradox, we have followed eighteen natural villages (more than 800 households) in Guizhou province (the poorest in China) and conducted four waves of census-type surveys since 2004. I treat these villages as my observatory: going there every year, staying and eating in farmers' homes. This provides both objective and subjective measures, and could be very useful for future research. Thank you.

General Discussion

Daniel Cohen suggested that in terms of policy implications, the objective is not to tell people "you don't have the right to do that," but at least to demonstrate that it can be a mistake to move to cities. What about a policy that would advise the Chinese authorities to "subsidize the girls," as so many outcomes seem to be linked to the sex ratio imbalance? Ada Ferrer-i-Carbonnel wondered how long it takes people who move to cities before they adapt to their new reference group? Claudia Senik wondered whether within-household migration decisions and insurance mechanisms could explain some of John's findings. For example, one could imagine that certain members of the household remain in the rural area, where they are happier, and some members move to urban areas where they are less happy but earn more money, which allows them to send remittances to the countryside. This intra-household division of labor would explain why people move to urban places, even if this does not make them personally happy. Another likely phenomenon is inter-temporal planning: migrants may sacrifice themselves for the sake of the next generation. In a way, Xiaobo has encompassed all these elements within his model of the marriage market, but these are elements that are worth taking explicitly into account.

John Knight thought that Xiaobo raised an important question: why is it that when rural people move to the city they become less happy? Can it be rational? Psychological research has shown that people are better at forecasting their income than their aspirations. They might realize that they are going to raise their income by migrating but what they cannot forecast is that, once they are settled in the city, their reference group will change and their aspirations will also change as a result. There is another possible explanation: Claudia's suggestion that people look to the long run. In a society in which the saving rate is about 25 percent of household income, it is plausible that people take a long-run view. They may care as much or more about their future welfare and the future welfare of their children than about their own current welfare. John also appreciated Xiaobo's point about social competition. There are several testable hypotheses in what he has suggested. Son preference is relevant for subjective well-being. For instance, some of John's earlier research inquired why it is that in rural China households with a son have higher conditional income than households with a daughter. There are two explanations: the selection hypothesis and the incentive hypothesis. The former is that richer households are better able to abort daughters, and the latter that people with a son have greater incentives to accumulate more for their son. We have devised several tests and found evidence in favor of the incentive rather than the selection hypothesis.

The suggestion was made that religion might be the best policy intervention. Whatever has been found for other countries, John and his co-authors could find no significant effect of religion on happiness in their Chinese dataset.

Xiaobo's point about people valuing status goods is interesting. If conspicuous consumption contributes to social status, it is predictable that happiness is more responsive to consumption than to (less observable) income. Most happiness functions contain income rather than consumption. However, the authors tried both but obtained very similar results.

The questions of choice and change of reference group are interesting but are as yet not much explored in the happiness literature. How rapidly do migrants change reference groups from the village to the city? The answer would require further research; however, it is notable that the coefficient on average city income per capita is significantly negative for the migrant sample as a whole and for the subsample with duration of residence in the city above the median (7.5 years), but not significantly different from zero for the group with below-median duration.

5

Income Comparisons in Chinese Villages*

Andrew E. Clark and Claudia Senik

5.1 Introduction

One of the mainstays of the recent resurgence of interest by economists in subjective well-being has been its relationship with income. This has, in particular, revolved around issues of causality (Gardner and Oswald, 2007; Pischke, 2010; Roberts, 2012) and income comparisons (Easterlin, 1974; Clark et al., 2008). With respect to this latter topic, income comparisons can be made to others who appear in the individual's reference group (social comparisons), or to oneself in the past (adaptation). The great normative interest in these two issues is their centrality to the question of whether higher incomes will make individuals happier. Were the causal relationship to run from well-being to income, or were both income and well-being to be caused by a third variable (parents' characteristics, for example), then the answer would be No. If there is adaptation, the answer is Yes, but not permanently. If there are social comparisons, then my higher income will make me happier, but reduce the well-being of all those who compare to me: at the aggregate level, higher incomes for all then may not lead to greater happiness for all (Easterlin, 1995).

The importance of this question has by now led to a considerable body of work. This research has used direct evidence on subjective well-being measures (such as job and life satisfaction, or happiness) to show that these are indeed often positively correlated with own

* This chapter would not have been possible without the continuing support of Xiaobo Zhang (IFPRI), to whom we are extremely grateful. We also thank Yuvraj Pathak for research assistance, and Ada Ferrer-i-Carbonell for having the good grace to discuss a very preliminary version of the chapter.

income but negatively correlated with the income of some plausible reference group. The latter can be defined at some aggregate geographical level (for example, Luttmer, 2005; Ferrer-i-Carbonell, 2005), by the income of other people who share some of the individual's characteristics (such as age, sex, and education: see Clark and Oswald, 1996; Senik 2004), by what the individual expected to earn (McBride, 2010), or even by the individual's partner (Clark, 1996).

The analysis of subjective well-being data is not the only way to proceed in this respect. Alternative approaches include the analysis of individual observed behavior, experimental approaches, asking individuals to choose between hypothetical alternatives,[1] and neurological experiments. Some of these are surveyed in Clark et al. (2008).

Overall, although the debate continues, much of this work has concluded that well-being is at least partly relative with respect to income. The open question remaining is whether the relative income effect is small enough to ignore, or rather is prevalent enough to substantially change our policy conclusions.

It is easy to criticize any empirical work, and research on well-being is no exception in this respect. One of the serious drawbacks in this literature has been the identification of the reference group. We only very rarely know to whom individuals actually compare, and as such simply have to impose a reference group in order to carry out empirical analysis. Even when we do know to whom individuals compare (as in Senik, 2009; Clark and Senik, 2010), the income of the reference group is not adequately measured.[2]

A second sticking point is that almost all of the analysis that has been carried out to date concerns rich countries. But most people in the world do not live in rich countries. The constraint here is most likely one of data availability.

The current chapter is able to overcome both of these problems. In particular, we use panel data from a number of Chinese villages. These villages are fairly isolated, so that the income of others in the village is a natural yardstick for reference group income. In addition, all

[1] Individuals report preferences for lower absolute incomes. When they are asked to choose between situations A (your yearly income is $50,000; others earn $25,000) and B (your yearly income is $100,000; others earn $200,000), individuals have a marked preference for A over B. This taste for relative position differs by domain: in Alpizar et al. (2005) it is stronger for cars and housing, and weaker for vacations and insurance.

[2] One possibility is to ask individuals about their reference group and then ask them how much their reference group earns (or where they stand in relation to this reference group), as in de la Garza et al. (2010). There is however a potential associated problem of endogeneity here, whereby individuals might imagine that others earn more because their own current level of well-being is relatively low.

households within the village are interviewed, so that we have complete information on the income distribution. This allows us to not only compare the individual to the mean income in the village, but also to calculate their exact rank in the village income distribution. As will be seen below, this is a key distinction.

The remainder of the chapter is organized as follows. Section 5.2 considers some of the existing evidence on well-being and income comparisons in China, and Section 5.3 then presents our data set. Section 5.4 discusses our main empirical results regarding comparisons to others within the village and comparisons to oneself in the past. Last, Section 5.5 concludes.

5.2 Existing Literature

There are at least two reasons to be interested in China. The first is that is the most populous country, accounting for over 19 percent of the world's population. The second, in the context of the current chapter, is that is has experienced almost unprecedented levels of economic growth over the past twenty-five years, on the order of roughly 10 percent per annum in real GDP per capita.[3] This has led to rises in real GDP per capita of an order of magnitude in the space of only one generation.

We would like to know how these movements in income have translated into well-being. What might be the consequences of such growth for subjective well-being? While Chinese economic performance over the past thirty years has been very impressive, a parallel can be made with the postwar experience of another Asian country: Japan. In the 1950s/early 1960s, Japan was a relatively poor country, but then experienced unprecedented growth. Between 1962 and 1987 Japanese GNP per capita (in real terms) rose 3.5-fold, growing from 22 percent of the United States level in 1962 to a figure of 77 percent in 1987. Easterlin (2005) and Sacks et al. (2011) have discussed the well-being impact of this growth.

Cross-country aggregate regressions of average well-being on real income per capita typically reveal a positive concave relationship: greater real GNP per capita goes hand-in-hand with higher average happiness scores. In the early 1960s, Japan had real GNP per capita

[3] Chow and Li (2002) report an exponential rate of growth of real GDP of 9.7 percent between 1978 and 1998, over half of which is due to capital growth, and a third of which reflects increased productivity.

somewhere between that of Cuba and Poland, and was in the middle of such a curve (see Figure 1 of Easterlin, 2005). As income rose in Japan, it might be expected that the Japanese would become substantially happier, following the cross-section concave relationship. Easterlin considers annual indices of life satisfaction which he maps to real GNP per capita over the 1958–87 period. The time-series relationship between well-being and income in fact turns out to be essentially flat (although see Sacks et al., 2011, for a critical discussion of this result). Rising income within the country then did not bring rising average happiness, despite the strong positive cross-section relationship across countries. This is, of course, what we understand by the Easterlin paradox.

We will not be able to map out such time-series relationships here, due to a lack of sufficiently long-run data.[4] However, we can use regression analysis applied to a short panel dataset in China to see if there is any evidence of the social comparisons and adaptation which are often suggested as explanations for the Easterlin paradox.

We first know that we can reproduce the typical positive within-country cross-section relationship between well-being and income for China. Figure 5.1, taken from Clark and Senik (2011), depicts the income decile–happiness gradient in China in 2007 (based on World Values Survey data). The fact that in a given society the rich are happier than the poor is a well-established and undisputed empirical finding in this literature, and here China seems to be no exception.

There have been a number of recent contributions which have considered the determinants of well-being in China, some of which have taken comparison effects into account. Appleton and Song (2008) conclude that the life satisfaction reported by urban Chinese is affected by status considerations, and Smyth and Qian (2008) analyze data from thirty-one Chinese cities in September 2002, finding that the log of average monthly income in the city in which the respondent lives is negatively correlated with happiness, controlling for own income. Gao and Smyth (2010) appeal to two different datasets to present some evidence that job satisfaction is negatively related to reference group income, where this latter is either average income in the firm in which the respondent works, or the predicted income of "people like me" (as in Clark and Oswald, 1996).

[4] Inglehart et al. (2008) present a series of graphs plotting average happiness (on a one-to-four scale) against time in different countries, based on the first four waves of the World Values Survey. That for China is negative, although not spectacularly so. Easterlin, in this volume, provides further evidence of a lack of happiness growth over time in China.

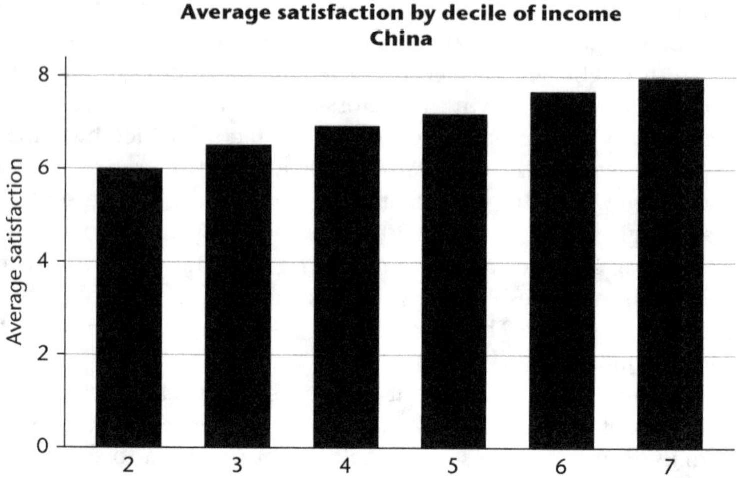

Figure 5.1. Income and happiness in a Chinese cross-section, 2010 Guizhou data

One of the key contributors to this literature has been John Knight, who has written a series of papers using Chinese data from the 2002 CHIP national household survey. Unusually, this survey included not only questions on subjective well-being but also direct questions about whom individuals considered as their reference group. Knight et al. (2009) use cross-section data on 9,200 Chinese households to show that comparisons in China are essentially local, in that 70 percent of individuals see their village as their reference group. Further, conditional on both own and village income, those who say that their own income is much above the mean level in the village also report higher happiness scores. Knight and Gunatilaka (2010*a* and 2010*b*) also underline the importance of relative income, and the role of changing reference groups, in China.

This evidence suggestive of income comparison effects in well-being in China mirrors work on observable behavior, which has underlined the importance of status. For example, Brown et al. (2011) use data from a Chinese household panel, and show that spending on banquets, funerals, and gifts is consistent with status-seeking behavior. A number of related contributions underline the importance of status in China via the marriage market. The sex imbalance in the Chinese marriage market makes rank very pertinent for parents who have sons, with knock-on effects on parents' labor supply (Wei and Zhang, 2010) and housing investments (Wei et al., 2012), for example.

We here contribute to this literature on income comparisons in China. Inspired by Knight's work, the reference group we retain is the village. The dataset that we use is eminently suitable for this purpose. First, it comes from twenty-six fairly remote villages, in which it is easy to argue that the income of the other villagers is indeed salient for comparison purposes. Second, all households within each village are surveyed, affording us a complete picture of the household's position in the local income distribution. The data is described in the next section.

5.3 Data and Methods

We here appeal to data from the IFPRI (International Food Policy Research Institute) "Public Policy and Rural Poverty" Program Survey. This survey was jointly conducted by IFPRI, the China Academy of Agricultural Sciences, and Guizhou University. Mainland China (excluding Hong Kong and Macau) consists of twenty-two provinces, five autonomous regions, and four municipalities. The IFPRI survey was carried out in Guizhou province, which is located in China's south (see Figure 5.2). Guizhou is relatively undeveloped and has the lowest per capita GDP among Chinese provinces.

The Guizhou data is extremely useful for the analysis of income comparisons for a number of reasons. First, the dataset is panel, with waves in 2004, 2007, and 2010. Second, at each wave individuals are interviewed within households, and serious attempts are made to interview all of the households within twenty-six different villages in Guizhou. As such we have almost complete information on the village income distribution, and the relative remoteness of the villages from each other makes the village a natural reference group, as argued earlier. Last, in the 2010 wave, the head of household provided information on various measures of satisfaction, including satisfaction with income.

We therefore have satisfaction at one point in time, in 2010. As such, we cannot appeal to standard panel data techniques. We can however introduce a lagged independent variable, and consider satisfaction in 2010 as a function not only of income in 2010 but also of income in 2007. This will allow us to address the issues of both comparisons to others (in the same village) at a point in time and comparisons to oneself in the past (three years earlier).

The measurement of income in rural China is not the same as in OECD countries. Household income was constructed here as an aggregate of

Figure 5.2. Map of China showing Guizhou province

a number of different components. First, the individual income of all household members was calculated by summing up the wage income earned from regular job, income from odd jobs, and self-income. These individual incomes were then added up by household to yield total household wage income. Additional earnings at the household level from a) agricultural produce, b) livestock and poultry produce, and c) any other source of income were then added to household labor income. In the 2010 round of the survey, income from gifts received by the household, both cash and in kind, was also included in the aggregate household income. The final household income figure does not include the assets owned by the households. Household assets were similarly constructed by summing up the values for variable, fixed, agricultural, and livestock and poultry assets at the household level

Average household income in 2010 was 16157.75 Renminbi (about $2,400, using an exchange rate of 6.7). This income was very unequally distributed. The 2010 D9/D1 figure in the Guizhou data is 14.3, and the Gini coefficient is 0.547. By way of comparison, the highest OECD Gini coefficients are around 0.5 (found in Chile and Mexico); the figure in the US is 0.4, in France 0.29, and in Denmark 0.25.

There are twenty-five villages in the 2010 wave. Table 5A.1 shows the number of households interviewed per village. The smallest village has thirty-six households interviewed, and the largest 256.

Our key dependent variable is satisfaction with income. Each head of household is asked "Are you satisfied with your current income?," where the replies are on five-point ordered scale from "Not Satisfied" to "Very Satisfied." Table 5A.2 shows the distribution of the replies to this income satisfaction question. As can be seen, Guizhou villagers are not particularly satisfied with their income, and we see a priori only little evidence of Sen's "Happy Slaves" here. Over 40 percent of respondents are in the bottom satisfaction category, which is the mode, and the median response is only two on the one-to-five scale. The mean satisfaction score is only slightly over two. Given that Cummins (2003) suggests that in many cases average subjective well-being is somewhere around 75 percent of the scale maximum, this is a remarkably low figure.

There is however a certain amount of variation in this satisfaction figure, and it is this that we would like to investigate. We have two empirical questions. First, we would like to establish the relationship between own household income and income satisfaction. Second, and perhaps more importantly, we want to see which aspects of the distribution of household income in the village matter for income satisfaction, conditional on the household's own income. The empirical results follow in the next section.

5.4 Chinese Comparisons

5.4.1 *Comparing to Neighbors: Basic Results*

The first column of Table 5.1 shows the basic relationship between income satisfaction and a number of demographic indicators. These are all linear regressions, with clustering at the village level, estimated on the 2010 Guizhou data. Income satisfaction does indeed rise with own income. We use log income, rather than the level, here as this specification is preferred by the data (and this is the typical functional form that appears in the literature). This income effect is conditional on the level of education, and in column 1 of Table 5.1 there is something of a positive relationship between education and income satisfaction. Dropping education as a right-hand-side variable does increase the size of the coefficient on own income here, but not very much so. We find no evidence of a gender effect (47 percent of the household heads are women in this regression sample), nor a relationship with age. Last, given household income, income satisfaction falls with the number of children, which is arguably uncontroversial (as is often found in existing work).[5]

Column 2 of Table 5.1 adds the log of median village household income to the regression. The estimated coefficient on this new variable is positive and significant: conditional on the household's own income, income satisfaction is *higher* in richer villages. This finding thus runs contrary to the idea that individuals compare to their neighbors, so that they are more satisfied when their neighbors are poorer. Research suggesting such comparisons has been found in American (Luttmer, 2005), Canadian (Helliwell and Huang, 2010), Latin American (Graham and Felton, 2006), and South African (Kingdon and Knight, 2007) data.[6]

However, not all existing research has identified such comparison effects. Clark et al. (2009) use Danish register information on income in small neighborhoods (typically of a few hundred households), matched to ECHP data on satisfaction with economic conditions. They find that, conditional on own household income, respondents report higher satisfaction levels when their neighbors are richer. Altruism is one possible explanation of such a positive correlation; another is local public goods, such as infrastructure or lower crime rates, which are associated with local income levels.

Column 3 of Table 5.1 attempts to separate out these contrasting relative income and local public good effects by introducing the household's normalized rank in the village income distribution. This normalized rank is calculated as the rank in the village divided by the number of households in the village: the normalized rank is just over zero for the poorest household in the village, and one for the richest household. Such measures of income rank have previously been appealed to in the context of economic satisfaction (Clark et al., 2009), job satisfaction (Brown et al., 2008), life satisfaction (Boyce et al., 2010), and effort at work (Clark et al., 2010). When rank is added to the regression (in column 3 of Table 5.1), the coefficient on median village household income becomes more positive (as a standard omitted-variables argument would suggest, if individuals enjoy being

[5] All of the results reported in this chapter can be reproduced using a measure of equivalent income, where household income is divided by the square root of the number of individuals in the household.

[6] When we include median income in the regression, the coefficient on own income is no longer statistically significant. This might be an indication that village resources and community solidarity are predominant in the determination of household income satisfaction.

Table 5.1. Income satisfaction: own and village income

Log household income	0.071 (0.018)***	0.057 (0.040)	−0.033 (0.080)
Male	−0.006 (0.043)	−0.001 (0.025)	−0.001 (0.026)
Age	−0.002 (0.007)	−0.002 (0.005)	−0.002 (0.005)
Age-squared/1000	0.050 (0.065)	0.051 (0.054)	0.048 (0.053)
Married	0.004 (0.059)	0.002 (0.066)	0.002 (0.065)
Did not graduate from primary school	0.103 (0.062)*	0.093 (0.069)	0.098 (0.069)
Primary school graduate	0.206 (0.080)**	0.199 (0.097)*	0.200 (0.096)**
Did not graduate from junior high	0.138 (0.077)*	0.121 (0.106)	0.126 (0.106)
Junior high graduate or above	0.125 (0.072)*	0.097 (0.082)	0.099 (0.082)
No. of children	−0.040 (0.016)**	−0.039 (0.034)	−0.042 (0.033)
Log median village		0.233	0.300
Household income		(0.120)*	(0.136)**
Village normalized income rank			0.368 (0.365)
Constant	1.329 (0.217)***	−0.657 (0.898)	−0.639 (0.904)
Observations	2802	2802	2802
R-squared	0.01	0.02	0.02

Notes: Robust standard errors in parentheses.
* significant at 10%; ** significant at 5%; *** significant at 1%

high rank). The estimated coefficient on rank itself is positive, but is not significant.

The empirical results in Table 5.1 might be thought of as suggesting that income comparisons are primarily a rich-country phenomenon. As discussed in Clark and Senik (2011), this is a critical piece of information for development policy purposes. So far, Chinese income growth would seem to be a good thing for all concerned. There are no negative externalities from others' higher income: if anything, the spillovers seem to be positive.

Table 5.2. Income satisfaction: non-linear rank effects

Log household income	0.033 (0.042)	−0.040 (0.061)	0.051 (0.040)	−0.044 (0.060)
Log median village household income	0.250 (0.121)**	0.307 (0.136)**	0.236 (0.119)*	0.310 (0.135)**
Top 10% village normalized income rank	0.155 (0.082)*	0.238 (0.101)**		0.220 (0.105)**
Top income rank in village			0.372 (0.269)	0.342 (0.292)
Bottom 25% village normalized income rank		−0.216 (0.122)*		−0.222 (0.121)*
Constant	−0.625 (0.897)	−0.423 (0.877)	−0.635 (0.900)	−0.401 (0.880)
Observations	2802	2802	2802	2802
R-squared	0.02	0.02	0.02	0.02

Notes: Robust standard errors in parentheses.
* significant at 10%; ** significant at 5%; *** significant at 1%.
All regressions include the other control variables in Table 5.1.

5.4.2 *Non-linear Rank Effects*

It is worth mentioning one potential drawback of much of the existing literature: it has considered rank as a cardinal variable, so that moving from the 20th to the 10th percentile is just as important as going from the 70th to the 60th, or indeed from the 100th to the 90th. However, some rank movements (those at the extremes of the distribution, perhaps) might be thought of as being more important than others. This is what we investigate in Table 5.2.

The first column of this table introduces a dummy variable for being in the top income decile in the village (rather than just the continuous rank variable which appeared in column 3 of Table 5.1). Being in the top decile in the village does indeed attract a positive significant coefficient in the income satisfaction regression. Equally, in column 2, being in the bottom 25 percent of the village income distribution is associated with lower income satisfaction. Both of these correlations are conditional on both the household's own income and village median income.

As we know the entire village income distribution, we can experiment with many different kinds of rank variables. Column 3 of Table 5.2 shows that a dummy variable for having the highest income of any household in the village attracts a positive coefficient, which is indeed larger in size than that of being in the top decile in the first two columns. However, this coefficient is not significant at standard levels (due to the large standard error, reflecting the fact that we only have one observation on the top earner in each of the twenty-five different villages).[7] These conclusions as to the potentially non-linear effects of rank survive when all three of our dummy variables are introduced together in column 4 of Table 5.2.

5.4.3 *Heterogeneity*

We can also investigate heterogeneity in some of these relationships, by interacting the various income variables in Table 5.2 with individual characteristics.[8] Some suggestive relationships ensue. In particular, immigrants to the village seem to be more sensitive to the negative effects of low rank. On the contrary, men are significantly more sensitive to high rank than are women. Last, interactions with education did not reveal anything of note with respect to the rank variables. However, these did show that the positive coefficient on median village income was found only for the lowest-educated (illiterate or did not graduate from primary school), which is consistent with local public goods being essentially redistributive, or with those at the lower end of the income distribution taking others' income in the village as a signal of their own expected future income (as in Senik, 2004).

5.4.4 *Habituation in Panel Data*

As noted in Section 5.3, we have here panel data on Chinese households, who were interviewed in 2004, 2007, and 2010. As the question on the dependent variable, income satisfaction, was only asked in 2010 we cannot estimate a panel well-being equation. However, we can introduce lagged explanatory variables into the regression. We now do so with respect to income in order to investigate potential adaptation to income: for a given level of 2010 income, does higher income in 2007 imply lower income satisfaction in 2010?

The results are presented in Table 5.3. In column 1 of this table there is no evidence of habituation to income for this Chinese sample. On the contrary, past household income is positively associated with current income satisfaction.

[7] Experiments with a dummy variable for having the lowest income did not reveal any results of interest, however.

[8] These tables are not produced here, for space reasons, but are of course available on request.

Table 5.3. Income satisfaction and adaptation

Log household income	−0.013	0.004	−0.002
	(0.076)	(0.079)	(0.080)
Log median village household income	0.108	0.208	0.204
	(0.137)	(0.167)	(0.167)
Top 10% village normalized income rank	0.191	0.189	0.310
	(0.126)	(0.126)	(0.165)*
Bottom 25% village normalized income rank	−0.089	−0.064	−0.204
	(0.144)	(0.144)	(0.168)
Lagged log household income	0.217		
	(0.045)***		
Lagged top 10% village normalized income rank		0.130	0.215
		(0.171)	(0.170)
Lagged bottom 25% village normalized income rank		−0.272	−0.411
		(0.094)***	(0.116)***
Top 10% village normalized income Rank both now and past			−0.457
			(0.256)*
Bottom 25% village normalized Income rank both now and past			0.448
			(0.188)**
Constant	−0.676	0.250	0.327
	(1.217)	(1.225)	(1.222)
Observations	1456	1456	1456
R-squared	0.05	0.04	0.04

Notes: Robust standard errors in parentheses.
* significant at 10%; ** significant at 5%; *** significant at 1%.
All regressions include the other control variables in Table 5.1.

Column 2 continues this exploration of the role of the past in individuals' current subjective evaluations, but now introducing past income rank, rather than past income level, into the analysis. Both current and past top decile attract positive coefficients, although neither is significant. With respect to low rank, past low rank attracts a negative and significant estimated coefficient.

It is worth noting that there is a substantial amount of income rank mobility in this dataset, so that individuals who are high (or low) ranked in 2010 were not necessarily so in 2007. In the regression sample in column 2 of Table 5.3 we have 147 individuals who were in the top income decile in 2010: only forty-four of these (30 percent) were in the top income decile three years earlier. Equivalently, only

36 percent of the 329 individuals in the bottom 25 percent in 2010 were also found there in 2007. Both the high and low rank dummies are significantly correlated between 2007 and 2010, but with relatively low correlation coefficients of 0.16 and 0.19 respectively.

Finally, column 3 investigates a new kind of adaptation that has not to our knowledge been investigated in the context of subjective well-being: adaptation to rank. This is carried out by interacting the current and lagged dummy variables for high rank to see if the positive well-being return of high rank today is smaller if the individual was also high rank in the past. An analogous operation is carried out with respect to low rank.

Both of these interactions attract statistically significant estimated coefficients. The results suggest that being in the top decile in 2010 only has a well-being impact for those who were *not* in the top decile in 2007 (the sum of 0.310, 0.215, and –0.457 is statistically zero). Equally, those who both are now and were in 2007 in the bottom quarter of the village income distribution report levels of income satisfaction that are *ceteris paribus* equivalent to those of individuals who were out of the bottom quarter in both years (0.204–0.411 + –0.448 = 0, statistically). As such, although we cannot identify any adaptation to income levels, we do find evidence that is consistent with adaptation to rank in the village income distribution.

5.4.5 *Subjective Income Rank*

Last, the Guizhou data includes direct information on the individual's subjective evaluation of their income rank in 2010. Individuals are asked: "Within your village what socioeconomic level does your family's income place you?," with responses on a five-point scale from "Much below average" to "Much higher than average." The distribution of answers appears in Table 5A.3. Less than 10 percent of respondents consider themselves to be above average.

Combining the top two responses into one category, subjective income rank predicts income satisfaction, even when we control for both the household's own income and for the household's income rank. The results here appear in Table 5.4. The omitted income rank category is "Much below average."

What Chinese villagers perceive as their income rank is therefore something partly different from their objective position in the village income distribution. Reassuringly, subjective income rank and our objective calculation of the normalized income rank in the village are correlated. The average normalized income rank of those who report

Table 5.4. Income satisfaction and subjective income rank

Log household income	−0.051 (0.060)
Subjective rank *"Higher than average"*	0.862 (0.218)***
Subjective rank *"Average"*	0.517 (0.135)***
Subjective rank *"Below average"*	0.087 (0.146)
Log median village household income	0.260 (0.136)*
Top 10% village normalized income rank	0.150 (0.108)
Bottom 25% village normalized income rank	−0.187 (0.115)
Constant	−0.165 (0.892)
Observations	2794
R-squared	0.08

Notes: Robust standard errors in parentheses.
* significant at 10%; ** significant at 5%; *** significant at 1%.
All regressions include the other control variables in Table 5.1.

their position as "Higher than average" is 0.57 (i.e. they are on average at the 57th percentile); that of those who say "Below average" is 0.49, and that for individuals who say their income is "Much below average" is 0.39. However, the fact that subjective rank remains important even controlling for the objective rank in the village suggests that something else is at play. In particular, changing reference standards may explain why fewer than 10 percent of villagers see their income as above average. The identification of the relationship between such objective and subjective measures likely represents an important task for future work.

5.5 Conclusions

Despite the intrinsic interest in the drivers of well-being, and the possibility that comparisons (of income or something else) matter, there are still significant gaps in our understanding. In particular, despite the fantastic growth in the literature over the past fifteen years or so, we still know far less about the developing world than we do about OECD countries.

This chapter has considered income comparisons in China, using a novel panel data set in which all households in a number of Chinese villages in Guizhou province are interviewed. This allows us to see whether individual well-being is affected by the income of others in the same village.

Our first set of results suggest only a minor role for income comparisons. Individuals are more satisfied with their income when their neighbors are richer, rather than the other way around. Our complete information on the village income distribution allows us to pick out the household's exact position, so that we can consider the household's percentile position rather than just a measure of centrality of others' incomes, such as the mean. However, the normalized measure of the household's rank in the village income distribution has no significant impact on income satisfaction (controlling for own income and village median income).

We do find evidence of income comparisons when we treat rank non-linearly. In particular, it seems that having low (bottom 25 percent) or high (top 10 percent) income rank does matter for satisfaction (suggesting that moving through the middle of the income distribution actually does not make that much of a well-being difference).

We also consider adaptation, and find no evidence of adaptation to income levels. However, the data does suggest that there is adaptation to income rank, so that currently being top-ranked matters less for well-being when the household was also top-ranked in the previous wave of the survey.

Last, subjective income rank is correlated with actual income rank, but not perfectly so. As the former is an important driver of well-being, it would seem useful to understand why individuals do not perfectly perceive their position in the village income distribution.

Overall, these results provide some additional evidence that income comparisons take place, even in relatively poor countries. Our finding that in China these comparisons (both to others and over time) seem to operate via income rank rather than income level are, we think, new. In addition, we believe that there is much more to be said about the possible non-linear effects of rank. We here suggest that the bottom quarter and the top 10 percent matter more than just a simple continuous measure of the household's rank in the village income distribution. In this case the analysis of well-being arguably needs to pay more attention to the two ends of the income distribution, perhaps both in level and rank terms, rather than settling for simple measures of centrality.

References

Alpizar, F., Carlsson, F., and Johansson-Stenman, O. (2005). "How Much Do We Care about Absolute versus Relative Income and Consumption?" *Journal of Economic Behavior and Organization*, **56**, 405–21.

Appleton, S., and Song, L. (2008). "Life Satisfaction in Urban China: Components and Determinants." *World Development*, **36**, 2325–40.

Brown, G., Gardner, J., Oswald, A.J., and Qian, J. (2008). "Does Wage Rank Affect Employees' Well-being?" *Industrial Relations*, **47**, 355–89.

Brown, P., Bulte, E., and Zhang, X. (2011). "Positional Spending and Status Seeking in Rural China." *Journal of Development Economics*, **96**, 139–49.

Boyce, C., Brown, G., and Moore, S. (2010). "Money and Happiness: Rank of Income, not Income, Affects Life Satisfaction." *Psychological Science*, **21**, 471–75.

Chow, G., and Li, K.-W. (2002). "China's Economic Growth: 1952–2010." *Economic Development and Cultural Change*, **51**, 247–56.

Clark, A.E. (1996). "L'utilité est-elle relative? Analyse à l'aide de données sur les ménages." *Economie et Prévision*, **121**, 151–64.

Clark, A.E., Frijters, P., and Shields, M. (2008). "Relative Income, Happiness and Utility: An Explanation for the Easterlin Paradox and Other Puzzles." *Journal of Economic Literature*, **46**, 95–144.

Clark, A.E., Kristensen, N., and Westergård-Nielsen, N. (2009). "Economic Satisfaction and Income Rank in Small Neighbourhoods." *Journal of the European Economic Association*, **7**, 519–27.

Clark, A.E., Masclet, D., and Villeval, M.-C. (2010). "Effort and Comparison Income." *Industrial and Labor Relations Review*, **63**, 407–26.

Clark, A.E., and Oswald, A.J. (1996). "Satisfaction and Comparison Income." *Journal of Public Economics*, **61**, 359–81.

Clark, A.E., and Senik, C. (2010). "Who Compares to Whom? The Anatomy of Income Comparisons in Europe." *Economic Journal*, **120**, 573–94.

Clark, A.E., and Senik, C. (2011). "Will GDP Growth Increase Happiness in Developing Countries?" In R. Peccoud (Ed.), *Measure For Measure: How Well Do We Measure Development?* Paris: STIN, 97–170.

Cummins, R. (2003). "Normative Life Satisfaction: Measurement Issues and a Homeostatic Model." *Social Indicators Research*, **64**, 225–56.

de la Garza, A., Mastrobuoni, G., Sannabe, A., and Yamada, K. (2010). "The Relative Utility Hypothesis with and without Self-reported Reference Wages." Collegio Carlo Alberto, Carlo Alberto Notebooks 159.

Easterlin, R. (1974). "Does Economic Growth Improve the Human Lot?" In P.A. David and W.B. Melvin (Eds.), *Nations and Households in Economic Growth*. Palo Alto: Stanford University Press, 89–125.

Easterlin, R.A. (1995). "Will Raising the Incomes of All Increase the Happiness of All?" *Journal of Economic Behavior and Organization*, **27**, 35–47.

Easterlin, R. (2005). "Diminishing Marginal Utility of Income? Caveat Emptor." *Social Indicators Research*, **70**, 243–55.

Ferrer-i-Carbonell, A. (2005). "Income and Well-being: An Empirical Analysis of the Comparison Income Effect." *Journal of Public Economics*, **89**, 997–1019.

Gao, W., and Smyth, R. (2010). "Job Satisfaction and Relative Income in Economic Transition: Status or Signal? The Case of Urban China." *China Economic Review*, **21**, 442–55.

Gardner, J., and Oswald, A.J. (2007). "Money and Mental Well-being: A Longitudinal Study of Medium-Sized Lottery Wins." *Journal of Health Economics*, **26**, 49–60.

Graham, C., and Felton, A. (2006). "Inequality and Happiness: Insights from Latin America." *Journal of Economic Inequality*, **4**, 107–22.

Helliwell, J.F., and Huang, H. (2010). "How's the Job? Well-being and Social Capital in the Workplace." *Industrial and Labor Relations Review*, **63**, 205–27.

Inglehart, R., Foa, R., Peterson, C., and Welzel, C. (2008). "Development, Freedom, and Rising Happiness: A Global Perspective (1981–2007)." *Perspectives on Psychological Science*, **3**, 264–85.

Kingdon, G., and Knight, J. (2007). "Community, Comparisons and Subjective Well-being in a Divided Society." *Journal of Economic Behavior and Organization*, **64**, 69–90.

Knight, J., and Gunatilaka, R. (2009). "Income, Aspirations and the Hedonic Treadmill in a Poor Society." University of Oxford, Discussion Paper No. 468.

Knight, J., and Gunatilaka, R. (2010*a*). "Great Expectations? The Subjective Well-being of Rural-Urban Migrants in China." *World Development*, **38**, 113–24.

Knight, J., and Gunatilaka, R. (2010*b*). "The Rural–Urban Divide in China: Income but not Happiness?" *Journal of Development Studies*, **46**, 506–29.

Luttmer, E. (2005). "Neighbors as Negatives: Relative Earnings and Well-being." *Quarterly Journal of Economics*, **120**, 963–1002.

McBride, M. (2010). "Money, Happiness and Aspirations: An Experimental Study." *Journal of Economic Behavior & Organization*, **74**, 262–76.

Pischke, S. (2010). "Money and Happiness: Evidence from the Industry Wage Structure." LSE, mimeo.

Roberts, C. (2012). "Wealth and Well-being: Lessons from Indian Debt Relief." Harvard University, mimeo.

Sacks, D., Stevenson, B., and Wolfers, J. (2010). "Subjective Well-being, Income, Economic Development and Growth." NBER Working Paper No. 16441.

Senik C. (2004). "When Information Dominates Comparison: Learning from Russian Subjective Panel Data." *Journal of Public Economics*, **88**, 2099–133.

Senik, C. (2009). "Direct Evidence on Income Comparison and their Welfare Effects." *Journal of Economic Behavior and Organization*, **72**, 408–24.

Smyth, R., and Qian, X. (2008). "Inequality and Happiness in Urban China." *Economics Bulletin*, **4**, 1–10.

Wei, S.-J., and Zhang, X. (2010). "Sex Ratios, Entrepreneurship, and Economic Growth in the People's Republic of China." IFPRI, mimeo.

Wei, S.-J., Zhang, X., and Liu, Y. (2012). "Status Competition and Housing Prices." NBER Working Paper No. 18000.

Discussion: Ada Ferrer-i-Carbonell

This chapter provides very interesting and promising empirical evidence that will help us to understand human preferences and behavior. In addition, it does so in a very interesting and relatively unknown (from a behavioral perspective) country. The chapter examines the importance for self-reported satisfaction of own current income, income in the past, income of the reference group, and rank of the individual within the income distribution of the reference group. This chapter is a very interesting piece of work that, in addition, has promising further dimensions to be explored.

The Reference Group

The dataset used in the chapter overcomes two important drawbacks of many other papers dealing with the importance of the reference group: namely, it has information on all incomes of everybody in the reference group. In other words, one has complete information about the reference group. The chapter assumes that the reference group is composed of all individuals in the village. One could of course generate smaller reference groups within the village (for example by using individuals' socioeconomic characteristics). The first question is whether indeed individuals compare themselves to *only* village members and to *everybody* in the same village. Would people not compare themselves to family members that have emigrated to other villages or to the cities? Is there so little contact between the different villages or with old village members that have left for the cities that makes no sense to include them in the reference group? Do people compare with similar people also in other villages or only with people inside the same village? The chapter assumes that individuals compare themselves with everybody from the same village. This imposes strong exogeneity of the reference group. In other words, not only do individuals' happiness or personality traits not play any role in determining the reference group, but also individuals' socioeconomic characteristics, such as income and wealth, are not allowed to influence the reference group formation. Perhaps this is not a strong assumption, to the extent that (i) the villages are very isolated, even from old members that have emigrated to other villages or to the cities, and (ii) there is very little heterogeneity within the village and between the villages around.

The Data

The data set is interesting, rich, and unique. It is based on a sample of rural villages, where income in kind (home production) is a very important part of income. Therefore, it is very important to know, first, how income is collected in the data (does it include home production?) and, second, what is the exact phrasing of the income satisfaction question? Are people asked about their satisfaction with income or does the questionnaire use another wording, such as satisfaction with consumption? Do respondents understand that they are being asked about their financial situation? Do they understand that home production is included in this income definition?

Since the data include many individuals who report a life satisfaction of 0 or 1, it may be a good exercise to see whether the results change when using a binary probit econometric approach.

Results

One of the lessons we learn from the chapter is that there are no happy slaves (in Sen's words). This can mean either that people do not adapt very much, that people do reasonably adapt but only sometimes and depending on who and in which situation they are, or that they only adapt after a certain amount of income, i.e. they adapt when they have *enough*. This last point is related to the Easterlin paradox.

The chapter finds that satisfaction is positively correlated with the median income of the village. This result could be driven by the fact that this group is geographically defined (and thus captures regional amenities); it could also relate to the fact that the median income correlates very well with the capacity that other members of the village have to help the respondent if confronted with economic difficulties. It would be interesting to know what happens to the median income coefficient if you allow the reference group to depend on the socioeconomic characteristics of the respondent. For example, the reference group would include only those who are similar to the respondent in some relevant characteristic, such as income.

Including the median income of the village in the satisfaction question makes the own income coefficient statistically insignificant. This is a very interesting phenomenon for which I have not found an explanation. While it makes sense that living in a region where everybody is rich makes you happier (either because of amenities or because of cooperation), I cannot understand why individual own income turns insignificant. Actually, own income has a smaller coefficient than the median income of the village. One possible explanation for this is related to measurement error. Imagine that the income distribution within the village is very compressed and that income is measured with error. In this case, the median income of the village could be a better proxy for own income than the reported level. The measurement error in reporting income is more probable if, as in the present case, income in kind (which is difficult to measure) is a very important dimension of income in rural villages. In the chapter the empirical analysis is also presented by dividing the sample into various groups. For some sub-samples (immigrants) the coefficient of own income even turns negative when introducing the median income of the village into the regression.

In the regressions, the authors do not find the asymmetry effect of income comparisons that is usually found in western countries, where people in the top of the income distribution do not get much happiness from that, while people at the bottom are unhappier. This difference could be an interesting feature of non-western countries. I would like to see the rank effect in all the different deciles instead of only for the top and the bottom. Perhaps there are some differences here.

The result when past income is introduced into the regression is also surprising. While the coefficient of past income is positive and significant (this denotes that there is no habituation in the sample), including past income in the regressions makes all the other income coefficients (median income and current income) become insignificant. The positive effect of past income is very interesting and may denote that adaptation only occurs after one has achieved a certain income level (a concept similar to the Easterlin paradox). It is however surprising that the current income coefficient becomes insignificant when the regression includes past income. This surprising result also happens when rank is introduced into the satisfaction equation: people do care about their past rank, but not about their current rank. Could it be that income is better measured in the 2007 dataset? One could check, for example, whether there are large income changes over time.

Subjective Rank

This work can be extended by further exploiting the subjective dimension of the data set, as the authors initiated in the chapter. In the last regressions of the chapter one can see that subjective rank is statistically significant and is a very important determinant of happiness. This data can allow us to understand how people assess their rank and why people make mistakes in doing that. (i) Do respondents make a mistake when reporting their place in the rank? Or (ii) are researchers making a mistake, assigning individuals to the wrong reference group? Are the mistakes that people make correlated with the size of the village, the number of immigrants in the village (about which individuals do not know much), or with the income distribution (or polarization) of the village? There are a large set of questions that can be answered with this data and that would help to understand reference group formation, individuals' preferences, and human behavior.

General Discussion

Martin Ravallion wondered how much power there is in the dataset to identify comparison effects. This region of southwest China is really poor, and fairly uniformly so. So is there sufficient variance in the data? In Malawi, Martin found no sign of comparison effects among poor people; poor people living in a rich village are happier, and not the reverse. John Knight was pleased to discover this second generation survey but was dubious about using income satisfaction as the dependent variable. This is because his own work found that a high proportion of respondents were dissatisfied with their income, while they were satisfied with their life. The other thing is that the villages seem very small. He found in Africa a positive coefficient in small neighborhoods, but in more extended areas, the coefficient became negative. So it is possible that in the Chinese data, the small size of the villages produces this positive effect. Xiaobo Zhang thought the question about income was very similar to the World Bank questions. He also mentioned that the value of home production was available in the survey. He stressed the importance of social spending that people incur to improve their social rank, which explains why they feel stressed when they are at the bottom. There is more social pressure among poor people than among rich people. Andrew Clark pointed out that the effect of social comparison considered is within villages rather than between villages. Concerning the mistakes made by people concerning their subjective ranking, indeed, only 9 percent of respondents say that they stand above the average... so there is a reason why people underestimate their own income relative to others, which does not seem to be pure measurement error.

Appendix

Table 5.A1. Number of households interviewed per village, 2010 Guizhou data

No. of households	Percentage
36	1.1
40	1.3
45	1.4
48	1.5
56	1.8
61	1.9
63	2.0
72	2.3
86	2.7
89	2.8
102	3.2
112	3.6
123	3.9
125	4.0
129	4.1
147	4.7
161	5.1
167	5.3
168	5.3
184	5.8
213	6.8
218	6.9
221	7.0
230	7.3
256	8.1

Table 5.A2. The distribution of income satisfaction

	Frequency	Percentage
Not satisfied	1,295	42.1
Not too satisfied	896	29.2
Average	481	15.7
Rather satisfied	374	12.2
Very satisfied	28	0.9
Total	3,074	100.0

Table 5.A3. The distribution of subjective income rank

	Frequency	Percentage
Much higher than average	9	0.3
Higher than average	261	8.4
Average	1,335	42.9
Below average	1,088	35.0
Much below average	420	13.5
Total	3,113	100.0

6

Happiness and Economic Growth: A Panel Discussion

Stéfan Lollivier, Conal Smith, Martin Ravallion, and Richard A. Easterlin

6.1 Stéfan Lollivier

I will present some investigations of the French Social Statistics Institute about the Stiglitz recommendations. I will then present preliminary results. What are the recommendations about quality of life from the Stiglitz commission? There are three kinds of recommendations. The first one is about national accounts, the second one is about sustainability, and the third one is about quality of life. I will only speak about the quality-of-life recommendations today, and present them briefly here:

- Quality of life depends on people's objective conditions and capabilities.
- Quality-of-life indicators should assess inequalities in a comprehensive way.
- Surveys should be designed to assess the links between various quality-of-life domains for each person. This information should be used when designing policies in various fields; statistical offices should provide information needed to aggregate across quality-of-life dimensions, allowing the construction of different indexes. I will present some indexes today.
- The last recommendation is about measures of both objective and subjective well-being providing key information about people's quality of life. Statistical offices should incorporate questions to capture people's life evaluations, hedonic experiences and priorities in their surveys.

What are the dimensions of quality of life in the report? There are exactly nine dimensions: material living conditions, health, education, productive and valued activities, governance and basic rights, leisure and social interactions, natural and living environment, economic and physical safety, and overall experience of life. I will not discuss these recommendations too much: I prefer to use my time to talk about implementation.

In Europe and France, we want to quickly implement the Stiglitz recommendations. In Europe, there has been a sponsorship between Eurostat and INSEE, with four Task Forces. The third one, which I co-chaired, proposes recommendations to implement quality-of-life indicators in Europe for the short term and for the Eurostat middle term (2015). In France, INSEE have begun to integrate some variables in existing surveys. Moreover, a specific new multimodal survey has been implemented. In addition, many studies about quality of life have been published in France. Other related work here includes the *France Portrait Social*, and information on bad housing conditions, subjective dimensions of well-being, and the quality of time in the French 2010 *Time Use Survey*. I will now present the multimodal quality-of-life survey and some of its preliminary results.

We tried to gather many questions coming from existing surveys into one unique survey, in order to cover most dimensions of quality of life in the same questionnaire. Questions about living conditions came from EU-SILC and the European Quality of Life Survey (EQLS) 2007; questions about environment and insecurity came from EU-SILC and EQLS 2007; questions about labor satisfaction came from EQLS 2007, taking into account the recommendations of the French "collège Risques psychosociaux"; questions about health came from EU-SILC; the usual questions about welfare (Gallup-type questions); new questions from the WHO5 module about stress; and questions about confidence in society and public decision-makers (adapted from EQLS 2007). This survey was implemented last year. It is a multimodal survey (internet + paper), concerning 10,000 people aged 18 or more. They were contacted by mail. They could answer by Internet or return a paper questionnaire. The response rate was 38 percent.

The first step was to build synthetic indicators for all the dimensions of quality of life (except for education and productive and valued activities). Indeed, the survey provides many items and allows the computation of a synthetic indicator for every dimension of quality of life by aggregating and cumulating items. Finally, every dimension of quality of life is summarized by one synthetic indicator; this is a very standard method for the computation of indicators and I will not discuss it much. What is new in our survey is that we collected items for most of the dimensions of quality of life described in the Stiglitz report and not only one or two of them, as is usually the case. Figure 6.1 shows an example: the results are normalized, so for all the population the average synthetic indicator is 1 for every dimension. When the indicator is over 1, the sub-population is in a good position; when it is less than 1, people are in a bad position. Here, poor people are in a worse position than are the rich, and this is true in all dimensions, not only for financial restrictions (see, for example, social links). The first decile of income is in a very bad position concerning stress, but there is not such a gap with respect to confidence in society. Another example, as can be seen in Figure 6.2, relates to urbanization between rural and large (over 200,000 people) agglomerations. Although the gaps are not as large as was the case for income, they are significant for housing conditions, insecurity, and environment.

I now consider welfare and the last recommendation of the report about quality of life. In the survey, a Gallup-type question about welfare

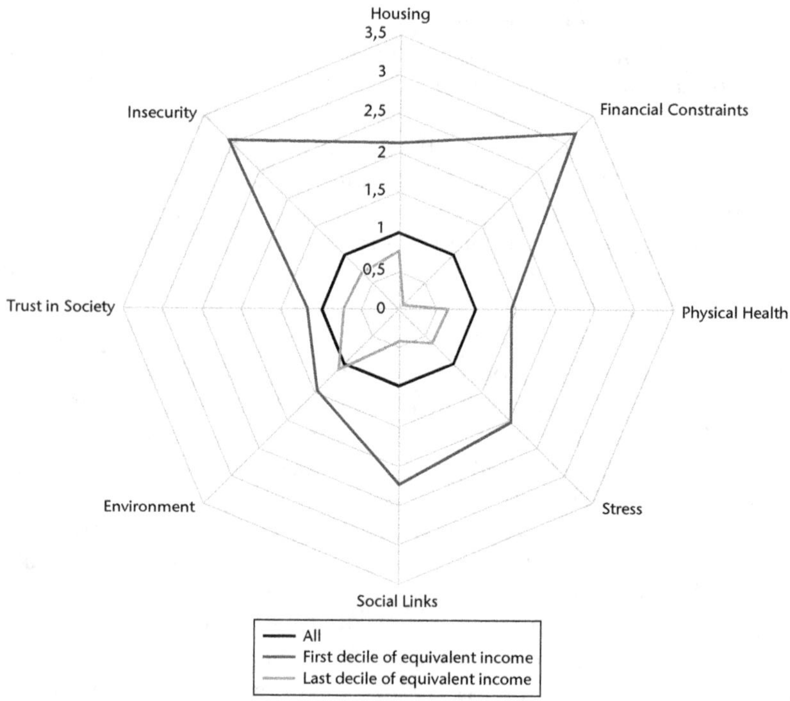

Figure 6.1. Quality of life, rich versus poor, INSEE

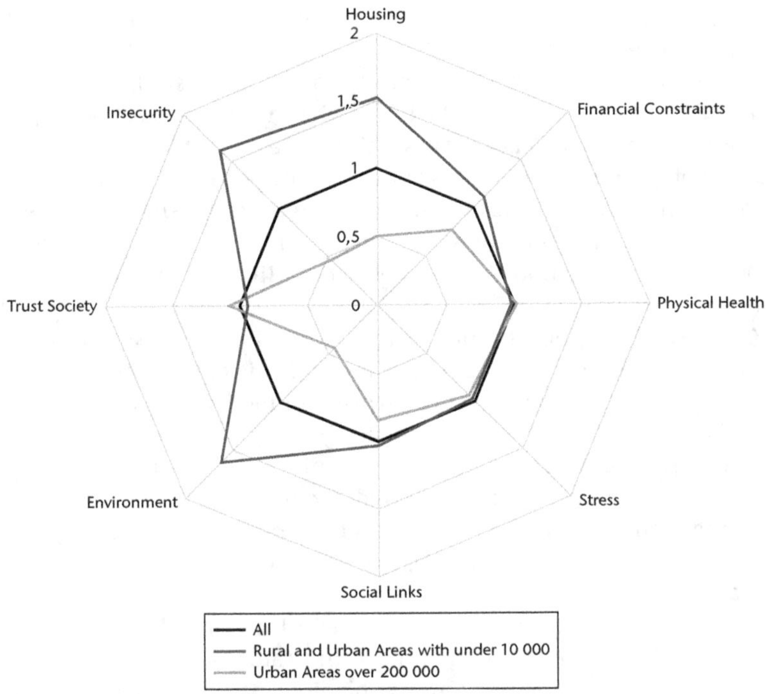

Figure 6.2. Quality of life, urbanization, INSEE

is asked: "Please rate your life satisfaction, on a scale from 0 to 10, from the worst to the best possible." The scale from 0 to 10 corresponds to the OECD recommendations. First, let us consider this welfare question as explained only by the usual socio-demographic variables: we find very standard results, a sharp rise with income decile, which is larger at the beginning of the distribution and flatter for higher levels of income. Satisfaction is higher for the under-25s and over-65s, and for those with high education. Satisfaction is lower in greater Paris, but there is no effect of gender and country of birth. What is more interesting is a mix of the usual socio-demographic variables and quality-of-life indexes in the same regression. Considering welfare explained by quality-of-life indexes and the usual socio-demographic variables, there is almost no effect of socio-demographic variables: only the quality-of-life indicators are significant. The most significant are social relationships, financial restrictions, and stress. Less correlation is observed with physical health, housing difficulties, and insecurity, and there is no link with environmental conditions and confidence in society. In fact, confidence in society is related with almost nothing.

We define "low welfare" as corresponding to answers which are below 5 on the 0–10 life satisfaction scale; this concerns about 7 percent of the sample. The most significant explanatory indicator of quality of life for low welfare is "poverty" in social links, much above financial restrictions, housing difficulties, physical health, and stress. Socio-demographic variables are not significant in this regression, especially income (conditional on quality-of-life indicators). This was, for me, a surprise.

Concerning happiness and quality of life, happiness is defined as high welfare, at 9 and 10 on the scale, and this covers about 13 percent of people. This was another surprise for me. The most significant explanatory variable in the regression is stress (if you are stressed, you cannot be happy!). The other significant variables are social links and physical health, followed by financial restrictions and housing difficulties. There is no effect of confidence in society and environment conditions and still no effect of the socio-demographic variables.

I have here discussed only very preliminary results, with some surprises. For example, quality-of-life indicators are very important when we try to explain welfare with micro data, rather than usual socio-demographic variables. There were other surprises, such as the importance of stress in the understanding of high welfare. But in most statistical offices, we usually include no questions about stress, which is not a good idea if we consider these results.

6.2 Conal Smith

I want to make two points. One concerns policy and the other concerns measurement. The mission of OECD is about policy advice and we have concerns about measurement, especially on subjective well-being. There are two broad approaches to explain the Easterlin paradox: one focuses on the impact of behavioral factors, i.e. relative income and adaptation to circumstances—this explains why a rise in income does not generate a rise in subjective well-being over the long run. The other is that several factors compensate for each other and leave life satisfaction unchanged. We have discussed both types of phenomena today. For instance, Richard Easterlin emphasized China's unemployment rising over time as an offsetting factor. Much of the literature and the presentations today focus on behavioral explanations, which is intellectually interesting and tells us a lot of things about the welfare function. But from a policy point of view, there is a real interest in offsetting factors and in assessing the exact trade-offs. For example, if at the OECD we tell governments they should implement structural reforms, say on labor markets, to increase growth, it is crucial to know how large the welfare gains of economic growth are, and what will be the expected costs associated to uncertainty in the labor market. I have one picture here (Figure 6.3); illustrating part of the story on the potential size of offsetting forces. It shows cross-sectional regressions over OECD countries, showing relative effects of different determinants of well-being relative to a doubling in income. The key thing we know from the literature on subjective well-being is that non-income drivers of life satisfaction are very large relative to income. It is important from a policy perspective to know this part of the story.

Let's now talk about measurement. Subjective well-being has been used as a synonym for life satisfaction and possibly as an evaluation of living standards. But we know, partly from the psychology literature, that subjective well-being is a multidimensional concept. And depending on the measure you use, you can tell a very different story. For instance, a famous stylized fact is that having children has no effect on your life satisfaction. But if you consider measures of meaning

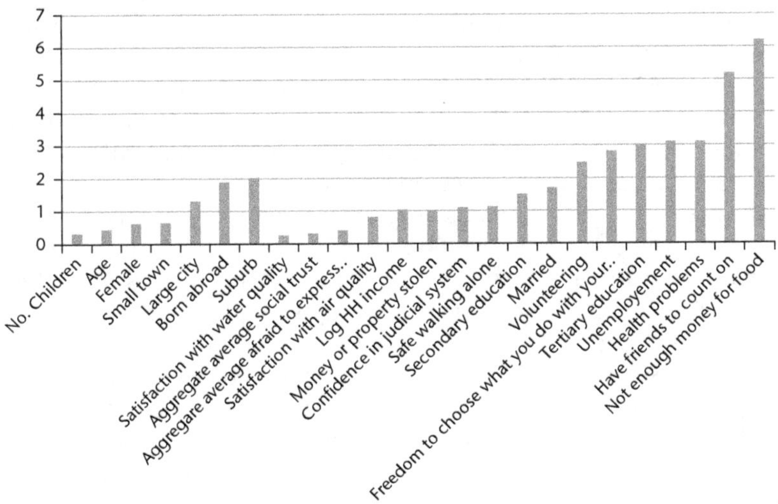

Figure 6.3. Relative effect sizes of different variables on satisfaction, OECD 2012

and purpose of life, then you find a large impact from having children. Hence, we cannot focus simply on measures of life satisfaction.

6.3 Martin Ravallion

About directions for future research. My take, as a development economist, is that subjective well-being is not a very promising approach for monitoring longer-term development progress. I am quite skeptical, basically because of what I said this morning: economic development is a process of structural change, which changes people's reference groups and scales. It changes how you think of the world where you live when you move from a village, where the reference group is very narrow, to a city with a very vast set of people at different levels of living. In that process, the scale of subjective well-being that we use is surely going to change. So, this makes me skeptical about long-term welfare comparisons in developing countries.

These data do provide a potential new window for policy analysis. But they also raise some concerns that we don't know much about. I would like to see more research testing these data and trying to understand better some of the things that we heard about today. We really need much more testing. I think the incentives in economics do not give a high return for this kind of work, though this seems to be changing. Heterogeneity in scales, as emphasized this morning, is a real problem. I think we need to develop these kinds of tests. There are many future applications.

Policy analysis will be turning more and more to subjective welfare regressions. This kind of regression does contain important information that is missing from objective measures. Standard objective data sources provide an incomplete picture of welfare. Subjective self-assessments provide valuable new information. As I reported this morning, the one test I have done, and the only test so far it seems, suggests that these regressions are quite robust to cross-sectional heterogeneity in scales. But we need more tests in other settings.

Another thing is that I would like to see more work that uses subjective measures in evaluating policy. I guess 10 percent of the things we do in the name of development economics get properly evaluated. And I think this is probably an overstatement. That is probably the upper band of the kind of evaluations that are done in the World Bank. There is the prospect to use subjective welfare in that task.

The problem in practice is that we often do not have a baseline survey. Unfortunately we often don't observe the situation before the intervention. There is a solution; you have treatment group and comparison group but no baseline data. So just ask: "recall how your life satisfaction has changed over time since the project began." You don't need baseline data, because recording the change of subjective well-being becomes a kind of difference-in-difference estimation. That is promising, but does it work? Long-term recall of welfare changes has been used in a number of studies, but few tests exist.

In China, we did a ten-year evaluation. At the end, I designed a subjective recall "report card" on thirty dimensions of welfare for both the treatment and comparison groups. I asked people, "How has your living standard changed?" Alas, I found in this case that the subjective recall of the household's overall standard living contained only a weak signal of changes in consumption based on contemporaneous surveys. These subjective recall data are so contaminated with noise that there was a weak relationship between subjective recalls and objective measures (the change in consumption). There were clear signs of telescoping in the recall responses. The telescope is that people don't exactly know when the event has occurred. You remember this happened, but you don't exactly remember when it happened. The bulk of the benefits occurred in the earlier half of the recall period, which was given too little weight by respondents in treatment villages. So subjective records of change in living standards have no useful information about baseline welfare and there is no ability to deal with this selection bias. Of course, this is just one study. We need more tests of these data.

So I have described two tests on how we might use subjective data in policy analysis. One is very encouraging and one is discouraging. I would like to see more tests of this sort. Thankfully the marginal cost of doing such tests in the context of a full-scale evaluation is not too high.

6.4 Richard A. Easterlin

I have only a few brief remarks to make. If improving human well-being is the objective of policy, then the issue, as I see it, is what is the best measure of human well-being?

We now seem to be prepared, at least at the margin, to consider measures of well-being beyond real per capita income as approximated by GDP per capita. The evidence for China is that if we look at so-called objective measures such as income, or educational attainment and life expectancy, they have all improved. In contrast, subjective measures of well-being, such as overall satisfaction with life, have not. If we ask most economists how well-being has changed in China they will typically say: "income is four times higher than it used to be, the Chinese are better educated and live longer than they used to; hence, they are better off." But when the Chinese themselves are asked how they feel about their lives, they report, on average, no increase in satisfaction—indeed, if anything less satisfaction than two decades ago. Who are we to believe—the social science "experts" who themselves decide what measures capture people's feelings of well-being, or the statements of the people who are themselves the subject of study? My judgment is that we need to listen to what people say. When we do, we learn quite a bit about desirable policies.

People in general, and policy makers in particular, need a unitary measure that indicates the change in *overall* well-being, not a measure limited to one aspect of life, or a bundle of different measures that go in various directions and give conflicting signals. GDP is only about the material dimensions of life. The value of the measure of life satisfaction is that it takes account, not only of material circumstances, but of the impact on peoples' lives of changes in their health, in their family circumstances, their employment conditions, and so on. We need to know about people's satisfaction with these numerous domains of their lives, and this is what a subjective measure like life satisfaction tends to encompass.

Moreover, subjective measures suggest policy conclusions that are not trivial. The evidence for China is very clear that the social safety net is very important, and that jobs are very important. Unfortunately, we in the West are now living in a policy world where unemployment is easily tolerated—a world that doesn't care very much about full employment and job security. Perhaps, the use of subjective well-being as a guide to decision-making might move policy in a direction more meaningful to people's lives.

7

Concluding Remarks. How Inequality Matters to Well-being: Agency, Adaptation, and Changes versus Levels

Carol Graham

All of the chapters in this volume take on an important and long-debated question in economics: the effects of inequality on individual welfare. There are several reasons why the inequality question is so complex. One is that the effects of inequality on well-being vary depending on what it signals. In some contexts, inequality is a signal of future mobility and opportunity; in others it signals persistent disadvantage for some cohorts and advantage for others.

In addition, inequality has both over-time and cross-cohort dimensions. Initial increases in inequality in the development process, for example, are often a sign of change and growth and can provide incentives for productivity and innovation.[1] In contrast, persistent inequality, which signals permanent disadvantage for some cohorts, can ultimately discourage them from investing in their own future and that of their children.[2]

Martin Ravallion, in his chapter in this volume, describes the concerns for relative deprivation and the reference group effects that often influence poverty assessments as "spurious social effects." From the perspective of objective, income-based poverty measurement, they are. Yet they are also phenomena that people care deeply about and which can have effects on their well-being and related behaviors

[1] See Birdsall and Graham (2000) and Hirschman (1973).
[2] See Birdsall, Ross, and Sabot (1995).

and outcomes.[3] Not surprisingly, these concerns are attenuated by the development process, a process which often results in changing distributions and heightened expectations.

These concerns (or spurious social effects) are difficult to measure. Inequality more generally is an institutional arrangement which most individuals are powerless to change. Thus the information in standard revealed preference-based data, such as that based on consumption choices, does not shed much light on its effects on well-being.

The extent to which inequality matters to people, meanwhile, is mediated by their point of reference. Analysis of country-level measures of inequality, for example, rarely yield significant results, as most people do not use their country as a benchmark of comparison. Instead, people are more likely to compare their rank in the distribution to others in their profession, in their neighborhood, or in their age and education cohorts. Thus the particular unit of analysis that is chosen can make a large difference to the results.

Finally, discussions about inequality often elicit strong ideological positions, with liberals (in the American sense of the word) inclined to think of inequality as a negative result of unequally shared opportunities, and conservatives (again in the American sense of the word) inclined to think of inequality as just rewards for differential efforts in the labor market.

The complexities surrounding inequality introduce uncertainty about what to measure, how to measure it, and what it all means. It is precisely the kind of question where survey data, and in particular well-being data, can shed some light. In this chapter I attempt to complement the results that are presented in the other chapters of the book with some insights from my empirical work on inequality and well-being. That work is largely but not exclusively based in Latin America, a region with a long trajectory of high and persistent levels of inequality. I focus on three organizing themes: the extent to which inequality is a signal of future mobility and opportunity; adaptation and agency issues; and the well-being effects of changes versus levels in the development process.

[3] There is some research which suggests that higher levels of well-being are, on average, linked to positive behavioral outcomes, such as healthier living and better performance in the labor market. See Diener and Chan (2010), de Neve and Oswald (2012), and Graham, Eggers, and Sukhtankar (2004).

7.1 Relevant Conceptual Distinctions in the Measurement of Well-being

A wide body of research shows that there are two distinct, albeit related, dimensions of well-being.[4] How people think about and evaluate their lives as a whole, as measured by evaluative metrics, reflects a more global view and may also be related to longer-term behaviors, such as investments in health and education. This dimension of well-being, which in previous work—as a rogue economist stepping into philosophers' territory—I roughly categorize as "Aristotelian," also encompasses eudaimonic concepts—such as the extent of purpose and meaning that people derive from their jobs, their relationships, and their lives. It is, in my view, inherently related to the opportunities that people have to exercise choice and to pursue fulfilling lives.

The hedonic dimension of well-being, which I categorize as "Benthamite," is more directly related to the environment or context that people live in—the quality of their jobs, their immediate state of health, the nature of their commute to work, and the nature of their social networks—and is reflected in positive and negative affective states, among other things. Daily experience is linked to health status and other outcomes via channels such as worry and stress on the one hand, and pleasure and enjoyment on the other. Evaluative well-being, meanwhile, is more likely to reflect people's longer-term outlooks about their lives as a whole. Paul Seabright, in his discussion in this volume, makes a related distinction between assessments of the temperature of bath water at the moment, and the broader set of variables that come to play when people think of their lives as a whole. [5]

The dimension of well-being that respondents emphasize/value the most may be mediated by their agency and capacity to control their own lives. Kahneman and Deaton, for example, find that income correlates much more closely with evaluative well-being than with hedonic well-being in the United States.[6] The correlation between hedonic well-being and income tapers off at roughly $75k or median income, but that between income and evaluative well-being continues in a linear fashion. After a certain point, more income cannot make people enjoy their daily lives more (although insufficient income is clearly linked to suffering and negative moods), but higher levels of

[4] Diener (2011), Kahneman et al. (2006), and Graham, 2011.

[5] See Clark and Senik in this volume; see also Dolan (2012) and Graham (2011).

[6] Kahneman and Deaton (2010).

income offer people many more choices about how to live and what to do with their lives.

Similarly, Eduardo Lora and I find that the most important variable for the reported life satisfaction of the "poor" (respondents below median income) in Latin America, after having enough food to eat, is having friends and family to rely on in times of need.[7] In contrast, the most important variables for the life satisfaction of the "rich" (respondents above the median) are work and health. It is likely that friends and family are the vital safety nets that make daily life tolerable for the poor, while work and health are what provide respondents a greater capacity to make choices in their lives.

Individuals who focus primarily on daily experiences—due to low expectations, lack of agency, or imposed social norms—may have less incentive to invest in the future. In rapidly growing developing economies, I find lower levels of reported well-being (evaluative well-being) among respondents with relatively high levels of income mobility than among poor rural respondents with no mobility. In the U.S., I find that the obese have lower levels of well-being than the non-obese, but the negative effects are mitigated if they are in high-obesity cohorts—cohorts which also have lower levels of income mobility. It seems that people are better able to adapt to unpleasant certainty and retain relatively high levels of well-being (and likely higher in the hedonic dimension than in the evaluative dimension) than to live with uncertainty, even that which is associated with progress.[8]

Individuals who have a longer-term focus and are more achieve ment-oriented, meanwhile, may at times sacrifice daily experiences for longer-term objectives and anticipated well-being (evaluative) in the future. The extreme manifestation of this is those who choose to migrate to another country to provide their children with opportunities, or to participate in social unrest for a broader societal objective. My initial research with Julie Markowitz (2011), based on intent-to-migrate data from Latin America, finds that individuals who plan to migrate are actually less happy (in the subjective well-being sense) than their like-traited cohorts who do not intend to migrate (this is discussed in greater detail later in the chapter). Thus some of what studies of migrants in their place of destination pick up as lower levels of well-being related to migration may actually be a result of the unhappiness that led to migration in the first place.

[7] Graham and Lora (2009).

[8] Graham (2008, 2011b) and Graham, Higuera, and Lora (2011).

In my view, these different dimensions of well-being—and in particular the issue of agency and the challenges of acquiring it—are relevant to understanding the effects of inequality on well-being. There are several examples of this in the chapters in this volume. The unhappiness of migrants in China and their concern with rank and income differentials, likely due to rising aspirations and changing reference norms, is a good example.

7.2 Inequality and Well-Being: Why the Signals Matter

One reason why there is so much debate about the relation between inequality and well-being is that it is mediated by what inequality signals in particular contexts. Theoretical work by Benabou and Ok (2001), for example, highlights the importance of individual attitudes about upward mobility (prospects of upward mobility or the POUM hypothesis) and posits that, at least in the U.S., public perceptions of inequality are that it is a sign of future mobility, and voters will not vote for redistribution because they do not want to tax themselves in the future. Indeed, Benabou and Ok posit that the majority of voters think that they will be above mean income in the future, even though that is a mathematical impossibility.[9]

Empirical data on well-being and inequality bear their hypothesis out. Alesina, di Tella, and MacCulloch examined the relationship between inequality and happiness in the U.S. and Europe. They find that inequality has a modest negative effect on well-being in Europe, with the effects being the strongest for the poor. In the U.S., in contrast, they find that the only group that is made unhappy by inequality are left-leaning rich people! In another exercise, Peyton Young and I looked at attitudes about redistribution and inequality at the time of the Bush tax cuts (2002–3) and were surprised to see that polls showed that while only one half of the top 1 per cent of Americans in the income distribution actually benefited from the tax cuts, 19 per cent of Americans thought they would when they were proposed.[10]

These attitudes likely stem from a long-held perception, beginning with de Tocqueville, of America as the land of opportunity. And for many decades, empirical data on mobility bore that perception out. More recently, though, a number of studies have suggested that mobility rates in the United States are among the lowest in OECD countries,

[9] Benabou and Ok (1998).

[10] Alesina, DiTella, and MacCulloch (2004) and Graham and Young (2003).

and that mobility is increasingly determined by access to high-quality tertiary education, which is in turn correlated with parental incomes. Yet it seems that public perceptions have not caught up with changing trends, and Americans remain remarkably tolerant of high and increasing rates of inequality.[11] There are some signs that may be changing, as in the Occupy Wall Street movement and some of the other discussions surrounding the financial crisis. However, we do not yet have updated data on public attitudes to inequality.

Rather ironically, in Latin America, where mobility rates have increased and poverty and inequality rates have decreased in recent years, public perceptions have not caught up.[12] Andrew Felton and I looked at the relationship between inequality and well-being in Latin America, based on a large-scale data set, the Latinobarometro.[13] In contrast to the findings for the U.S., we find that inequality (defined as each respondent's distance from average income for their country, controlling for average per capita income in each country) has strong negative effects on the happiness of the poor and positive effects on the happiness of the rich (see Table 7.1). Average per capita income does not have significant effects on happiness, meanwhile.[14]

Figure 7.1 provides an illustration of the results, via a comparison of Honduras and Chile. Even though average per capita income is almost twice as high in Honduras as it is in Chile, it does not have significant effects on happiness. Instead, because there is a larger gap between the average Chilean poor respondent and mean income than there is for the average poor Honduran, the latter is happier than the former! This is likely a result of narrower income differentials. Some may also be a result of lower aspirations in Honduras (which is discussed in the next section).

[11] Haskins and Sawhill (2009), among others.

[12] See Lopez-Calva and Lustig (2010) and Lustig (2011).

[13] The Latinobarómetro (1997–2008) survey consists of approximately 1,000 annual interviews in each of eighteen countries in Latin America. The samples are conducted by a prestigious research firm in each country, and are nationally representative except for Chile, Colombia, and Paraguay. The survey is comparable to the Eurobarometer survey for European countries in design and focus; both surveys are cross-sections rather than panels. A standard set of demographic questions are asked every year. The usual problems with accurately measuring income in developing countries where most respondents work in the informal sector and cannot record a fixed salary are present. Many surveys rely on reported expenditures, which tend to be more accurate, if less good at capturing the assets of the very wealthy. The Latinobarómetro has neither, and instead relies on the interviewer's assessment of household socioeconomic status (SES) as well as a long list of questions about ownership of goods and assets, upon which we compile our wealth index. The index is based on ownership of eleven types of assets, ranging from drinking water and plumbing to computers and second homes.

[14] Graham and Felton (2006).

We also looked at respondents in different sized cities (small—less than 5,000 inhabitants, medium—from 10,000 to 100,000 inhabitants, and large—over 100,000 respondents) to see if our results varied when we used different reference groups. We found, indeed, that the unhappiness effects of inequality were greater in larger cities, as one would expect, as both wealth differences and aspirations are greater. In addition, we found that the only context where average incomes were important to well-being was small cities (see Table 7.1). One can imagine that in smaller places, where people are more connected with each other and poverty is still a widespread concern, higher levels of average incomes may have positive spillover effects which counter the usual comparison effects. The effects of relative income differences were still negative for those below mean income in the small cities, however.

In Latin America, despite remarkable progress in reducing poverty and inequality, public attitudes have not caught up. As a result, inequality still seems to signal persistent disadvantage for the poor and persistent advantage for the rich, in sharp contrast to the U.S. even though, again, the empirical data in the U.S. does not support the public perception of inequality as a sign of opportunity. One reason for this misalignment between perceptions and actual trends in both

Table 7.1. Average versus relative wealth. Ordered logit estimation of a 1–4 scale of happiness.

	Average wealth calculated by:					
	Country	Country	Country city size	Country city size	Country city size	Country city size
Wealth	0.112 [5.44]**		0.112 [6.9]**		0.097 [7.96]**	
Average wealth	−0.052 [−0.70]	0.059 [0.78]	0.054 [0.92]	0.058 [0.99]	−0.081 [−2.19]*	0.016 [0.42]
Relative wealth		0.112 [5.44]**		0.112 [6.9]**		0.097 [7.96]**

Notes:

Demographic variables in all regressions: age, age squared, years of education, marital status, gender, health status, employment status (including whether unemployed, self-employed, retired, and student).

Explanatory variables include country (columns 5 and 6), and city-size dummy variables (all columns), and cluster controls, as appropriate for each particular regression specification.

Values in parentheses denote t-statistics.

* significant at Solo; ** significant at 1%.

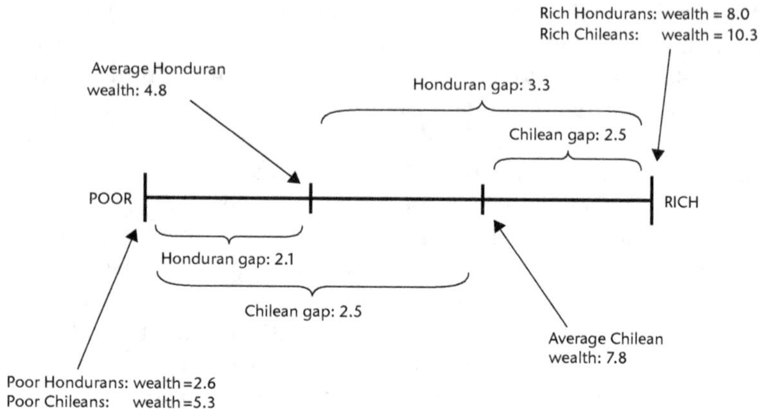

Happiness Gap = wealth gap * coefficient ÷ 4

Calculated Happiness Gap

	Poor	Rich
Chile wealth gap	–2.489	2.521
Honduras wealth gap	–2.142	3.261
Chile-Honduras difference	0.347	0.740
difference * coefficient/4 = Honduran happiness differential	0.43%	0.93%

	Mean happiness (1–5 scale)			Mean wealth (1–11 scale)		
Wealth quintile	Chile	Honduras	Overall	Chile	Honduras	Overall
1	2.54	3.11	2.73	5.26	2.64	3.12
2	2.74	3.15	2.85	7.00	4.00	5.00
3	2.77	3.17	2.91	8.00	5.00	6.00
4	2.94	3.13	2.97	9.00	6.00	7.46
5	3.08	3.30	3.08	10.27	8.04	9.63
Total	2.79	3.17	2.88	7.76	4.78	5.81

Figure 7.1. Happiness gap in Honduras and Chile
Source: Graham and Felton (2006).

contexts is the complexity of most income inequality data, which may make it quite difficult for the average citizen to discern.

These findings resonate with those of Clark and Senik in this volume. They find that average Chinese village income is positively correlated with financial satisfaction but, being in a low rank in the distribution, is negatively correlated. Earlier work by John Knight also comes to mind. He finds that rural respondents in China typically compare their financial situation to that of their own household in the past year, while urban respondents compare their situation with the average for their city. Recent migrants, meanwhile, who have recently switched reference groups, are the most bothered by inequality, likely because their knowledge of how large the gap is between them and the average is fairly new. [15]

Some new work by Sandu Cojocaru, based on a comparison of Western and Eastern Europe and using the Life in Transition survey, tests the signaling hypothesis explicitly. He compares respondents based on their past mobility trends and on their attitudes regarding the fairness of the distribution. He finds that respondents with a recent trajectory of upward mobility are less likely to support redistribution, as are those who believe that success is a result of hard work (as opposed to due to luck and connections).[16] Cojocaru also tests the mediating effects of different reference norms. He finds that an externally imposed (by the researcher) reference group (distance from the Census Enumeration Area mean income) has inconsistent effects on reported well-being. In contrast, a self-assessed reference group—the respondents' reported position on a notional societal economic ladder—has a strong and significant correlation with well-being.[17] The Economic Ladder Question asks respondents to rank their position in society compared to the rich (at the top) and the poor at the bottom.

As with any study based on perceptions and well-being, there is an endogeneity problem, as less happy respondents may be more likely to perceive injustice or to compare themselves negatively with others. As a robustness check, Cojocaru uses an instrumental variables strategy, based on the interviewer's assessments of each household's rank in their community, and his findings still hold. In this instance, what inequality signals, as well as the reference group that is chosen, seems to be an important mediating channel for its effects on welfare.

Cojocaru's findings are analogous, in a way, to the trends across Democrats and Republicans in the United States, with Democrats more likely to perceive outcomes to be a result of systemic bias rather than personal effort and more likely to be concerned about injustice, while Republicans are more likely to believe that outcomes are a result of personal effort in the labor market. Not surprisingly, Democrats are both less happy about inequality and less happy in general than are Republicans.

All of this suggests that inequality has varied effects on well-being, which are very much mediated by what inequality signals, as well as

[15] Kingdon and Knight (2007) and Knight and Gunatilaka (2010).

[16] Cojocaru (2012).

[17] The variable is actually the respondent's core in the last year of the survey minus the respondent's score in the first year of the survey.

the reference group that is utilized. In smaller (and likely poorer) reference groups, higher levels of average income seem to have a stronger positive signaling effect as opposed to negative comparison effect, even though the usual concerns about rank still hold. In larger reference groups, such as big cities, where social connections are weaker (and resources are surely less likely to be pooled) and where income variance is much greater, comparison effects seem to overwhelm any positive effects of higher average income levels, and concerns about rank continue to hold and may even be more important as real and perceived income differences are greater.

7.3 Adapting to Unpleasant Certainty

Another theme that runs through much of my work on well-being, and is relevant to the discussion here, is that of adaptation. People seem to be able to adapt much better to unpleasant certainty than to uncertainty, even that which is associated with progress. We find, for example, that during the economic crisis in the U.S., there were very large and negative effects of well-being at the time of the free-fall in the markets. National average happiness fell by 11 percent in six months. Given that average national happiness levels in the U.S. were flat for over three decades of strong growth performance, this is an impressive drop. Equally remarkable, though, as soon as the markets established some semblance of stability in March of 2009, average happiness levels recovered to and surpassed their pre-crisis levels, even though the same respondents reported having less income than they had before the crisis.[18]

We find similar effects in the health realm. Based on data for Latin America from the Gallup World Poll and additional information on respondent's answers to the EQ-5D index question, we calculated the life and health satisfaction effects of various conditions (the EQ-5D index is based on five questions about whether respondents have problems with mobility, self-care, the usual acts, pain, and anxiety, with responses ranging from no problems to extreme problems). We find that respondents seem to be much better able to adapt to physical injuries and limitations and return to their pre-injury levels of well-being than they are able to adapt to conditions associated with

[18] See Graham, Chattopadhyay, and Picon (2010) and Deaton (2011). Deaton finds that the inclusion of political questions prior to the happiness questions during some parts of the Gallup Survey biased happiness responses down prior to the crisis. Even applying Deaton's corrections, though, we get a similar U-shaped trend in happiness levels in our analysis of the data.

constant uncertainty, such as chronic pain, anxiety, and uncontrolled epilepsy.[19]

Norms and expectations also seem to mediate the adaptation phenomenon. We find, for example, that respondents in Guatemala are more satisfied with their health than are those in Chile, even though objective conditions in the former are at roughly sub-Saharan African standards and those in Chile are at the top of OECD country standards. Yet respondents in Guatemala have different norms with regard to what is good health, which in turn mediate their expectations. Respondents in Kenya, meanwhile, report to be as satisfied with their health as are those in the U.S., which again makes no sense based on objective conditions, but does if one considers differences in norms.

A similar phenomenon occurs in the income realm. We examined life satisfaction across respondents in Peru and Russia, some of whom were upwardly mobile and some of whom were not. We found, rather remarkably, that over half of those respondents with upward mobility (who were more likely to be urban) had lower levels of life satisfaction than poorer respondents with no mobility. We explain the difference between our "happy peasants and frustrated achievers" based on the higher expectations of the latter, as well as the precarious and uncertain context in which they made their gains. We also find that the frustrated achievers were more concerned about inequality than were our non-frustrated respondents. While it may well be that less happy people are more likely to be unhappy with any gains that they make, as well as more concerned about inequality and unfairness, it is also likely that changing norms and expectations, as well as increased awareness of how even wealthier urban respondents live, drive some of the frustration.[20]

Indeed, we tested the reference norms that each group used as a comparator and found that the frustrated achievers were more likely to compare themselves to others in their country, while the non-frustrated rural respondents were more likely to compare themselves to others in their community. Angus Deaton's work, meanwhile, suggests that much of what studies of well-being pick up as negative effects of relative income is simply an over-time effect of people adapting to higher levels of income and expecting more income, as well as comparing themselves to others who have also gained.[21]

The previous section suggests that gradual changes in distributive trends are not easily perceived by the public, not least as they

[19] Graham, Higuera, and Lora (2011).
[20] Graham and Pettinato (2002).
[21] Deaton (2012).

are typically very gradual, at least in stable economic times. In contrast, changes in individual positions in the distribution, as well as increased awareness of existing differences related to those changes, seem to have much more direct effects on perceptions and welfare. And very visible examples of distributive injustice, such as the exposure of corruption in the privatization process or, as in the case of the recent U.S. financial crisis, in the causes and consequences of financial sector management, seem to spark more public reaction or discontent. The widespread protests in cities around the world following the crisis—from Occupy Wall Street, to the London riots, to the protests in Greece, among others—are good examples.

In the same way that people seem to be able to adapt to poor norms of health or to stable if unpleasant situations of poverty, they seem to also be able to adapt to persistent if unfair distributions. Latin America is a case in point. Even if remarkably high and persistent levels of inequality have had negative effects on individual well-being over time in the region, they have rarely resulted in concerted public action for change. In contrast, visible changes, which make people aware of distributive issues as well as more concerned about potential injustice in the future, seem to have much greater effects. The public protests surrounding visibly botched and unequally shared gains of particular privatizations, such as in Argentina and Bolivia in the 1990s, are suggestive here.[22]

Clark and Senik's chapter in this volume provides an example from a developing economy with very rapid and very uneven economic growth, precisely where changes in the distribution are likely to be noticeable. Their research is based on a panel study in a very high inequality province in China. They find very little evidence of a "happy peasant" adaptation phenomenon (what they call Sen's "happy slaves"), and instead that the coefficients on both village income and past income are positive for financial satisfaction, while that on rank is insignificant. In contrast, being in a low rank does have a significant and negative effect on financial satisfaction, and immigrants in particular are unhappy about being in the lower ranks.

7.4 Changes versus Levels Effects

A related issue is something that I have termed changes versus levels effects in the development process. While, on average, people are happier when they have higher levels of income and in contexts

[22] Graham (1998).

with higher levels of GDP per capita, the process of change related to achieving higher levels of prosperity—e.g. the process of acquiring agency—seems to be an unhappy one.

In addition to the individual-level "happy peasants" and "frustrated achievers" phenomenon, Eduardo Lora and I identified a trend that we call the paradox of unhappy growth. Looking across 122 countries in the Gallup World Poll data set for 2006–7 we find that, controlling for average levels of GDP per capita, which have a positive effect on reported life satisfaction, higher rates of growth are negatively correlated with life satisfaction (see Table 7.2).

When we split the sample into countries above and below the median income level for the sample, and above and below median growth rates, we find that the results are driven by fast-growing middle-income countries. If one considers the changes taking place in countries such as China, which is the subject of much of this volume, as well as in other fast-growing countries such as Brazil and Korea, this paradox makes sense. While levels are indeed improving as a result of growth over time, the initial stages of rapid growth are often accompanied by uncertainty, changing rewards to different skill sets, and increases in inequality, all of which seem to drive unhappiness.

John Knight's chapter in this volume describes how trends such as these are undermining happiness and the benefits of growth in

Table 7.2. The paradox of unhappy growth

The relationship between income per capita, economic growth, and satisfaction	122 countries	
	GDP per capita	Economic growth
Life satisfaction	0.788**	−0.082***
Standard of living	0.108***	−0.018***
Health satisfaction	0.017*	−0.017*
Job satisfaction	0.077***	0.006
Housing satisfaction	0.084***	−0.006

Source: IADB-RES using Gallup World Poll, 2007.

—OLS regression: dependent variable is average life satisfaction per country; growth rates are averaged over the past five years. N = 122.

—GDP per capita: the coefficients are the marginal effects: how much does the satisfaction of two countries differ if one has 2× the income of the other?

—Economic growth: How much does an additional % point of growth affect satisfaction?

—The life satisfaction variable is on a scale of 0–10: all others are the percentage of respondents that are satisfied.

—Gratham and Chattopadhyay find similar effects for Latin America, based on individual data rather than country averages.

China. Indeed, they are now the focus of government concern. Mean happiness levels are higher in rural areas even though urban income levels are three times the levels of rural income. He attributes these results to the insecurity in which urban migrants live, to their higher aspirations, to changing reference norms, and to the withdrawal of the security that comes from rural community support mechanisms. Related work by Namrata Chindarkar, also on the well-being of urban migrants in China, finds significant and negative well-being effects of the *hukou* system, which limits the access of new migrants to good schools and other amenities that are available to established urban residents.[23] The negative effects of *hukou* discrimination are above and beyond those of the income differentials between migrants and their non-migrant counterparts.

The U-shape in well-being that Richard Easterlin highlights in this volume also fits this story. He finds that average well-being levels fell in China with the initial stages of growth in the 1990s and then increased after the year 2000 (with the year depending on the source of the survey data). Clark and Senik's results on China, meanwhile, are also suggestive here. While past income and average village level incomes are positive for well-being, low-level rank in the village distribution is negative for well-being.

We recently attempted to test whether change produces unhappiness or whether unhappiness is necessary to produce change. In most places where migrants are compared to non-migrants in their place of destination, migrants are less happy than non-migrants. Yet it is not clear whether migrating produced the unhappiness, due to changing reference norms and loss of safety nets, or whether unhappiness produced the decision to migrate.

Julie Markowitz, Namrata Chindarkar, and I (in two separate papers) explored intent-to-migrate data from Latin America. We find a significant frustrated achievers effect. Those migrants who intend to migrate from the region are, on average, wealthier and more educated than the average. At the same time, they are less happy and more critical of their economic situation compared to the past and compared to others.[24] Thus in this instance, it seems that unhappiness (and concerns about relative status) seem to drive migration, and may at least in part explain the unhappiness of migrants in their destination point compared to non-migrants.

[23] Chindarkar (2012).

[24] Chindarkar (2012) and Graham and Markowitz (2011).

In a later and still preliminary exercise, we created a pseudo panel of recent migrants in the U.S., based on the New Immigrant Survey, and matched them with our intent-to-migrate cohorts in Latin America. We find that recent migrants are slightly less happy than non-migrants in the U.S., but (after a few years in the U.S.) the mean happiness levels of the U.S. migrants are higher than those of the respondents who reported to intend to migrate *ex ante*. While far from a perfect exercise, this suggests that unhappiness and concerns for relative status may drive change rather than change simply resulting in unhappiness.

What is also clear is that over time there is a clear positive relationship between well-being and the higher levels of prosperity (and available opportunities) that those changes are intended to achieve. What is less understood is if the concerns for rank and other relative income differences that underlie the migration decisions—and that may have been heightened by the new reference levels of income that migrants usually encounter—also dissipate over time. There is some evidence—as in the case of U.S. Democrats and Republicans—that some cohorts are more inclined to be concerned about inequality and injustice regardless of the context. At the same time, the immigration evidence suggests that some of these concerns—or at least the welfare effects of income differentials—may dissipate over time, particularly as conditions stabilize.

7.5 Conclusion

It is not surprising that the results of analysis on well-being and inequality are mixed, given the complexity of measurement and the many different channels at play. These mixed results in turn complicate the debate on the relationship between income and well-being. Yet despite the measurement and interpretation complexities, distributive justice and income differentials seem to be phenomena which people care deeply about, and which, in turn, influence behavioral outcomes.

My objective in this chapter was to provide some insights from the perspective of the different dimensions of well-being, with one being how people experience their lives and the other being how people evaluate their lives as a whole, a dimension which is more likely to capture aspirations and norms. I framed the discussion around three related themes that run through my research: what inequality signals; adaptation and agency issues; and changes versus levels in the development process. All of these perspectives suggest that concerns about relative income differences and about distributive justice matter to well-being, and in particular the evaluative dimension of well-being that encompasses individuals' capacity to make choices and seek opportunities. How much it matters, though, varies across both contexts and time.

My results, as well as the more general discussions throughout the volume, highlight the various ways in which inequality and well-being relate, and how, in turn, that relationship can mediate the more general relationship between well-being and income. While the debates on both these relationships are far from resolved, the contributions in the volume provide striking evidence of the role of inequality—and, in particular, how concerns about distribution and the channels through which they affect well-being are heightened by the process of development and change. As I noted throughout the chapter, the higher levels of prosperity that the development process seeks to achieve are indisputably associated with higher levels of well-being. Yet the process of change, and the necessary search for agency that accompanies it, is not necessarily a happy one, due both to uncertainty and to the changes in distribution that typically accompany it.

References

Alesina, A., Di Tella, R., and MacCulloch, R. 2004. "Inequality and Happiness: Are Europeans and Americans Different?" *Journal of Public Economics*, **88**, 2009–42.

Benabou R. and Ok E. (2001). "Social Mobility and the Demand for Redistribution: The POUM Hypothesis", *Quarterly Journal of Economics*, **116** (2), 447–87.

Birdsall, N. and Graham, C. (eds.) (2000). *New Markets, New Opportunities? Economic and Social Mobility in a Changing World* (Washington, D.C.: The Brookings Institution Press).

Birdsall, N., Ross, D., and Sabot, R. (1995). "Inequality and Growth Reconsidered," *World Bank Economic Review*, **9**, 55–79.

Chindarkar, N. (2012). "Essays on Subjective Well-being: Applications in International Migration, Poverty Alleviation Programs, and Inequality of Opportunity," PhD Dissertation, School of Public Policy, University of Maryland, May.

Cojocaru, S. (2012). "Essays on Inequality, Social Mobility, and Redistributive Preferences in the Transition Economies," PhD Dissertation, School of Public Policy, University of Maryland, May.

Deaton, A. (2012). "The Financial Crisis and the Well-being of Americans," *Oxford Economic Papers*, **64**, 1–26.

DeNeve, J.-E. and Oswald, A. (2012). "Happiness Pays: Measuring the Effect of Subjective Well-being on Later Income Using Sibling Fixed Effects," Royal

Economic Society 2012 Annual Conference paper, University of Cambridge, March 26–28.

Diener, E. (2012). "Do Hedonic Measures Differ from Cognitive Evaluation Measures of Well-being?" Background paper for National Academy of Sciences Panel on Well-being Metrics, May 2012.

Diener, E. and Chan, M. (2010). "Happier People Live Longer: Subjective Well-being Contributes to Health and Longevity," Mimeo, Department of Psychology, University of Illinois, October.

Dolan, P. (2012). "NAS SWB Position Paper," Background Paper for NAS Panel on Well-being Metrics, May.

Graham, C. (1998). *Private Markets for Public Goods: Raising the Stakes in Economic Reform* (Washington, D.C.: The Brookings Institution Press).

Graham, C. (2008). "Happiness and Health: Lessons—and Questions—for Policy," *Health Affairs*, **27**, 72–87.

Graham, C. (2011a). *The Pursuit of Happiness: An Economy of Well-being.* Washington, D.C.: The Brookings Institution Press.

Graham, Carol (2011b). "Adaptation amidst Prosperity and Adversity: Some Insights from Happiness Studies from around the World," *World Bank Research Observer*, **27**, 105–37.

Graham, C., Eggers, A., and Sukhtankar, S. (2004). "Does Happiness Pay? Some Initial Evidence from Panel Data for Russia," *Journal of Economic Behavior and Organization*, **55**, 319–42.

Graham, C. and Felton, A. (2006). "Does Inequality Matter to Individual Welfare: An Exploration Based on Happiness Surveys in Latin America," *Journal of Economic Inequality*, **4**, 107–22.

Graham, C., Higuera, L., and Lora, E. (2011). "Which Health Conditions Cause the Most Unhappiness?" *Health Economics*, **20**, 1431–47.

Carol G. and Lora, E. (eds.) (2009). *Paradox and Perception: Measuring Quality of Life in Latin America* (Washington, D.C.: The Brookings Institution Press).

Graham, C. and Markowitz, J. (2011). "Aspirations and Happiness of Potential Latin American Immigrants," *Journal of Social Research and Policy*, **2**, 1–17.

Graham, C. and Pettinato, S. (2002). "Frustrated Achievers: Winners, Losers, and Subjective Well-being in New Market Economies," *Journal of Development Studies*, **38**, 100–40.

Graham, Carol, Soumya Chattopadhyay, and Mario Picon (2010), "Does the Dow Get You Down? Happiness and the U.S. Economic Crisis," The Brookings Institution, mimeo.

Graham, Carol and Young, Peyton (2003). "Ignorance Fills the Income Gulf," *The Boston Globe,* 23 June.

Haskins, Ron and Sawhill, Isabel (2009). *Creating an Opportunity Society* (Washington, D.C.: The Brookings Institution Press).

Hirschman, A. (1973). "Changing Tolerance for Inequality in the Course of Economic Development," *Quarterly Journal of Economics*, **87**, 544–66.

Kahneman, D. and Deaton, A. (2010). "High Income Improves Evaluation of Life but not Emotional Well-being," *Proceedings of the National Academy of Sciences*, **107**, 16489–93.

Kahneman, D., Krueger, A., Schkade, D., Schawrz, N., and Stone, A. (2006). "Would You Be Happier If You Were Richer? A Focusing Illusion," *Science*, Vol. **312**, No. 5782, June.

Kingdon, G. and Knight, J. (2007). "Communities, Comparisons, and Subjective Well-being in a Divided Society," *Journal of Economic Behavior and Organization*, **64**, 69–90.

Knight, J. and Gunatilaka, R. (2010). "Great Expectations? The Subjective Well-being of Rural-Urban Migrants in China." *World Development*, **38**, 113–24.

Lopez Calva, L. and Lustig, N. (eds.) (2010). *Declining Inequality in Latin America* (Washington, D.C.: The Brookings Institution Press).

Lustig, N. (2011). "Fiscal Policy, Fiscal Mobility, the Poor, the Vulnerable, and the Middle Class in Latin America," Mimeo, Inter-American Dialogue and Tulane University, October.

Name Index

Footnotes are indicated by the page number followed by "n" and the note number.

Subject Index

Figures and Tables are indicated by page numbers in italics.

Subject Index

The manufacturer's authorised representative in the EU for product safety is Oxford University Press España S.A. of el Parque Empresarial San Fernando de Henares, Avenida de Castilla, 2 – 28830 Madrid (www.oup.es/en or product.safety@oup.com). OUP España S.A. also acts as importer into Spain of products made by the manufacturer.

www.ingramcontent.com/pod-product-compliance
Lightning Source LLC
LaVergne TN
LVHW011511200926
848484LV00001B/14

* 9 7 8 0 1 9 8 7 2 3 6 5 3 *